Overcoming Tradition and Modernity

Overcoming Tradition and Modernity

The Search for Islamic Authenticity

Robert D. Lee

Colorado College

WestviewPress

A Division of HarperCollins*Publishers*

Published in 1997 in the United States of America by Westview Press, 5500 Central Avenue, Boulder, Colorado 80301-2877, and in the United Kingdom by Westview Press, 12 Hid's Copse Road, Cumnor Hill, Oxford OX2 9JJ

Library of Congress Cataloging-in-Publication Data
Lee, Robert Deemer, 1941–
    Overcoming tradition and modernity: the search for Islamic
authenticity / Robert D. Lee.
        p. cm.
    Includes bibliographical references (p.   ) and index.
    ISBN 0-8133-2797-0 (hc).—ISBN 0-8133-2798-9 (pbk.)
    1. Islam—20th century.   I. Title.
BP163.L36 1997
297´.09´04—dc21   97-7391
                                                                                  CIP

The paper used in this publication meets the requirements of the American National Standard for Permanence of Paper for Printed Library Materials Z39.48-1984.

10   9   8   7   6   5   4   3   2   1

Contents

Acknowledgments

For a project in gestation nearly twenty years, my debts are so many and diverse I find it difficult to reconstruct them. I'm not even sure where it all started. Perhaps it was in Cairo in fall 1977, when I interviewed Egyptian leaders about the concept of development. Then, as at several later stages, I depended upon the support of my home institution, Colorado College.

As I began to explore the concept of authenticity in the early 1980s, my colleague Timothy Fuller helped guide me toward fruitful sources. As I struggled to clarify my thoughts, Joseph Pickle and Douglas Fox of our religion department provided important suggestions.

Teaching at a place where undergraduate education is one's foremost responsibility, I doubt I would ever have managed to complete the project without a sabbatical year and two unpaid leaves spent in Florence, Italy. Jean Blondel of the European University Institute and his seminar in comparative politics provided welcome intellectual stimulation. Michael Beard, also on sabbatical, turned up in Florence and offered encouragement as well as a reading of an early version of the Iqbal chapter. He later read more. I owe the Associated Colleges of the Midwest for the chance to help direct its programs in Florence in 1991–1992, and I am especially indebted to Janet Goodhue Smith of the ACM, whose friendship made all three of those stays so enjoyable and productive.

When Mohammed Arkoun asked whether I would translate his book *Overtures sur l'Islam* from French to English, I hesitated to accept the assignment for fear it would further delay the appearance of this book. In fact, the collaboration with Professor Arkoun and Barbara Ellington at Westview Press provided just the sort of stimulus I needed to finish the larger project. I am grateful to Professor Arkoun, in particular, for his judicious analysis of what I had written about him and for his tolerance of my questions and doubts. He tried to explain his position without dissuading me from mine.

Omar Dahbour and John Riker provided much-needed comments on the first two chapters. William Shepard went far beyond the call of duty in his close reading of the chapter on Sayyid Qutb. My colleagues in political science at Colorado College have all listened to me expound my ideas on authenticity at departmental luncheons; they have always been merciful, tolerant, and insightful. It goes without saying that the remaining weaknesses and defects of this book are not anyone's fault but my own.

When it takes twenty years to produce a small manuscript, the suffering of a family, which usually figures in such accounts, is probably attenuated. I am nonetheless grateful to my wife, Susan A. Ashley, who has read everything on more than one occasion and has embarrassed me into rethinking countless ideas, and to our sons, William and Matthew, who have thrived in Italian schools and on Italian soccer fields when called upon to do so. I might have gotten this done sooner if I had watched less soccer over the years, but I have no regrets.

I do regret that my father, Deemer Lee, who died when I was just beginning to imagine this manuscript, did not live to see it completed. Publisher of a small-town newspaper, he always thought I should be a writer, not a college teacher, constrained on a daily basis to what he regarded as the much less satisfactory realm of verbal communication. If I have written in a clear and straightforward way about complicated matters, some of the credit surely goes to him and the early encouragement he gave me. If I have failed to do that, I guess it will show that he was right about the fuzzy-headedness of academics.

Robert D. Lee
Colorado Springs

one

◈

The Concept of
Authenticity

"AUTHENTICITY" HAS BEGUN TO RIVAL "DEVELOPMENT" as a key to understanding the political aspirations of the non-Western world. In the 1960s and 1970s, the new states of Africa and Asia wanted more capital, more schools, better communications facilities, more industry, more transfer of technology—more of those things deemed essential to an imitation of the Western pattern of economic development. Western theories of modernization both described these demands and fostered them. But the Iranian Revolution of 1978–1979 diminished the plausibility of development theory and practice as a universal phenomenon. Development became suspect for its origins in the West, its devastating social consequences, its inability to deliver long-promised doses of well-being, and its indifference to cultural distinctions. In many places besides Iran, the demand for development lost ground to the cry for authenticity.

In its most generic sense, individual authenticity means that I as a person should be who I am and not someone else. I should not follow external recipes for ethical behavior and success but should be guided by the innermost instincts of my being. By extension, societies must collectively set agendas that reflect not the theories of international planning agencies but the cultural heritage of their own peoples. They must be true to themselves, even if this means revolt against the world-yoking rationality of social engineers. Peoples must fashion their own political, economic, and social systems to fit their own culture.

Such a notion of cultural authenticity can, however, conflict with the freedom of choice implied by individual authenticity. Individual authenticity requires radical rejection of external standards, whether these be the

1

product of cultural tradition or modernity, the logic of Aristotle or the rationality of Islamic establishment, the dictates of parental guidance or the conventions of high society. Authenticity elevates the importance of particular circumstances of time, place, and culture in explaining identity. My authentic being depends upon my family, my language, my religion, my place on the map, and my position in the flow of history. All these factors precede the consciousness of the Cartesian cogito. The particular context from which I derive my originality is itself the product of past human action and creativity. To lead an authentic life means to be free to fashion my own world and therefore to create myself from the context I am dealt, without either denying my existential condition or being resigned to it.

The authentic self is necessarily unique; no two persons share exactly the same presence in the world. Does not uniqueness necessarily imply radical disjunction from all other human beings? Unless I can feel at one with others who share my context and particularity, how can I construct a world that I recognize as my own? Would a world in which all human beings strive to live authentic lives be a world of multiple particularities locked in perpetual conflict? If the drive for authenticity is itself universal, can one imagine a set of minimally constraining circumstances in which multiple versions of authenticity could coexist without war? Does the idea of authenticity contain within it not just the promise of enhanced consciousness of difference but also the potential for a level of commonality in the substrata of existential diversity? Most advocates of authenticity, although they reject Cartesian rationality, suggest the existence of a mystical human bond deep beneath the surface of things, but they differ on how and when such a bond may assert itself. Most contemporary Middle Eastern advocates of authenticity suggest the possibility of moving from individual to cultural authenticity as a foundation for group action.

By intensifying the burgeoning Islamic interest in authenticity, the Iranian Revolution of 1978–1979 affected politics in almost every other Middle Eastern country. Most radical groups, including the assassins of Anwar al-Sadat, have couched their demands in the language of Islam[1] and have become known as "fundamentalists" or "Islamists."[2] Such groups have captured the word 'aṣāla (authenticity) and have made the term anathema to some of their more secularized, development-oriented opponents. The word "authenticity" has thus tended to become identified with efforts to establish Islamic governments and societies in the Middle East. In the minds of many scholars and laymen, both in the Middle East and the West, cultural authenticity has become synonymous with reaction and fanaticism.

Yet the debate about Islam in Middle East politics is only one part of a larger discussion of authenticity that began two centuries ago in the West.[3] Although this study will focus on four efforts to understand authenticity in Islamic terms, it seeks to place these efforts in the context of a debate about authenticity that began with Jean-Jacques Rousseau; ran through Friedrich Nietzsche, Johann von Herder, Martin Heidegger, Jean-Paul Sartre, Antonio Gramsci, Frantz Fanon, Aimé Césaire, Léopold Senghor, and Julius Nyerere; and led directly to the work of Charles Taylor.[4] A recent outpouring of literature[5] shows that any effort to dismiss authenticity as the exclusive preserve of Islamists, however much they would welcome the identification, would be wrong.

In the Third World, the demand for authenticity reflects the failure of a developmentalism that arose to cure the faults of colonialism, of a liberalism that was supposed to accompany development, and of a modernism that purported to provide the irrefutable logic upon which colonialism, developmentalism, and liberalism were based. Yet the quest for authenticity also seeks to escape the dilemmas of subjectivism, relativism, and meaninglessness that are often linked to postmodern vistas on human affairs. Advocates of authenticity assert the existence of a standard against which attitudes and behavior can be evaluated. They assert the possibility of freely chosen norms to replace the external norms derived from the dominant perspective of Western civilization. The search for authenticity, while dedicated to the destruction of modern impediments to human fulfillment, is equally committed to a program of reconstruction and refounding. It is a search for new, more robust, more legitimate foundations. The Middle East just happens to be an area of the world where foundations—the remnants of colonialism, a vicarious liberalism, a smattering of maverick socialism, a stagnant Islamic tradition, a fractured set of ethnic loyalties—have been shaky and legitimacy in short supply.

The pursuit of authenticity has gathered momentum as a product of both concrete circumstances of dissatisfaction with modernization and an intellectual critique of development and liberalism. Can this radical discontent be transformed into institutions legitimated by the seal of authenticity? Must one assume that such institutions would be illiberal and would pursue policies diametrically opposed to those linked to developmentalism? The development of the free market system appears to be pulling the world closer together. Do the politics of authenticity necessarily imply a contrary tendency toward fragmentation into more and more heterogeneous cultural groups, which have less and less in common? Does a world in search of authenticity create intolerant nationalisms, oppressive majorities, or even a "clash of civilizations," as Samuel Huntington has argued?[6] Or does it portend a coming together on new foundations as the context of authenticity itself expands toward universality? Which versions of authentic thought can be most plausibly reconciled with liberal democracy, with international tranquillity? These are some of the questions this study will address.

These are questions whose contemporary relevance is particularly acute in the Middle East. An early proponent of authenticity, Muhammad Iqbal, the Indian poet-philosopher of the early twentieth century who is widely regarded as the intellectual father of modern Pakistan, sought to discover what was authentically Eastern about himself and his society, as distinguished from the forces of Western civilization he felt pressing in upon him. This book focuses primarily on the work of Iqbal, together with that of Sayyid Qutb, the Egyptian Islamist hung by Gamal 'abd al-Nasir in 1966 for his denunciation of the Egyptian regime; 'Ali Shari'ati, the Iranian radical Islamist popularizer who died before the revolution began; and Mohammed Arkoun, the Algerian Berber who is professor emeritus of Islamic thought at the Sorbonne. They all drew upon the efforts of Western thinkers to move beyond the predominant Western mode of thinking. They describe a world so deeply marked by Westernization that the restoration of the status quo ante is unthinkable. All object to a dualistic portrait of the world: a modern, dynamic West, on the one hand, opposed to an East steeped in unchanging religious tradition, on the other—a caricature dear to Orientalists (at least according to Edward Said) and to root-and-branch modernizers but not an image congenial to the search for authenticity. The question of authenticity emerges in a world where modernization has already become so generalized that the choice between East and West, traditional and modern, has already been foreclosed. The question is one of being modern in a way I can call "my own," and it is a question that affects both West and East.

The Onrush of Modernity

Political historians treat the "modern period" in European history as beginning with the rise of national states in the sixteenth and seventeenth centuries. The modern European economy, with its origins in the revival of cities in the medieval period and the Scientific Revolution of the Renaissance, grew rapidly in the eighteenth and early nineteenth centuries as a result of the Industrial Revolution. It was only in the wake of the French Revolution, the development of political parties in the fledgling United States, and the English reforms of the mid–nineteenth century that the modern polity began to take shape. The erosion of "traditional" European society, anchored by the Roman Catholic Church, accelerated during the eighteenth and nineteenth centuries under the forces of urbanization, mass education, improved communication, and Enlightenment thinking.

The force of modern European civilization carried into the Americas and then into the rest of the world on a wave of imperialism. Napoleon's conquest of Egypt in 1798 symbolized European power but, more important, propelled Egypt and the Middle East toward wide-scale social, economic, and political changes. The Ottoman Empire, impressed with European military power, had already begun tentative efforts to modernize its army. Then Muhammad 'Ali in Egypt, profiting from the power vacuum left by French withdrawal, launched an ambitious program of imitative industrial, military, and educational reform. The rush toward modernity understood as the European way of life had begun and would not relent, both because the European powers sought economic and political advantage and because local statesmen and potentates sought to promote their own power and interests either in cooperation with the Europeans or in opposition to them. The "traditional" way of life based on agriculture, nomadism, and crafts, on landed and military elites, and on the centrality of popular religion began to erode, as had "traditional" European society a century or more before.

Resistance in the name of "tradition" largely died with the nineteenth century. Uprisings under the banner of tribal alliance, as with 'Abd al-Qadir in Algeria, or in the name of Islam, as with the Mahdiyya in the Sudan or the Sanusiyya in Libya, dumbfounded Europeans and delayed the onrush of modernity but did not block the spread of European imperialism. By the turn of the twentieth century, the power of the Vieux Turbans—those nostalgic for pre-European society—had already become marginal in most of the Middle East. In Iran, when the shah invited a foreign company to manage tobacco sales and exports, the protests of indignation came as much from modernists, such as merchants of the bazaar offended by the threat to their business or intellectuals scandalized by the exercise of despotic power, as from those ulema who were willing to play politics and defend a way of life. In fact, the actions of those ulema choosing to play activist roles rather than to follow the Shi'a tradition of political passivity (i.e., waiting for the return of the hidden Imam) may provide the best testimony of the degree to which the maintenance of tradition had already been compromised.

The social changes resulting either directly or indirectly from the projection of European power destroyed tradition, if tradition is understood to mean a lifestyle characteristic of an era before the advent of the Europeans. Life in eighteenth-century Egypt differed, of course, from patterns of living only a century before and certainly from those of the Fatimid Caliphate or those in Egypt at the moment of the Islamic invasion. Nowhere was "tradition" unchanging, nor was it utterly given to religious rather than secular logic, entirely diffuse in its allocation of roles rather than differentiated, completely particularistic in its orientation rather than universal, or wholly ascriptive rather than achievement oriented in distributing social roles.[7] Nor should "tradition" in this sense be confused with the Islamic *turāth*, a term often translated as "tradition" and used to mean the entirety of the Islamic experience; contemporary

Arab thinkers, including Hasan Hanafi of Egypt, have used the term *turāth* to represent a concept of an evolving religious tradition prescribing norms but not necessarily reflecting words recorded in archives or practices ingrained in daily life; it is constantly under construction.[8]

The proponents of *turāth* have been seeking to liberate Islam from dependence on the hadith, the so-called "traditions" or sayings of the prophet Muhammad and his close companions. They also wish to avoid linking Islam to the traditional way of life in a particular place and time such as eighteenth-century Egypt. Rather, influenced no doubt by many of the writings analyzed in this volume, scholars such as Hanafi and Mohammad al-Jabiri of Morocco seek to define an "authentic" Islamic tradition (*turāth*) that has little to do with "tradition" in the sense of a pre-European lifestyle. That pre-European "tradition" continues to recede toward the margins; the erosions of tradition in the last thirty years, whether one looks at Egypt, Iran, Yemen, Algeria, or Kuwait, may have been as devastating as the previous 150 years.

Rupert Emerson argued that the last word on European imperialism, once national independence had been achieved everywhere, would be that it had carried the benefits of Western civilization to the rest of the world.

> A plausible case can . . . be made for the proposition that the future will look back upon the overseas imperialism of recent centuries, less in terms of its sins of oppression, exploitation, and discrimination, than as the instrument by which the spiritual, scientific and material revolution which began in Western Europe with the Renaissance was spread to the rest of the world.[9]

In the long run his prediction may prove correct, but thus far, the benefits, however real if measured by such standards as economic productivity, general health of the population, and literacy rates, must be balanced against heavy costs. Radical disjuncture between old ways and new, fragmentation of lives and of families, dependence of villages on central cities and of central cities on foreign models, radical inequalities between elites prepared to profit from the new circumstances and those not yet favored in the development process, marginality of traditional minority ethnic groups in the new nation-states, political instability or political authoritarianism produced by institutional incapacity to respond to mushrooming demands, a sense of psychological alienation from traditional lifestyles (on the part of the young, the educated, the favored) and new patterns of behavior (by the old, the minorities, the countryside)—such are the costs, and the list could be extended. Most analysts of the Iranian Revolution see the forced pace of modernization, followed by a slowdown in the late 1970s, as responsible for producing dislocations, inequities, and disorientation that contributed to the regime's vulnerability.

Similarly, modernization appears to have widened rifts in Algerian society and to have contributed to the political instability of that country.[10]

The nationalist elites that assumed power in the postcolonial era did not succeed in harnessing the forces of modernization. Algeria, Egypt, Syria, Iraq, and Libya eventually embraced forms of Arab Socialism, which was supposed to produce modernism in a fashion consistent with Arab customs and traditions, but the impulses of all these regimes were fundamentally secularizing, bureaucratic, and authoritarian. None of them paid much more than lip service to Islam, and none achieved the degree of economic and social progress, much less the sort of liberal democracy, that Westernized elites had expected. The Arab defeat at the hands of Israel in 1967 signaled the failure of the progressive Arab states and opened the door to fresh demands for authenticity.

The cry for authenticity does not usually reflect a wish to halt the spread of modernity and restore a traditional society that disappeared long ago. Rather, it wants the tiger tamed; it seeks a modernity rendered less arbitrary, less vicious, more comprehensible, and above all, more productive of lifestyles people would recognize as spiritually as well as materially satisfying. At the popular level, the demand for authenticity constitutes a response to a set of social conditions produced by the onrush of modernity that has encompassed the globe in the last century. On an intellectual level, it is also a rejoinder to the ideas upon which modernization policies have been founded.

The Limits of Developmental Thinking

Modernization theory ever since Marx and Weber has assumed a single model of historical change based on rational access to objective knowledge and "de-magification of the world."[11] Daniel Lerner, working from one of the first examples of survey research to touch the Third World, posited critical psychological changes linked to improving communication as key to the transformation toward modernity.[12] W. W. Rostow wrote about stages of economic growth; his "Non-Communist Manifesto" suggested that increased world prosperity would, à la Seymour Martin Lipset, increase the probability that democratic political arrangements would occur.[13] Karl Deutsch proposed indices of social mobilization to chart the course of social change to facilitate broad comparisons.[14] Samuel Huntington added his caveat that social modernization might actually tend to generate political instability in the short run; the emergence of democracy could be expected only in a more distant future—after interludes of authoritarianism, under which institutions could be strengthened.[15] Dependence theorists took exception to such generalizations but added one of their own: that only nation-states free of dependence on the external world could achieve genuine development. Yet these theorists offered no challenge to the notion that development is a universal process, marked by increasing economic productivity, social mobility, and political participation.[16] Autonomous states would necessarily choose this one and only process.

To be sure, many scholars sought to show why different cultures might respond in different fashion to the pressures of modernization. Peoples with hierarchical authority structures in tribe and family would be in a position to decree a policy of modernization. Those cultures marked by a lack of overarching political authority, such as the segmentary cultures of precolonial North Africa, might, however, be affected more slowly than those in which centralized institutions had adopted and promulgated change. But the segmentary societies, with less centralized capacity for resistance, might adapt to change more easily. Highly fragmented states might find nation-building difficult but might find democracy somewhat easier to implement than countries where a single ethnic group dominated political institutions.[17] Peoples with high quotients of Protestant values buried in their children's literature might respond more quickly to the incentives of the market system.[18] All these observations suggest that culture conditioned, retarded or accelerated, and bent or shaped but did not divert the process of modernization from its fundamental course.[19] Marxists and non-Marxists were equally fervent in embracing the idea of a single path toward modernity, even though they differed about the appropriate instruments for pursuing that objective.

Even as universal propositions about development were being articulated, doubts had begun to arise within the West about the degree to which the chosen indicators of modernization coincided with a higher quality of life. Higher GNP at the expense of the environment began to appear an illusory gain; east-central Europe was an example. Greater homogenization of culture at the expense of regional diversity provoked protests in France, Britain, Canada, Italy, and many other so-called developed countries. The spread of television did not seem to guarantee greater citizen knowledge or citizen involvement. Crime, homelessness, and the destruction of families threatened the good life in the West, even as the Western recipe was being propagated in the East.

These unintended consequences caused theorists of development to become more cautious in their prescriptions for the Third World. To blunt criticism, they began to avoid the details of what modernization might mean by speaking of first addressing "basic needs": food, shelter, health, education.[20] But even that proposition revealed itself as laden with confusion. Does a given people need two thousand calories or does it need food that has always been deemed appropriate to its culture? What sort of shelter do people need? Does health mean access to replacement surgery or just to clean water? How much of what sort of education is enough to meet "basic needs"? Even the basic needs approach, as an effort to limit the universal prescriptiveness of development theory to the lowest common denominator of policy, foundered on the reality of cultural diversity.

What might be termed the democratic strain in development theory sought to accommodate diversity by arguing that development is self-development and therefore reflects whatever a group of people perceives as beneficial. At a Middle East Institute conference on development in 1963, Chester Bowles, undersecretary of state and then ambassador to India in the Kennedy administration, said: "The only realistic program we can promise with any hope of success is the fundamental one of helping people to help themselves evolve something they are willing to defend themselves."[21] William H. Lewis, a historian of Africa then serving in the Department of State's Bureau of Research and Analysis, in talking about northern Africa, argued for development planning that would begin at the village level. The key questions, more pressing for him than which projects should be undertaken, were: "(1) Who should establish the priorities? (2) Who is to decide what is of value in a people's traditions? (3) What means—suasion, coercion, etc.—should be applied in pursuit of modernity?"[22] Merely posing such questions implies that development might mean different things in different countries or even in different regions of the same country.

The democratic strain in development thinking resurfaced at another Middle East Institute conference on development thirteen years later, in 1976. Afif T. Tannous, consultant on Middle Eastern development for the U.S. Department of Agriculture, called for beginning development based on knowledge of the "expressed needs" of the people. "We must begin with what they want to be done," he said. The planning process must be turned upside down.[23] At the extreme, such thinking suggests there is no universal definition of development. A community might decide to "develop" by forgoing new roads, sticking with Qur'anic schools, rejecting state help with irrigation, and preferring improvement of the public water supply over a system that would pipe water into houses. It might choose to protect patterns of family, religious, and community life by forgoing the lure of material improvement.

The improbability of such a scenario betrays the weakness and even hypocrisy in the democratic strain. Most communities had no mechanism for choice: effective mayors, city councils, leaders of stature, or even persons sufficiently sophisticated to articulate options and project consequences. (Even highly trained social scientists have proved incapable of foreseeing consequences.) Where political structures might have permitted choice and action, the structures were scarcely democratic. Illiteracy made participatory democracy unknown and unthinkable. Elites in capital cities could always, therefore, act in the name of "the people," over and against local notables, who might be claiming to protect their communities.[24] National elites therefore make choices for the nation. Trained in the ways of Western social science, they have confidence in their superior knowledge of national and international circumstances and their capacity for judgment; their conceptions of development coincide quite broadly with the very universal models the "democratic strain" would seek to undercut. Even the notion of people making their own choices in democratic fashion reflects the idea that participation is an element in the syndrome of traits we regard as modern. To suggest that people must choose is already to presuppose that they would Westernize. Development that was, by hypothesis, potentially different for every culture turned out to be surprisingly uniform and thoroughly Western in inspiration, even though advocates could not agree precisely on the set of ideals that should shape it.

Ever since revolution shook Yemen in the 1960s, all Middle Eastern governments have embraced modernization, understood to mean economic growth and social mobilization, whether they called themselves socialists or capitalists, liberals or monarchists. In addition, the republican regimes have all embraced the concept of popular sovereignty. All states have, in some measure, invoked development theory to legitimate their policies, thereby endorsing widespread social change. They have sometimes reaped the benefits but, more frequently, especially in the resource-poor countries, have suffered from their own inability to produce the "good life" as defined in the West on a timetable of their own making. Developmentalism has only rarely been able to deliver the goods in sufficient quantities to persuade people to overlook increasing inequities, corruption at the highest levels, hypocrisy about adherence to democratic ideals, and general feelings of dislocation and alienation.[25]

The socialist regimes that emerged in the 1960s carried the greatest hopes of the modernizers and turned out to be the greatest disappointments. The Nasirist commitment to Arab Socialism changed the conditions of life in much of rural Egypt, but it also generated an inefficient state sector managed by an autocratic political elite that brought the country near to economic ruin in 1967, when the Israelis completed the economic devastation with a military blow. Socialism in newly independent Algeria floundered in both the agricultural and industrial sectors under the tutelage of an ideological, secular elite. In Syria and Iraq, the Ba'ath Party promised commitment both to Arab nationalism and Arab Socialism but, despite some notable economic achievements, delivered examples of separate national development under highly autocratic regimes. The Israeli victory over Egypt, Jordan, and Syria in 1967 constituted visible evidence for many in the Arab world that Arab nationalism (the United Arab Republic, Ba'athism, as well as individual nationalisms) and Arab Socialism were unequal to the task of supplying economic progress, social mobilization, and participatory politics. Not surprisingly, the responsibility for confrontation with Israel shifted to the Palestinian guerrilla groups, and the groups evoking "authenticity" began to gain support in the internal politics of Arab countries.

Although Turkey has moved haltingly toward more democratic political arrangements and Israel meets many of the criteria for labeling it a "liberal democracy," most Middle Eastern countries have responded with the maintenance or even accentuation of autocracy. The monarchies, where development theory has been combined with indigenous formulas for governing—embracing and denying theory at one and the same time—have proved stable despite what Huntington called the "king's dilemma":[26] They must modernize but must not let modern ideas reach the political realm, if they wish to retain their power. Journalists and academics consistently marvel at these regimes for their ability to survive despite predictions based in modernization theory; hypothetically, they ought to have disintegrated long ago.

The cry for authenticity arises not just because social change has swept the Third World and produced dislocation and alienation along with benefits but also because the theories that justify and legitimate such change have not provided solutions that take culture seriously. Where there has been success, it has come despite theory rather than because of it. That is, development theory itself has not provided helpful notions of what it would mean for a country to develop in ways adapted to its own culture. The impulse toward authenticity among Middle Eastern intellectuals stems in considerable measure from their dissatisfaction with mainstream development theory propounded by generalists. The twenty-year-old debate about Orientalism has served not just to crystallize this dissatisfaction but to extend the category of villains to include the students of culture, the area specialists, the so-called Orientalists.

The Critique of Orientalism

Western scholars of the Middle East have necessarily approached the object of their study from the cultural and philosophical matrix of Western civilization. This is but a truism. In the nineteenth century, their penchant for philology clearly reflected the long-standing Western interest in texts. Equipped with knowledge of languages, such as Arabic, Ottoman Turkish, and Persian, they discovered civilizations they saw as strikingly different from their own. As Edward Said has argued, their writings portrayed an Orient of their own making: mystical, sensual, timeless, despotic, exotic, eloquent, hospitable, glamorous, arational, and utterly un-European.[27] Orientalism, according to Said, magnified the gulf between East and West, a gulf only Orientalists themselves could bridge. Akbar S. Ahmed has written:

> In the very premise of orientalism something central and indispensable is absent: it is the notion of a common universal humanity embracing people everywhere irrespective of colour and creed. By denying a common humanity orientalism corrodes the spirit and damages the soul, thus preventing a complete appreciation or knowledge of other people. In this light orientalism is either cultural schizophrenia or a complex form of racism.[28]

Orientalists were interpreters of East to West, but increasingly they also become interpreters of the East to itself, as Middle Easterners studying in Europe absorbed European methodology and the philosophies in which it was embedded. The Orient's contemporary tendency to glorify its past and to denigrate its current condition reflects, in part, the work of the Orientalists.

In dissecting Orientalism, Said attacked not just the methodologies of Western social science but its epistemological foundations. Only by assuming the existence of an observable truth accessible to a mind unaffected by cultural origins could the Orientalist presume to describe the East in objective fashion. To understand the "essence" of Islamic civilization the mind must be capable of seizing the essence of things, their nature and their purpose. (Said calls Orientalism a "static system of 'synchronic essentialism.'"[29]) But Western thought since Kant, and especially since Nietzsche, has become more and more skeptical of the human capacity to know something in essentialist fashion either through reason or observation. For Said, Orientalism represented an effort by the West to master the East intellectually through the application of logic and reason, in order to discover the essence of Islamic civilization. The Western analysts drew upon the work of Muslim medievalists to substantiate their vision of a religiously dominated society, to lay out a coherent picture of Islam as a way of life.[30] In doing so, Orientalism created an iron cage in which Muslims found themselves imprisoned.

The West spawned both Orientalism and its (implicit) critics. Kant had already cast doubt on the ability of the mind to know the essence of any external object; Islamic civilization obviously constituted such an object, albeit a complicated one. Rousseau had seen the dangers of reason; in *Julie, ou la Nouvelle Héloïse* he portrayed the heroine, Julie, as trapped in a semi-utopian life that was entirely reasonable, but utterly stagnant, unfeeling, unbearable. Nietzsche moved beyond Rousseau's romanticism to denounce in more general fashion the constraints of Western logocentrism. The cry for authenticity stemmed, in part, from those like Nietzsche and Rousseau who would escape the straitjacket of tradition bolstered by deductive reason applied in universalistic, ahistoric fashion. By borrowing from Nietzsche and portraying Orientalism as an enterprise in mythmaking rather than science, Said unwittingly served the cause of those who would challenge European intellectual and political mastery of the East in the name of authenticity.

Said's attack on an essentialism underpinned by the tyranny of Western reason may go too far, however, to permit a concept of authenticity. If Orientalism is dismissed as mythmaking, might not the work of Islamic scholars—and, indeed, of anyone who suggests that ideas have validity beyond the time and place of their origin—be dismissed for analogous disregard of history? Or would Said be willing to accord greater truth value to the mythmaking of Islamic scholars who openly embrace revelation as a source?[31] If Orientalists have failed not for lack of honest, even sympathetic, effort but for their cultural origins and place in history, does this mean that a scholar situated in Cairo today is any better placed to understand what is essential to Egyptian Islam? Or does Said's analysis suggest the impossibility of any essential, foundational point of reference? And if this is so, then what would it mean to speak of any idea, practice, or belief as authentically Egyptian or Islamic? The advocates of authenticity seek to establish a secure identity for those whose political, economic, and intellectual life has fallen under the sway of the West. Said's critique of Orientalism, helpful in liberating the East from a stultifying essentialism and from rationalist, Western development theory, threatens to swamp it with a thoroughly secularist, social-scientific postmodernism. The demand for authenticity represents a desire to break with essentialist notions of truth, both traditional and modern, but not a willingness to part with the notion of truth altogether.

The Idea of Authenticity, East and West

Those who have nurtured the idea of authenticity in both East and West, from Jean-Jacques Rousseau to Charles Taylor and from Muhammad Iqbal to Mohammed Arkoun, have helped to define the boundary between what we have come to term the modern and the postmodern. All have criticized modernity for its uniformity, impersonality, superficiality, commercialism, self-interested individualism, and infatuation with technology. They see humanism gone awry in its failure to understand the historical circumstances in which humanism developed. As moderns, they see human beings as peculiar products of their circumstances and producers of their own history, but they stop short of a verdict that human beings may be utterly separate, incoherent objects in a world that defines them, driven to make choices for which they find verification only in myths of their own making.

The advocates of authenticity I have studied renounce the project of universally accepted foundations but seek to refound the human experience on a deeper, inner, nonrational source, which the individual sees as "authentic." They search for what "we" are, as opposed to what "they" would want us to be. The advocates of authenticity seek escape from the imprisoning logic of modernity without losing all restraint and succumbing to what they fear: postmodernist subjectivism and relativism. The truth they seek must be recognizable not just as "my own" (for then it might well be subjectivist) but as something that ties me to other human beings and gives us some ground upon which to build a life together anchored in legitimate institutions. To do that we must have some basis for common knowledge.

The quest for authenticity has taken both secular and religious forms. Aimé Césaire, the French dramatist-poet and politician from Martinique, and Léopold Senghor, the poet-president of Senegal from 1960–1981, looked to a concept of *négritude* that depended upon culture but not faith. The African Socialism of Julius Nyerere sought to build upon commonalities of tradition across ethnic and religious boundaries, but liberation theology, as expounded by Gustavo Gutierrez and others, sought to define an "authentic," revolutionary Christianity within the Catholic tradition to enable Latin Americans to "be themselves" and escape external constraints, including those imposed by the Catholic Church. Within Europe, Kierkegaard proposed a version of religious authenticity, but Rousseau, Nietzsche, Heidegger, and Sartre, all proponents of authenticity in one fashion or another, looked beyond religious definitions of the sacred. All proposed that to be regarded as authentic, action must reflect not universal moral judgments but individual choice within concrete circumstances.

In the Middle East, radical Islamists have come to dominate the conversation about authenticity. Like the proponents of liberation theology, they look to the past to discover an Islam they consider "authentic"—this-worldly, action oriented, conscious of circumstance—an Islam they invoke against existing political authorities, against the living tradition of Islam, and against ordinary citizens, most of whom consider themselves Muslim. This propensity for intolerance causes Mohammed Arkoun to dissociate himself from the term "authenticity," but in fact he, too, is engaged in the process of attempting to find a bedrock of truth upon which institutions can be built. For him, Muslims can find themselves by considering the totality of their historical experience, rather than just one strand of it, and by thinking of the ways in which that historical experience links them to Judaism and Christianity and, hence, to the Western world. The search for authentic Islam leads him beyond religion to the context in which religion becomes a defining aspect of the self. Arkoun seeks to avoid the secularism of modern Western thought, with its underlying contempt for religion, and the exclusivist claims of Islamist groups who would harness Islam for their own political purposes. I see Arkoun as a theorist of authenticity because he, like the Islamists, seeks not merely to contest the Western effort to define human beings without regard for cultural norms and particularities but to reestablish foundations. Like other proponents of authenticity, he critiques the foundations of modernity, but then, rejecting postmodern claims about the impossibility of objective knowledge, he seeks more limited, experiential bases on which to build.[32]

Authentic thought as I have understood it from the Western tradition and from Iqbal, Qutb, Shari'ati, and Arkoun may then be said to share the following characteristics:

1. It begins from a concept of the self as unique. Human beings are not first and foremost mind and consciousness but flesh and blood, born into particular families in particular social circumstances. Authentic thought starts from the assumption that human beings have nothing in common except the fact of their utter diversity. Yet it is assumed that there is something called the "self" (Iqbal's most famous book is *Secrets of the Self*;[33] Charles Taylor has written *Sources of the Self*[34]) that seeks by making choices to distinguish itself from that which is other than self. These choices, to be authentic, must reflect the particularities that constitute the context. In some sense, this process is inevitable. The self asserts itself in dialogue with those who surround it; it reflects the horizons of significance prescribed by the context, even if it ultimately rejects those horizons.[35] The sources of the self lie within, but the nature of what lies within necessarily takes its particularity from context.[36] Existential particularity is thus the bedrock of authentic thought.

2. Human activity has generated the diversity of circumstances that underlines human individuality. Authentic thought, in all its forms, insists that human beings fashion their history and, therefore, themselves. What makes human beings is not just what they think or believe but what they do. Sayyid Qutb distinguishes "authentic" Muslims from ordinary Muslims not so much by what they may believe or how faithfully they pray but rather by how they act (or fail to act) in the world. Muhammad and his followers created a new world by responding to revelation and circumstance. Authentic Muslims do not merely believe in justice as defined in the Qur'an; they insist on practicing it. They do not simply mouth the revolutionary principles enunciated by Muhammad; they seek to change the world in which they live by overthrowing regimes they deem unwill-

ing to implement those principles. If human beings did not bear responsibility for their own lives and therefore for human history as a whole, then it would make no sense to speak of authentic or inauthentic actions. They would be mere robots in the hands of God or tin soldiers buffeted by the forces of modernization. The question of authenticity arises from the acknowledgment of human control, however imperfect, of the course of history. Authentic thought presumes human autonomy.

3. Authentic thought constitutes a revolt against both modernity and tradition. Tradition suppresses human choice and saps human initiative. The very idea of tradition obscures the fact that the tradition was itself a product of human choice, now serving to constrain further choice. Whether it is Rousseau railing at the formal restrictions of eighteenth-century French society or the Ayatollah Khomeini trying to rewrite Shi'i history to combat the passivity and lethargy of the traditional mullah, advocates of authenticity have challenged traditions, religious or secular. But they have also challenged the secular rationalism of the Enlightenment, so essential to the concept of modernity. In its drive for universal explanations, the French Enlightenment tended to overlook the cultural origins of ideas, as Germans such as Herder were quick to point out. If universal rules defined what it meant to be a person, then what did it mean to be a German? Or for that matter, simply a person at all? Where was the authentic self? The romantics found it in mysticism, nature, action, and death. Without abandoning rationality altogether, which would conflict with fundamental assumptions about the self, the advocates of authenticity have argued rather that rationality begins to work within particular circumstances. Like the German historicists and the romantics, modern advocates of authenticity do not dismiss as untruth all that is not defensible in rational terms. They regard myth and mysticism as elements of a truth that probes beyond the reach of reason.

The process of searching for legitimacy and comparing behavior with a model constitutes an exercise in reason used to comprehend both myth and reality. The issue of authenticity cannot arise in traditional society, where tradition commands respect precisely because it is unexamined. The search for authenticity demands stripping away custom and convention, digging beneath the surface of things, getting beneath everydayness, recognizing the historicity of all ideas, seeing beneath the corrupting and commercializing impact of the market, peeling away external layers, penetrating the discreteness of objects to reveal their common being. Such a process requires the operation of reason to transform consciousness, but reason may lead to the embrace of the mystical and nonrational, the creative, the original, the heroic, and even the "traditional," which is no longer traditional by virtue of having been examined and reconstructed.

Artists and prophets, by searching deeply within themselves and by expressing themselves in language that soars beyond reason, may be the most effective communicators of authenticity. It is they who lead the way toward overcoming the dualities of mind and body, subject and object, thinking and action, reason and religion—those dualities that are the great shortcomings of the Western tradition and, especially, of the Cartesian equation of consciousness with being.

For many advocates of authenticity, death outranks consciousness as a measure of what it means to be human; in death, a human being would appear to be utterly unique, complete, unified by the stillness of both mind and body, relieved of thoughts and actions that alienate from others and from the self, at one with the universe. Advocates of authenticity, from the romantics to religious ideologues, have not shied from linking death with authentic fulfillment. Rousseau's Julie seems to have chosen that route. Heidegger wrote, "By its very essence, death is in every case mine, insofar as it 'is' at all."[37] Shari'ati described the experience of a pilgrim in Mecca: "He witnesses his own dead body and visits his own grave."[38] The result is superior knowledge of the self.

4. Authentic thought can devolve into radical individualism, cognitive subjectivism, and value relativism. Bassam Tibi has written, "If the project of modernity . . . [were] denied [as] the universal platform for a rational discourse to be shared by all humanity the result [would be] cultural fragmentation. . . . It would become difficult for people of different cultures to communicate their 'sciences' to one another, insofar as their findings would be downgraded to cultural beliefs."[39] If there is no basis for common scientific endeavor, the possibility of values that span cultures appears even more problematic.[40] And if all individuals are primordially products of unique cultures with distinctive cognitive and value principles, must not human communities be severely limited in their extent?

Taylor's answer is that individuals make choices in the context of given horizons of significance and in dialogue with other human beings without specifying how broad those horizons or dialogues might be. Iqbal tries to show that the idea of the self reflects a tie to God that ultimately links human beings. Qutb says "authentic" Muslims are those who, like the early companions of the Prophet, take stock of their circumstances and see that they must act together to achieve something. Shari'ati speaks eloquently of the pilgrimage to Mecca as a defining experience for the self but in the context of an awe-inspiring glimpse of human commonality.[41] Arkoun seeks to show that Muslims, Christians, and Jews have all emerged from a set of historical circumstances that shaped their belief structures and conditioned choices. All advocates of authenticity, having demonstrated the discreteness of the self, seek to reestablish some element of commonality and association. The notion of authenticity implies a standard or multiple standards against which behavior can be judged. The question is how broad those standards might be. Is there a single cognitive standard, as Taylor and Arkoun clearly believe? Does that standard carry into values? If value standards are multiple, do they unite Arabs and Berbers, Kurds and Turks? Do they extend to all Muslims or just to "authentic" Muslims, Shi'i or Sunni? If common cultural horizons encompass Jews, Christians, and Muslims, as Arkoun suggests, and if, as a consequence, Islam should be considered a part of the West, then how does one look for linkage between this West, more inclusively understood, and the rest of the world?

All variants of authentic thought contain an impulse toward unicity to counterbalance the underlying particularistic drive. All seek to demonstrate elements of commonality as characteristic of the human community and necessary to the human condition. These tendencies give rise to certain questions: Can some common ground for knowledge, if not values and community, be successfully reconstructed on the ruins of tradition and modernity? Are the counterbalancing forces of commonality sufficient to prevent the explosion of humanity into thousands of particularistic enclaves, each endowed with its own version of science, morality, and identity? Can the resulting cultural pluralism spawn a healthy political pluralism consistent with and supportive of liberalism, or must disorder be regarded as a more likely outcome?

The Politics of Authenticity

For the most part, exponents of authenticity, from Rousseau through Nietzsche and Heidegger to Nyerere, Khomeini, and Qutb, have been ambivalent about liberal democracy. Islamist groups in Egypt and Algeria challenge the state for what they regard as comportment and policies that are unbecoming to Muslims. Some elements are willing to profit from democratic mechanisms to promote their points of view, but their secular opponents, the incumbents, regard the Islamist challengers as illiberal in intent. The Khomeini regime maintained and even enhanced parliamentary institutions but also installed a Council of Guardians and a *faqih* (supreme jurist) to keep watch on the elected representatives. Nationalist groups in Eastern Europe and the former Soviet Union battle to establish "authentic" states; those battles have produced violence and the violation of human rights in Yugoslavia and elsewhere. The efforts to establish authentically Slovenian, Croatian, and Serbian states have destroyed the short-run prospects for some sort of liberal democracy in Yugoslavia as a whole.

By reinforcing claims to so-called primordial identities—"so-called" because they are nonetheless products of culture—the search for authenticity solidifies a basis for group action. It tends to legitimate the search for self-determination, which has, in the main, been destructive of order and intolerant of liberal democratic forms.[42] "Homogenous nation-states were revealed as a pipedream, and the illusion that liberal and national ideals could be fully accommodated within one political framework could thus be expected to fade away," wrote Yael Tamir.[43] She thinks that national group identities can be reconciled with the liberal state but only by splitting the concept of nation from that of the state; a liberal state might, in her view, encompass a set of mutually tolerant national identities. For her, national identities can provide vital emotional cement for the liberal state, but the tolerance required in her pluralist model has not been a notable characteristic of nativist and nationalist claims. Tolerance stems from a universalist perspective, in which one national identity preserves itself by tolerating others.[44]

Dominant elites have, of course, sought to use elements of authentic thought to sustain their hold on power and reinforce their nation-states. Senghor drew on *négritude*, Nyerere on African Socialism and democracy, Nasir on Arab Socialism, and Khomeini on the idea of the Islamic state. The nature of these regimes depended upon interpretations of national authenticity espoused at the expense of other conceptions. As Tamir has observed: "There is a dangerous dimension in claims about authenticity. These claims are commonly used to imply that there is one genuine interpretation of a national culture, whereas all the others are fictitious and invalid. Agents of revision are therefore likely to be called disloyal and their products inauthentic."[45] The effort to identify an authentic national culture has, in general, been linked with repression and illiberalism. The Nazi effort to define authentic German culture would be an extreme example. Some scholars, including Elie Kedourie, have argued that a misguided application of the nationalist imperative, which Kedourie links to the impulse for self-realization, sowed chaos in the Middle East by exacerbating tendencies toward particularism and rendering liberalism virtually impossible.[46] In contrast, the long-defunct Ottoman Empire, criticized by the Great Powers for violating the rights of minorities, has attracted relatively favorable mention for what, in the light of recent history, appears to be a rather successful experiment in transnational governance.

The identification of unique culture in a national setting normally fosters policies aimed at promoting authenticity. For example, the promotion of *ujamaa* (communitarian) villages in Tanzania even against the rising opposition of the peasantry reflected Nyerere's ideological position. Nasir promoted foreign policies consistent with his vision of Egypt as Arab in heritage, whereas his successor, Anwar al-Sadat, refocused Egypt on its pharaonic past and broke ranks with other Arab states by making a separate peace with Israel. Algerian nationalists promoted Arabic-language schools after independence in the hopes of reinforcing what they saw as authentic Algerian culture; Berber-speakers considered this emphasis as an act of hostility against their place in the nation-state. Revolutionary Iran insisted upon dress codes for women that coincided with a particular conception of national culture. In turning away from an Ottoman identity and eschewing Islam as a national principle, Mustafa Kemal relied on Turkishness as the basis for a state, and in doing so, he created a rationale for discrimination against Kurds. Policies inspired by the quest for authenticity have often served to augment the rights and benefits of politically dominant groups at the expense of minorities. The thrust has been illiberal.

Authenticity also tends to be undemocratic. The great champions of authenticity turn out to be heroic figures, prophets, poets, visionaries, intellectuals—those who are able to "see" beneath the surface of things and "feel" the quintessence of culture. The problem of authenticity arises because the masses have been misled into conceptions that do not coincide with their roots: They follow traditions whose origins and meaning they do not understand; they ape foreign ways without comprehending the reason for the development and meaning of such ways; they embrace universal reason without understanding its embeddedness in Western culture and its role in Western domination. Because the distinction between authentic and inauthentic implies a standard, those who understand the standard should be in a position to make decisions. There is necessarily a division between those leading "authentic" lives and those who do not. The presumption is that the inauthentic lack the right to full participation. The decision of the secularist Egyptian and Algerian regimes to deny their Islamist opposition the right to democratic participation reflects this assumption about the demand for Islamic authenticity.

Authentic thought carries a presumption of antipathy to both liberalism and democracy. Debates about Rousseau, Nietzsche, Heidegger, and Sartre often hinge on the validity of this presumption, but presumption does not, of course, constitute proof. First, no liberal democracy seems capable of dispensing entirely with appeals to nationalist sentiment; the need to develop popular affection for states based on arbitrary boundaries drives leaders to distinguish the "we" from the "they" and to define the "we" as something more than just citizens who happen to be living in a given territory. As long as the nation-state remains the primary mode of political organization, the use of authenticity may be vital to its defense.[47] For Westerners to embrace civil religion as consistent with liberalism but to denounce the use of natural religions or ethnic identities as rallying cries for political solidarity appears hypocritical. Second, not all arguments for authenticity can be equated. Rousseau is not Heidegger, and Arkoun is not Qutb. Arkoun's rejection of the "authentic" label reflects his discomfort at being categorized with Islamist ideologues. He seeks to establish grounds for refounding the Islamic experience in a fashion that does not marginalize any person or group and that implies the need for tolerance and democracy; he thinks in terms of an individual authenticity that presupposes a liberal context. Similarly, Charles Taylor expounds a version of authentic thought that he believes is consistent with liberalism. The presumption, then, must remain a presumption. This study seeks to evaluate the work of Iqbal, Qutb, Shari'ati, and Arkoun against the background of European philosophy and against this presumption of illiberal and undemocratic impulses.

၊ဗ

Despite the disimperialism of the postwar decades, the prevalent mode of thought about the non-Western world has remained thoroughly developmental and thoroughly Western in both the Middle East and the West. The development paradigm accounted for the direction of political life in countries from Latin America to East Asia. It was a paradigm on which Cold War rivals could largely agree. But then, as the Cold War itself was grinding to an end, the Iranian Revolution opened a gaping breach in theory. That event called attention to a series of phenomena that had been underrated or ignored and shifted attention toward a set of demands linked to the idea of authenticity. A world in search of development had never proved as prosperous, stable, democratic, or peaceful as proponents of the 1950s had hoped. Will a world increasingly driven by the demand for authenticity be as dangerous as many analysts of the 1980s and 1990s suggest?[48]

Notes

1. See Johannes J. G. Jansen, *The Neglected Duty: The Creed of Sadat's Assassins: Islamic Resurgence in the Middle East* (New York: Macmillan, 1986).

2. The word "fundamentalism" has generally been applied to Protestant groups with strong commitments to a literalist interpretation and implementation of text. I side with those who do not find this term helpful in describing a range of Muslim groups that have sought to make a political ideology of Islam, some of which would achieve their aim through existing governments and others of which advocate violent overthrow. I prefer the term "Islamist" to describe such groups—a term that does not suggest that they are more "fundamental" or literal in their reading of the Qur'an than other Muslims.

3. The classic studies are Lionel Trilling, *Sincerity and Authenticity* (Cambridge: Harvard University Press, 1972), and Marshall Berman, *The Politics of Authenticity* (New York: Atheneum, 1970).

4. Charles Taylor, *The Ethics of Authenticity* (Cambridge: Harvard University Press, 1991.)

5. Besides the Taylor book, recent publications include Robert Kuhry, *Authenticity: The Being of the Self, the World, and the Other* (Saratoga, Calif.: R and E Publishers, 1992); Patrizia Longo Heckle, *The Statue of Glaucus: Rousseau's Modern Quest for Authenticity* (New York: Peter Lang, 1991); Stuart Zane Charmé, *Vulgarity and Authenticity: Dimensions of Otherness in the World of Jean-Paul Sartre* (Amherst: University of Massachusetts Press, 1991); Linda A. Bell, *Sartre's Ethics of Authenticity* (Tuscaloosa: University of Alabama Press, 1989); and Alessandro Ferrara, *Modernity and Authenticity: A Study in the Social and Ethical Thought of Jean-Jacques Rousseau* (Albany: SUNY Press, 1993).

6. Samuel Huntington, "The Clash of Civilizations," *Foreign Affairs* 72, 3 (Summer 1993), pp. 22–49.

7. The reference is to Talcott Parsons and his pattern variables.

8. See, for example, Hasan Hanafi's *Al-turāth wal tajdīd* (Cairo: Al-markaz al-'arabī lil bahth wal nashr, 1980). For a comparison of Hanafi's ideas with those of Muhammad al-Jabiri of Morocco, see Armando Salvatore, "The Rational Authentification of *turāth* in Contemporary Arab Thought: Muhammad al-Jābirī and Hasan Hanafi," paper prepared for the annual meeting of the Middle East Studies Association, Phoenix, November, 1994.

9. Rupert Emerson, *From Empire to Nation* (Boston: Beacon, 1960), p. 6.

10. John Ruedy makes this point in *Modern Algeria: The Origins and Development of a Nation* (Bloomington: Indiana University Press, 1992).

11. Bassam Tibi, "Islam, Modern Scientific Discourse, and Cultural Modernity: The Politics of Islamization of Knowledge as a Claim to De-Westernization," paper presented at annual meeting of the Middle East Studies Association of North America, San Antonio, Tex., November 10–13, 1990, p. 2.

12. Daniel Lerner, *The Passing of Traditional Society* (Glencoe, Ill.: Free Press, 1964).

13. Walt W. Rostow, *The Stages of Economic Growth: A Non-Communist Manifesto* (Cambridge: Cambridge University Press, 1960); Seymour Martin Lipset, *Political Man* (Garden City, N.Y.: Doubleday, 1960).

14. Karl Deutsch, "Social Mobilization and Political Development," *American Political Science Review* 55 (September, 1961), pp. 493–514.

15. Samuel Huntington, *Political Order in Changing Societies* (New Haven: Yale University Press, 1968), chap. 1.

16. See, for example, James D. Cockcroft, André Gunder Frank, and Dale L. Johnson, *Dependence and Underdevelopment* (Garden City, N.Y.: Doubleday, 1972).

17. David Apter, *The Politics of Modernization* (Chicago: University of Chicago Press, 1965), chap. 3.

18. David McClelland, *The Achieving Society* (Princeton: Van Nostrand, 1961).

19. The work of Fred Riggs, e.g., his *Administration in Developing Countries: The Theory of Prismatic Societies* (Boston: Houghton Mifflin, 1964), looks rather exceptional in this context.

20. See Mahbub ul-Haq, *The Poverty Curtain: Choices for the Third World* (New York: Columbia University Press, 1976), and ILO International Labour Office, *Employment, Growth, and Basic Needs* (New York: Praeger, 1977).

21. Chester Bowles, "Urban and Rural Tasks in National Development," in *The Developmental Revolution: North Africa, the Middle East, and South Asia*, ed. William R. Polk (Washington, D.C.: Middle East Institute, 1963), p. 41.

22. William H. Lewis, "The Development Equation in Northwest Africa," in Polk, *The Developmental Revolution*, p. 84.

23. From my notes on the 1976 conference.

24. See Jean Duvignaud's *Change at Shebika*, trans. Frances Frenaye (Austin: University of Texas Press, 1977) for eloquent exploration of these themes.

25. See Akbar S. Ahmed, *Postmodernism and Islam: Predicament and Promise* (London: Routledge, 1992), especially chap. 3, for extended discussion of general alienation.

26. Huntington, *Political Order in Changing Societies*, chap. 2.

27. Edward W. Said, *Orientalism* (London: Routledge and Kegan Paul, 1978).

28. Ahmed, *Postmodernism and Islam*, p. 183.

29. Said, *Orientalism*, p. 239.

30. Philip Hitti, *Islam: A Way of Life* (Chicago: University of Minnesota Press, 1970).

31. I am grateful to Michael Beard for alerting me to this question.

32. See Mohammed Arkoun's *Rethinking Islam: Common Questions, Uncommon Answers*, trans. and ed. by Robert D. Lee (Boulder: Westview, 1994) for an introduction to his thought.

33. Mohammad Iqbal, *Secrets of the Self: A Philosophical Poem*, trans. R. A. Nicholson (New Delhi: Arnold-Heinemann, 1978).

34. Charles Taylor, *Sources of the Self* (Cambridge: Harvard University Press, 1989).

35. Taylor, *The Ethics of Authenticity*, chaps. 4 and 5.

36. John Riker wrote in a personal communication (June 1996): "Authenticity runs a fine line between accepting one's particular fatedness and having the freedom to be self-determining. The self-determination is an overcoming of binding social and political forces which can determine one."

37. Martin Heidegger, *Being and Time*, trans. John Acquarrie and Edward Robinson (New York: Harper, 1962), p. 287.

38. Ibid., p. 10.

39. Tibi, "Islam, Modern Scientific Discourse, and Cultural Modernity."

40. Ernest Gellner argues that the hermeneutical approach of postmodernism leads to both cognitive and value relativism. He regards cognitive relativism as counterfactual; some varieties of science have simply proven better than others, even though they may not produce absolute truth. He believes value relativism may be inescapable. See his *Postmodernism, Reason, and Religion* (London: Routledge, 1992) for a discussion of these issues from an anthropological perspective that is distinctively hostile to postmodernism.

41. See Ali Shariati, *Hajj*, trans. Ali A. Behzadnia and Najla Denny (Houston: Free Islamic Literatures, 1980).

42. See Kedourie, *Nationalism* (London: Hutchinson, 1960), p. 109: "The truth is that good government depends as much on circumstances as on a desire for freedom and there are regions of the globe which may never know its blessings. . . . In fact, it is these countries which most clearly show that nationalism and liberalism far from being twins are really antagonistic principles."

43. Yael Tamir, *Liberal Nationalism* (Princeton: Princeton University Press, 1993), p. 145.

44. I thank John Riker for calling my attention to this point.

45. Tamir, *Liberal Nationalism*, p. 50.

46. Elie Kedourie, "Minorities and Majorities in the Middle East," *Archives européenes de sociologie* 25 (1984), pp. 276–282.

47. See Tamir, *Liberal Nationalism*, p. 139.

48. See Huntington, "The Clash of Civilizations."

two

◈

Authenticity in European Thought

THE CONCERN FOR AUTHENTICITY AROSE IN EUROPE as a reaction to the Enlightenment and the Industrial Revolution. It has flourished as a result of enduring fears that social, political, economic, and intellectual modernity threatens the uniqueness of the individual, the sense of inwardness and self that escapes rational articulation, the capacity of human beings to control their destiny, and the rich diversity of European culture. From Rousseau and the romantics came a renewed sense of an inwardness that reason and reflection could help uncover but not explain. From Schiller came an emphasis on culture as a dividing force. Opposing the religious establishment and Enlightenment deism, Kierkegaard emphasized the lonely, irrational act of faith as the mark of an authentic Christian. With Nietzsche, the very idea of the self began to come unraveled in the corrosiveness of history, only to reemerge more willful and mystical, even heroic. Heidegger and Sartre both concerned themselves with the way in which the self relates to other objects and beings, seeking to reconstruct a world torn apart in the dissociation of subject and object that was characteristic of Enlightenment thinking. For them, authenticity meant not a romantic inwardness but an acknowledgment of one's freedom and responsibility in the world and of one's linkage beneath the veneer of language and reason to other human beings and the world of objects. Gramsci, from a Marxist vantage point, sought to demonstrate how the search for authenticity could foster group action.

Starting, then, with Rousseau in the eighteenth century and extending into our era, a number of Western writers have pursued the idea of authenticity, some more explicitly than others. At least four themes run through their treatments: a particularistic understanding of the human condition; an argument about human autonomy in shaping the world; radical rejection of both tradition and universal reason as adequate guides for human conduct; and an assertion of fundamental unity of being at some deeper, more "authentic" level. Of course, all these themes can be traced in some measure to earlier works; the introspection underlying the claim of particularity surely owes something to Socrates and Augustine, and Blaise Pascal had much earlier expressed doubts about either tradition or reason as sufficient grounds for truth. The notion of autonomy emerges gradually from the arguments of Machiavelli, Descartes, Hobbes, Locke, and Kant, even though authentic thought resists the universalizing tendencies of these thinkers. It is, therefore, not any one of the four elements that characterizes the case for authenticity in the nineteenth and twentieth centuries but a combination of them that does so.

The combination itself cannot be explained without reference to the Enlightenment and the Industrial Revolution and their persistent impact on Western civilization. The universalizing impact of Enlightenment thought and the leveling force of industrial and technological society have not ceased to provoke alarm in the West, and that is perhaps why those minority voices proclaiming the importance of authenticity have not disappeared. The authentic moment has been, moreover, prolonged and even revitalized by the attacks of postmodern thought on the very possibility of truth being something other than the product of human imagination. What started out as a strand of thought interested in combating one truth in the name of a deeper, more heartfelt, more primordial truth has become an effort to defend truth or truths against subjectivism, relativism, and thoroughgoing skepticism.

Particularity

The question of authenticity arose in Europe from the confrontation between individual and society. As urbanization, commercialization, and industrialization brought people into greater proximity and the bureaucratic state spread its tentacles, life seemed increasingly routinized and dominated by conventions, laws, rules, and traditions. Protestantism had sought to liberate the individual from dogma and formality but had itself fostered churches and states with new versions of official truth. The Enlightenment nurtured the spread of a new universality in science and philosophy. The greater the generality of a proposition, the greater its significance in the Enlightenment paradigm. But what, then, was the place of an individual, born into a concrete setting, endowed not just with reason but with feelings, capable of will and action even against the forces of nature and society? Kant argued that the will, though universal in its character, permitted the unique definition of the individual; by seeing the self as the defining unit, Kant opened the way for the sort of self-definition implied by cultural authenticity and nationalism.[1] Writers such as Rousseau, Wordsworth, and Schiller evoked individual authenticity by looking upon the self not as an abstraction but as a particular person grounded in an individual "sentiment of being"—hard, strong, autonomous, replete with earthy instincts and nasty thoughts. In a world drifting toward impersonality and universality, they saw themselves engaged in a struggle for the uniqueness of the individual, a struggle for authenticity.

The struggle presupposes a disposition for inwardness; a consciousness of physical as well as mental capacities; a sense of one's position in time, place, and society; a recognition of that which is undeniably felt but may not be subject to rational defense; and, in short, a concern for what distinguishes a single human being from all others. The disposition for inwardness reflects the Socratic impulse toward reflection and introspection. Yet Socrates talked more about issues of mind and spirit than about the physical circumstances of his existence. He did acknowledge his good fortune to have grown up and thrived in Athens, because his citizenship protected him in the search for truth. But with Socrates the search for truth, like the escape from the cave into the upper regions of life, always seems to carry him toward reflection on humankind, the universal characteristics of truth, and the universal sets of moral considerations that ought to guide human behavior. Socrates relentlessly pursued a truth he assumed to be universal. The particularity of his origins, his body, and even his mind in all its creativity, however decisive for Western thought, disappeared into the systematic philosophies of Plato and Aristotle, as Socrates himself might well have wished.

When Jean-Jacques Rousseau composed his *Confessions*, he claimed to be undertaking a thoroughly original project. But Augustine had already embarked on this road by providing a highly personal account of his own evolution as a particular person, endowed not just with intellect and virtue but with material existence in a concrete setting of temptation. For Augustine, there is a shamefulness about it all and ultimately an effort to renounce the particularity of existence for the undifferentiated Truth he discovers in the Christian faith. Spirit overcomes body and essence takes precedence over existence, whereas for Rousseau, reviving the confessional style some 1,300 years later, there is no escape from such individuality.

Rousseau was proud of himself, defects and all; his heroine, Julie, in *Julie, ou la Nouvelle Héloïse*, seems utterly without defects, but she is not without a sharp sense of her self, which she tries desperately to submerge in an effort to please her parents, to rationalize her entire household, and to placate her lover. She embraces both reason and faith in an effort to overcome her instinctual, passionate, physical, natural self, and when she fails to kill that self in such fashion, she kills it by falling into a stream and contracting a fatal illness. Unlike Socrates and Augustine, Rousseau sees inwardness as not simply a route toward a rational truth but as a fundamental test of the truthfulness of rationality. Lionel Trilling has written:

> The sentiment of being is the sentiment of being strong. Which is not to say powerful: Rousseau, Schiller, and Wordsworth are not concerned with energy directed outward upon the world in aggression and dominance, but, rather, with such energy as contrives that the center shall hold, that the circumference of the self keep unbroken, that the person be an integer, impenetrable, perdurable, and autonomous in being if not in action.[2]

Schiller argued that the Greeks had achieved a balance between universality and particularity: "Combining fullness of form with fullness of context, at once philosophic and creative, at the same time tender and energetic, we see them uniting the youthfulness of fantasy with the manliness of reason in a splendid humanity."[3] In its efforts to surpass the Greek effort, the Enlightenment had destroyed such balance in favor of the cultivation of abstract, universal ideas, Schiller said; the sensuousness of the Greeks had been lost. What he calls the speculative spirit, in its search for permanence in the realm of ideas, had become "a stranger in the material world."[4] But where then is individuality and imagination? He called for aesthetic education as a means of restoring the whole person, as a way to keep sensuous and formal impulses within bounds, the sensuous being based in existence and the formal, in the mind. This, he argued, is the basis for wholeness and creativity. The temporal quality of human life ensures uniqueness. And indeed, for Heidegger, death represents the most utterly personal, utterly authentic moment in a life. At that moment each life is a finite set of points, complete, unique. To live authentically means to live in full awareness of the temporal quality of human existence and the fundamental fact of death. "By its very essence, death is in every case mine, insofar as it 'is' at all."[5] And for Heidegger, it is anxiety in the face of death that most thoroughly reveals an individual's "ownmost" potentiality for Being. Only in confronting the utter particularity of existence—its "thrownness," as Heidegger put it—can the human self understand its commonality with other beings.

Particularity comes not just from the inside—from the "heart of darkness," the deep, prerational impulses of the self—but from the particularity imposed by others. In *Anti-Semite and Jew*, Sartre argued that Jews are necessarily Jews by virtue of the way the rest of the world, and anti-Semites most especially, view them. Authentic Jews respond not by denying the uniqueness attributed to them but by embracing the particularity. "In a word, inauthentic Jews are those persons whom others regard as Jewish and who have chosen to flee before that intolerable situation."[6] Thus Jews, like everyone else, enjoy freedom to embrace or to deny the identity that others have fashioned for them. Where anti-Semites go wrong, according to Sartre, is in claiming that Jews are essentially different; democrats, in contrast, insist that human beings are essentially the same. But Man as archetype does not exist, wrote Sartre—only concrete individuals and peoples who choose who they are as a function of their circumstances exist.[7] He suggests that liberalism must learn to accommodate concrete particularity by dropping its assumptions about a universal, unchanging human nature.

These sources of particularity—inwardness, the sentiment of being, the defining act of faith, the temporal quality of human existence, the qualities imparted by social circumstances—may contribute to group identity. The validity of any proposition depends first upon its truthfulness with regard to a single individual; unless a way of life is genuine for someone, it cannot be genuine for all. Deductions from human nature lead only to abstractions that lack meaning for the individual. Because every thrust toward authenticity incorporates nonrational elements, the validity of that effort does not necessarily extend beyond a single individual. Any extrapolation to a larger group depends upon induction from the particular with constant testing against the feelings, instincts, inspiration, and will of those concerned. Each individual must discover and verify the genuineness of apparent commonality or, quite to the contrary, discover that individuality must be defined against the group.

Opposition to alien forces provides an initial, apparent bond. A strong current of nativism runs through theories of cultural authenticity.[8] Foreigners and foreign domination constitute a first obstacle to authenticity and a first rallying point for the protagonists of revolution. Nationalism, with its claim that each people has the right to govern itself, is both a consequence of particularistic thinking and a further impetus for achieving group identity. But the physical liberation from foreign domination can only constitute the first step, insofar as foreign ideas continue to contaminate a people. For example, Gramsci applauds Machiavelli as a revolutionary who wanted an Italy free of foreign control, but he, Gramsci, insists that liberation must penetrate the hegemony of foreign ideas. Fanon calls for the expulsion of not just the colonialists but of the very idea of colonialism, with its insistence on the superiority of foreign ways. The struggle against foreigners must thus become a fight against the indigenous bourgeoisie as the perpetrators of foreign lifestyles and the servants of foreign economies. Heidegger suggests that truth cannot be broader than one's own people;[9] the problem is not only to delimit that people but to identify the most indigenous, genuine, reliable elements within that group to serve as the guideposts for the reconstruction of the society. The search accentuates the particularistic tendencies.

Any selection of a beacon group proceeds from a set of values that may be more or less restrictive. For Nietzsche, it is the extraordinary, philosophical, creative thinker who is able to throw off the chains of tradition and reason and to chart the way toward overcoming humanity as it has been understood. Legitimated by diverse theories, these groups elaborate a new matrix of values—new because they are dissynchronous with present practice but old because they are rooted in a past—for the society as a whole. For a thinker like Gramsci, it is the masses who retain the closest touch with their heritage and who understand their own needs.

Paradoxically, however, the particularity of the new cultural matrix varies inversely with the restrictiveness of the beacon group. The more egalitarian versions of authentic thought must struggle to break out of provincial, particularistic outcomes, whereas the more elitist versions, capable of producing ideas of greater generality, face the need to recruit nonelites to their cause, that is, to break out of the particularistic criteria by which the beacon group is designated. For example, Gramsci sees veracity as linked to numbers. What is correct for a people or a group of people is that which most of them perceive to be correct. But Gramsci also acknowledges that ordinary people tended to accept passively the "common sense" (often founded in the most superstitious sort of Catholicism) of their village and region. The great ideas elucidated by Benedetto Croce and other leading Italian liberals have left them unscathed. For Gramsci, the problem was to conceive of some movement of the masses from the "common sense" of a distant past toward the "good sense" of the present, without violating his own rule that only the people themselves can pass judgment on the authenticity of the solution. He therefore emphasizes the role of intellectuals who propose but also listen and the role of a party that responds as well as acts. Like others, he acknowledges that the Italian South deserves policies that may be inappropriate for the North. But therein lies his problem, for the preferences of Sicilians may not resemble those of Calabrians, and village X may not recognize the same "authentic" world as village Y. Where does the assurance lie that any of these groups will in fact be willing to part with the truths that currently regulate their lives? The future depends on the least reflective, least creative, least rational strata and depends upon the capacity of these strata to imagine a future diverse from the present and to struggle actively toward that image. Elites may propose, encourage, cajole, listen, and repropose, but only concrete individuals, neighborhoods, villages, and cities can impart the seal of authenticity to any set of social arrangements. By definition, for Gramsci, an authentic solution must enjoy class if not universal acceptance; but his thought provides no more guarantees than does the Communist Manifesto that preexisting particularities will dissolve into class consciousness at the behest of enlightened intellectuals.

Nietzsche represents the antipode of Gramsci. Far from viewing the "rabble" as the arbiters of truthfulness, he regarded them as incapable of penetrating the fog of illusion, of risking danger, of creating new values and acting autonomously—finding them incapable, in short, of the sort of behavior he regards as most genuinely human. The approval of numbers adds nothing to the authenticity of such activity. In fact, he said,

> One has to get rid of the bad taste of wanting to be in agreement with the many. "Good" is no longer good when your neighbor takes it into his mouth. And how could there exist a "common good"! The expression is a self-con-tradiction: what can be common has ever but little value. In the end it must be as it is and has always been: great things are for the great, abysses for the profound, shudders and delicacies for the refined, and, in sum, all rare things are for the rare.[10]

For Nietzsche, only the few achieve the full potential of which human be-ings are capable by overcoming the illusions that enslave them. Only free spirits can muster the understanding, courage, and will to break not sim-ply with the provincialism of morality in a given place and time but even with the provincialism of Western thought, predicated upon an imagined realm of ideals and truth that takes its strength in the fact that its founda-tion cannot be verified. Only the few can understand the internal contra-diction of the *ratio*, the unprovability by logic of the supremacy of logic. Even more important, only the few can confront the repugnant result of such reflections: the "eternal recurrence of the same." Escaping from the illusions of the past, the few discover that there is in fact no escape from either illusion or the past. Only those of the greatest will and courage can act creatively without assurance of a future different from past or present. It is thus the precious few, according to Nietzsche, who can rise above the temporal, geographical, and social particularity of the human condition, but what they discover, far from a recipe for the salvation from mankind, is that there is nothing else beyond individual volition, the will to power, that can scarcely be anything but particularistic.

Nietzsche's judgment about the insensitivity of the masses led him to-ward an elitism from which escape is perhaps not possible. For him, cul-tural authenticity and individual authenticity appear to be irreconcilable. To dilute ideas for mass consumption out of hypocritical concern for hu-man equality is to invite decadence. Nietzsche reproached Western civi-lization for engaging in such an enterprise at the expense of those intellec-tual elites capable of genuine creativity. Empathy for the less fortunate has produced only mediocrity. The elites must know how to suffer and to endure the suffering of others in the name of cultural achievement, which only emerges from challenge and stress. But Nietzsche offers no assurance that even elites, driven by their will to power, will rally to a single set of values. Instead, if Nietzsche offers any vision of politics, the cohesion of society would seem to depend upon forcible imposition of a single will, the greatest will, which nonetheless reflects a single, arbitrary vision of what it means to be human. Born in flight from the overpowering force of tradition and logic, nurtured in violent opposition, Nietzsche's individualism may depend upon coercion to fend off anarchy. The will to power, whether it produces tyranny or anarchy, seems to preclude any reduction of human estrangement.

The basic premise about the particularity of the self thus leads toward the delimitation of groups, themselves distinct by virtue of their innermost sense of themselves, their common imagination of themselves, their position in time, their perceptions of each other. But these groups necessarily depend upon individuals or subsets of themselves to provide direction, to indicate the nature of "authentic" values at the group level, unless one is to presuppose democratic choice. But can the "will of all," with its confusion of ideas and interests, ever be authentic? Can it ever produce truth? Can a group maintain its particularity in the everyday, interest-driven, compromise-oriented drive to create a majority in democratic competition? Among the writers most committed to authenticity in the Western tradition, only Sartre and perhaps Gramsci appear to think so. To construct a liberal theory on particularistic foundations is a challenge. To reconcile individual and cultural authenticity may be impossible.

Radicalism

The demand for individual authenticity requires a struggle against the forces that betray one's nature, originality, creativity, and being. Those forces have been identified with tradition, understood as "the handing on of formed ways of acting, a formed way of living, to those beginning or developing their social membership."[11] Proponents of authenticity tend to see human beings as prisoners of tradition, victims of the social rules by which they are constrained to live, mere puppets of conventions established in a distant and irrelevant past. Authenticity means liberation from such restraints and hence from tradition as a binding set of social practices inherited from the past. That liberation may nonetheless be conceived by proponents of cultural authenticity in the name of another concept of tradition, one that is justified by an "assumption of previous performance" in some time period remote from the present.[12]

In the *Persian Letters*, Montesquieu interlaced his commentary on French life with scenes from Usbek's harem in Isfahan. With Usbek himself absent and eunuchs in command, the fetters of harem life, the boredom of the women, the unnatural limitations on the activity of human beings become unbearable. Not even augmentations in the level of repression can restore a world to which Usbek himself, having glimpsed the hurly-burly of Europe, seems reluctant to return.[13]

Montesquieu contrasted the male-dominated world of traditional society, exemplified by the stultifying languor of the female harem, with the vigorous, egalitarian life in Paris, where the industrious could aspire to drive more horses than the noble of birth. There a person could be autonomous, follow his own instincts, profit from his own efforts, be his own person. Modern society appeared masculine by traditional standards, even though women could play a much wider range of roles there; traditional society—portrayed as the harem—connoted passivity, subordination, and dependence.[14]

Montesquieu's caricature of tradition outdoes the Parsonian model in its exaggerated simplicity. All societies, including the Persian society of the eighteenth century, seem to include elements that both Parsons and Montesquieu might acknowledge as modern. The growth of those elements might eventually mitigate the unnaturalness that Montesquieu saw in the traditional world. But for Rousseau, as well as for most of the theorists of authenticity who follow him, Montesquieu erred in thinking that capitalism, urbanization, and enlightenment would liberate humankind. Instead, the advent of modernity replaced one set of chains with another, the new set perhaps more devastating and insidious because anchored in reason rather than repetition.

The reign of the eunuchs in Usbek's harem appears patently unnatural to enlightened European eyes; the condition of the oppressors itself represents the deformity of mankind. In *Julie, ou la Nouvelle Héloïse*, Rousseau took pains to persuade his readers of an analogous cruelty and artificiality in the hierarchical, male-dominated society that prevents Julie from marrying her lover, Saint-Preux, who does not share Julie's noble status. Her father has already decided her fate. Julie loves against her conscious will; Saint-Preux cannot shake his love for Julie, despite his realization that it immobilizes him. But Julie cannot join him without doing violence to her father, to whom she feels a heavy obligation of traditional loyalty, notwithstanding her knowledge of his adultery and evidence of his cruelty. She herself remains prisoner of the traditional mindset; her plight seems as unreasonable and hopeless as that of Usbek's wives in Isfahan.[15]

However, Rousseau found no relief in modernity. To escape the potential wrath of Julie's father and upon Julie's orders, Saint-Preux travels from his native Switzerland to cosmopolitan Paris. Far from being impressed with the liberating impact of commercial activity, he finds people obsessed with trying to be what they are not. Parisians worry about how they dress, how they ride, and how they talk but not about who they are, where they are going, or what life means. The ultimate humiliation for

Saint-Preux comes when he accepts an invitation from officer friends to meet "ladies." He writes to Julie that he had doubts about the house when he arrived but hated to offend. Then the "water" with which he diluted his red wine turned out to be white wine, and the "ladies" obliged his "friends" by making sure that he compromised himself. He longed for the simple, natural life of the countryside, though not for the social strictures of rural society.[16]

Cannot reason discern a middle ground between the oppressiveness of tradition and the alienating frivolity of the modern city? Julie's designated husband, de Wollmar, turns out to be a reasonable man. Within a traditional marriage, he and Julie seek to construct the perfect household, where the management of the servants, the farming of the land, the education of the children and the interaction of family members are as honest, natural, and authentic as possible, consistent with the need for social order. Knowing of Julie's natural love for Saint-Preux, de Wollmar has him summoned to the estate and offered a permanent place in the household. He expressly leaves the two lovers alone to give them the confidence that they can acknowledge and continue their feelings for each other without, thanks to their own self-imposed autonomous and hence authentic restraint, causing Julie to violate her marriage vow to de Wollmar. In letters to an English friend and protector, Saint-Preux, given to philosophical pursuits, extols the logic and naturalness of it all.[17] And Julie herself plans to lay the final brick in this magnificent edifice by trying to satisfy Saint-Preux's sexual needs by encouraging him to marry another occupant of the household, her intimate friend and companion, Claire, who has lost her husband. All would live under the same roof; both love and propriety could be preserved.

It did not work. Julie herself could not bear it. Perhaps it was the thought of her lover married to Claire; perhaps it was the growing realization that, once completed, the rational world she had helped construct snuffed out the spontaneous, creative, physical feelings for Saint-Preux she had come to identify as the essence of her being. She begins to see that her creation has condemned her to a routinized life that satisfies her every ostensible need and desire but leaves her profoundly alienated from herself. "Happiness bores me," she says, not long before turning to suicide for relief. It was in some sense the only authentic act of self that remained within her powers. (Not surprisingly, the Greek root of the word authenticity means "to have full power over; also to commit a murder."[18]) Julie dies "happy to have bought at the price of my life the chance to love you forever without wrongdoing and to tell you so one more time," as she says in a last letter to Saint-Preux.[19]

For Rousseau, then, tradition represents only a symptom of a more general dilemma for the sensitive being who would be true to himself or herself. Society, any society, however modern and rational in its construction, traps individual human beings, even those responsible for its construction, in a web of restraints. Insofar as those restraints remain external, an individual may retain a sense of self-control and efficacy through struggle. But insofar as the limits are internalized, both in the perfectly traditional society and in the perfectly modern one, the struggle must be carried on within the individual. Modern human beings liberate themselves from the chains of a system whose legitimacy stems either from infinite repetition or from charismatic creation. They can define themselves against the mindless, foppish social conventions of the emergent capitalist economy but be nonetheless reduced in their essential freedom by the rationality of the institutions they are capable of generating. The internalization of the new norms produces either passive, uncreative, self-abnegating compliance or open revolt against the self as a product of the society.

European advocates of authenticity came to see reason as buttressing the social fabric in which human beings have imprisoned themselves. According to Rousseau, human beings remain "free, healthy, good and happy" as long as they remain self-dependent. The need to live in proximity to others lures them into a division of labor and the construction of social relations in which inequality, dominance, and subordination become essential characteristics.[20] The justification for these alienating relationships emerges in a set of philosophical ideas that distracts human beings from their plight by focusing their attention on another world, the world of ideals as opposed to reality, of essence as contrasted with existence, of subject as opposed to object.

For Sören Kierkegaard, Catholic traditionalism and Protestant rationalism constituted separate but equally effective dampers on authentic Christian faith. The Catholic tradition insisted that faith could be routinized and ritualized, depriving it of the qualities of individual choice and risk epitomized by the life of Jesus. He wrote about the age of revolution as a reaction against "fossilized formalism, which, by having lost the originality of the ethical, has become a desiccated ruin, a narrow-hearted custom and practice."[21] He surely meant the comment to apply to the Catholic Church, among other institutions of prerevolutionary Europe. Protestantism, by contrast, subordinated religion to reason, action to thought, and individual acts of faith to universal principles. In a long discussion of Abraham and his decision to sacrifice Isaac, Kierkegaard argued that Abraham exemplified Christian behavior by stepping beyond the universal, by following his faith against his reason.[22] Authentic Christian action does not depend on either reason or tradition, except insofar as the example of Jesus in defying both reason and tradition is regarded as exemplary.

Nietzsche argued that Western philosophy, beginning with Plato, gradually eroded the creativity and plurality of ancient Greek drama and myth with its ever-increasing insistence on cause-and-effect analysis and monotheism. The belief in cause and effect leads to a vision of history in which man has little control or, at best, few options; it renders seemingly inexorable and hence acceptable the process by which custom and institutions have deprived human beings of their self-dependence. Monotheism reinforces the notions of ideals, essence, and subject by proposing a realm of absolute truth; little does it matter, according to Nietzsche, whether that realm be accessible by faith alone, by reason in faith, or by reason alone. The internal contradiction of the Western *ratio* and its preoccupation with the search for the truth, which by its own methods can be shown to be unattainable, reveal tradition for what Nietzsche took it to be: the mask that Western man has imposed on himself (or rather that some men have forcibly imposed on others) to sustain a set of social arrangements and render legitimate a distribution of power.[23] The question for Nietzsche, and for other theorists of authenticity, is whether human beings can live without the traditional myths that have, while suppressing their independence and creativity, saved them from despair. What would be truthful behavior in the absence of customary truth? How can one accede to an authentic existence when the tentacles of inauthenticity reach to the core of the reasoning process one is accustomed to use to seek solutions and when the susceptibility of such a probe to reasonable solution may itself be an illusion of the Western tradition?

If traditional perspectives took their strength primarily from their logical persuasiveness, then they would be susceptible to modification by superior evidence and argument. However, tradition itself depends not on reason but on previous performance "or the assumption of previous performance"[24] and on some element of force for its preservation. Its principal practitioners, the masses, know no philosophy but behave as they do from common sense, which includes a healthy sense of not rocking the boat or stepping out of line. The intellectuals who defend any traditional order argue for its general utility, which inevitably includes their own position in the social hierarchy.[25] And even if they advocate reform, they employ tools selected from the workshop of the dominant intellectual tradition, all products of an array of forces protective of the existing order of things. Reformism strengthens the status quo by reducing the need for coercion in the maintenance of order but does not, by definition, challenge the coercive foundation of any dominant perspective.

The pursuit of authenticity thus requires escape not just from the prevailing intellectual tradition and not simply from the coercive power of the state but rather from a combination of mutually reinforcing ideas and forces. Nietzsche argued that violence permitted the installation of the *ratio* as the dominant mindset and continued to sustain both the linear view of causality and the distinction between essence and existence. The

Athenian state, the Roman Empire, the Catholic Church, the divine monarchies of early Europe, and even the liberal regimes of the nineteenth and twentieth centuries had inculcated the *ratio* and been sustained by it. Nietzsche asserted that the idea of the subject as an actor in history obscures the domination of thinking over other human instincts, of mind over body, of the spiritual over the material world, of master over slave.[26] The solution, Nietzsche suggested, lies not in a reversal in which the material world takes precedence over the spiritual or the slaves become the new masters but in overcoming the dualism that marks the Western tradition since Plato. Such a tradition, violently established and coercively sustained, can only be overcome by violence: Nietzsche's "free spirit" takes his liberty by acts that are repugnant and deleterious to the existing order. That which the society defines as evil necessarily becomes good to the free spirit, who has not escaped the pattern of retribution that Nietzsche saw as characterizing the struggle of master and slave through history. The free spirit still remains to that extent a prisoner of the history he seeks to escape. Violence is but a first step, however necessary, toward the liberation of the self.[27]

Not all theorists of authenticity accord equal importance to violence, but the need for some measure of violence emerges from the imprisoning nature of a tradition. For example, Fanon argued that the native can escape nativeness only through physical attack on the perpetrator of the violence suffered. Physical repression produces mental submissiveness that can only be overcome in acts of mental and physical aggression. Violence, in Fanon's eyes, can be the midwife in the rebirth of the genuine personality of the colonized. Rousseau, by contrast, suggested both the inevitability and the futility of violence; Julie's suicide culminated, and ended, her search for authenticity. Gramsci, convinced of the ultimate need for violent overthrow of the Italian liberal state, cautioned nonetheless that a "war of maneuver" could not be successful without prior "tactical battles" against the prevailing common sense of the masses. He felt that the great war of maneuver might serve little purpose unless it had first acquired meaning through the search for a new common sense. Seen as a partial cure for the psyche in Fanon and as a defeat for the self in Rousseau, violence constituted for Gramsci, as for Nietzsche, both a part of the logic of struggle and a fundamental characteristic of the situation from which human beings seek liberation.

Martin Heidegger, whose discussion of the word "authenticity" in *Being and Time* touched off much of the subsequent debate about the concept, has often been regarded as a conservative, a defender of tradition, though certainly not a defender of the philosophical tradition of rationality. But W. R. Newell has argued that Heidegger, too, should be seen as a "revolutionary." Tradition comes to constitute the rationale for everyday life, which is filled with routine, repetition, idle chatter, ordinariness. Tradition in this sense contradicts the very forces that created tradition.

> The community's reassumption of its destiny requires a new kind of radicalism which is both backward- *and* forward-looking. It requires the rejection of all existing political, social, cultural, and moral bonds in the name of a contentless communitarianism; a wholly abstract notion of "the people" rooted in a past so primordial as to bear little if any resemblance to what is regarded in everyday life, by custom, public, and intellectual opinion, as the people's past history.[28]

The appeal to the "primordial" is not, of course, an appeal to reason; like Nietzsche, Heidegger struggled to find language capable of describing the human condition without subordinating it to reason. Authenticity is a mode of being distinguished both from traditional behavior and from ethical conduct based in universal reason.

The call for authenticity is a call for struggle against an existing social order seen as inimical to the development of the true self, indifferent to mankind's potential, and repressive of human effort to realize that potential. That struggle requires volition as an antidote to passivity, action as opposed to mere thought, and even violence as opposed to persuasion, because the pillars of existing society, erected and sustained by force, cannot otherwise be moved. Against a status quo reflective of efforts at social engineering and dependent upon a cultural hegemony defended by Western-educated intellectuals, the struggle appears no less protracted and no less violent than when waged against a society steeped in tradition. The call to authenticity is a summons to struggle against the fatalism of the traditional world and against the passivity of a world swept toward modernity.

Autonomy

On the practical level, authentic thought calls for active struggle against an existing social order. Through the quest for authenticity, human beings emerge from their passivity to become architects and masons of their world. They seek to liberate themselves from a past of their own making that has escaped their control, to fashion a future that is tailored to their own needs, instincts, and wishes. In the process, they transform themselves. The practical call for radical change thus presupposes a philosophical understanding of history as a product of human action and of human nature as subject to manipulation from within and without. In a mechanistic world, human volition has no place, and the question of how human beings may seek their genuineness lacks meaning. In a world knowable only by social scientific method, man's role becomes imitator rather than creator, object rather than subject, dependent player rather than autonomous actor, victim rather than protagonist. In contrast, advocates of authenticity necessarily see human beings as autonomous and creative protagonists of history.

Fouad Ajami has noted that the determinism inherent in the dominant strand of Western thought, predicated on the presumed inevitability of human progress, resembles a predominant fatalism in the Islamic world of the past several centuries. "Both want to spare men and women the agony of choice and experience," he has written.[29] The search for authenticity cannot be reconciled with either religious fatalism or social determinism. Authenticity calls for choice and will to overcome the clutches of the inauthentic life; if existing conditions result from the inexorable forces of God or nature, then the question of their authenticity does not even arise. If inevitable, how could they be regarded as anything but genuine? Concern for authenticity reflects a conviction that the human will shapes human destiny.

The emphasis upon human agency permits comparison between ideas marked by contrasting views of metaphysics. The search for authenticity may be conducted either within a context of revealed truth or in a context of skepticism; in both cases, authentic conduct depends upon truthful action even though, and especially because, human beings do not have access to the truth, either because truth resides with God alone or because no belief in universal truth can be sustained. Authentic thought tends to emphasize human volition as the sole force of history. According to the theists, God is separate from human beings, who must strive to feel God's presence and exercise their powers of reflection to understand God's word, who must analyze their place in society and history and try to effect change in themselves and the world. Since history is driven by individuals who may themselves be no more than contradictory packages of instincts who act without precise external guidance, one cannot foresee the behavior of any individual, much less that of a society.[30] Reason is vital to the discovery and pursuit of truthful modes of conduct, but it cannot reveal the truth; human beings reason from a perspective inside history, from within a perspective conditioned by the historical moment. To suppose them capable of lifting themselves beyond history is to make human beings into God, a supposition that conflicts both with the initial assumption that humans and God are separate and with a skeptical view of universal truth. The radicalism of the authentic persuasion requires human autonomy.

Conceptions of human beings as builders of their world, without perfect reasoning powers to discern the optimal course of action, foster an emphasis on unity of thought and action. If human beings bear responsibility for their fate, then they must exert themselves to know the truth, whether that means seeking contact with God or wrestling with the fact that there may be no Truth. Under the same assumptions, they must put into practice those ideas that reason or inspiration may permit. Not to do so gives advantage to those who drift passively and thus betray their authentic, creative natures. Thought is an initial action. Action taken without reference to thought sacrifices the human ability to control fate. Human beings would once again become objects rather than subjects. Thought and action cannot be distinguished, because human beings are both subjects and objects: To understand them as subjects alone is to remove them from the social conditions that impinge upon their freedom; but to emphasize only their condition as objects of history is to deprive them of any freedom whatsoever.

Orthodox Marxism, with its insistence on inevitability and its relegation of thought to the realm of superstructure, is incompatible with assumptions about autonomy found in authentic thought, but the writings of the early Marx have become an important element in the attempt to reconcile subjectivity and objectivity. Marx started from an observation about the creative potential of human beings. Human beings realize their creativity through work; they are the work they do and become alienated from themselves as they relinquish control over the tools needed in production and, as a result, over the objects of their labor. To realize their potential, human beings must struggle to regain control of production and of themselves. The wheel of history turns relentlessly because individual human beings, seeking to overcome their alienation, move it forward with their own efforts to understand their predicament and act on the basis of their understanding. Their consciousness is necessarily "determined, finite, rooted in a preconstituted social world," not reflective of an external, general truth. But as conscious agents, they are a "dynamic, creative driving force of social transformation,"[31] capable of altering their own being by virtue of their capacity to change the circumstances that condition their conceptions of self. Reunited with the product of their activity, human beings achieve authenticity.

This is the Marx who inspired Gramsci to reassert the place of conscious, reflective, organized will in revolutionary theory, against the mechanistic interpretations of both idealism and orthodox Marxism. For Gramsci, the fact that human beings create their own history implies the absence of any history without human beings, as actors, writers, or at least storytellers. Every metaphysical conception, every version of human history, every political ideology can be traced to human activity under a specific set of conditions themselves reflective of previous thought and action. No ideas, including the orthodox Marxist insistence that only the evolution of material forces shapes class struggle and the flow of history, escape their ties to an epoch and circumstance.[32] To argue for the inevitable triumph of the proletariat implies the existence of some observer placed beyond human history, the god that neither Gramsci nor orthodox Marxists was prepared to accept. Moreover, relying on a misplaced faith in dialectical materialism and underestimating the extent to which dominant thought patterns had instilled passivity, Marx missed a key step in the revolutionary struggle: the need to foster a will for change.

Gramsci manifested faith not in the objective processes of history but in the existence of an individual subject, distinct from all other subjects and capable of understanding that distinction. (Gramsci called "objective" the verdict of multiple subjective appraisals.) He based his case for autonomy not on necessity but on plausibility. "Is it better," he asked,

> to think without having critical awareness, in a disjointed and haphazard way—that is, to participate in a conception of the world "imposed" mechanistically by the external environment, by one of the many social groups in which one is automatically involved from the moment of entry into the conscious world; or is it better to elaborate one's own conception of the world, consciously and critically, and thus, in conjunction with this work of your own brain, to choose one's own sphere of activity, participate actively in the production of world history, to be guided by oneself and not to accept passively and supinely the imprint of the outside world on one's own personality?[33]

Those capable of such reflection—the intellectuals—must reexamine the hegemony of their day, the ideas that sustain the configuration of power in a given society and a given time. With assistance from the intellectuals, ordinary people can reassess the "common sense" by which they live. If offered new perspectives, they will plausibly prefer those suited to their own age, condition, and personality. They will prefer "good sense"—active pursuit of a more authentic society—to the prevailing "common sense," based on routine and folk religion and conducive by its wisdom of passivity to the maintenance of the old hegemony together with the political order it sustains. Independent thought is thus the first concrete act of will in the construction of a new world and a new human species.

Not surprisingly, Gramsci often wrote of his regret that the Protestant Reformation and the Protestant ethic had not spread to Italy. He argued that a Protestant Italy would have been more likely to follow Machiavelli's advice by thinking and doing for itself.[34] Such an argument leaves him far from such writers as Pascal, Gutierrez, Qutb, or Khomeini—all exponents of an authenticity rooted in religious belief. But these writers do share Gramsci's emphasis on autonomy and his opposition to tradition.

The theme of autonomy in authentic thought runs even deeper in the existentialist strain than in the Marxist tradition of Western thought.

Kierkegaard's characterization of the "present age," his age, derided its passivity: "The present age is essentially a *sensible, reflecting age, devoid of passion, flaring up in superficial, short-lived enthusiasm and prudentially relaxing in indolence*" [italics in original].[35] For Kierkegaard, Christianity requires an act of individual will. Individuals must choose it. God speaks to all human beings, but he is so remote that human beings cannot know him or understand him. Truth is in this sense unavailable; neither aesthetic nor ethical wisdom is reliable, but human beings can nonetheless choose through a leap of faith to do God's will. Reason cannot ground their choice. In doing so they reject both radical optimism that individual action cannot compromise God's benevolent plan for the universe and nihilism, which would in its radical form assert that human actions do not matter, either.[36] For Kierkegaard, authentic Christian behavior springs from the acceptance of individual responsibility for both individual and collective destiny.

Jean-Paul Sartre's version of existentialism makes the acceptance of individual freedom the principal criterion of authenticity. Freedom comes from human consciousness, which provides the ability to transcend one's own physical, factical nature, in and of itself meaningless and even absurd, as well as one's social situation. Sartre himself grew up within bourgeois constraints that, like Rousseau, he identified with artificiality and the suppression of individual feeling. Like Rousseau, he turned to nature as a remedy, but unlike Rousseau, he found absurdity in the natural state of things and, again unlike Rousseau, he linked human freedom with the purposeful confrontation with nature: "Sartre's path to existential authenticity requires him to navigate between the dual threat and promise that lie within both civility and nature. Civility can be either a prison of bad faith or a refuge from the onslaught of nature. Conversely, what is nature can be a source of nausea that engulfs consciousness, or it can be an oasis in a desert of pretentious civility."[37] The fact that human beings must navigate this channel means they face choices; to accept that freedom is to behave authentically. To deny choice and see oneself as either a captive of natural forces or a prisoner of propriety is to demonstrate fear of freedom and hence bad faith. Stuart Zane Charmé has argued persuasively that Sartre's interest in groups such as Jews, American blacks, and homosexuals reflected his conviction that their examples helped amplify his sense of the range of human choice.[38] Their particularity enhanced his freedom.

Sartre, like other advocates of authenticity, presumed that human beings can act in ways that are not mere reflections of their circumstances. Authentic choice requires that they reason about the constraints imposed by their physical and social situations. But if existence comes before essence and individuality takes precedence over common abilities to reason, how can one account for this capacity for autonomous choice? Autonomous reason cannot account for autonomous reason.

The theists say God has provided the impulse for autonomous choice: Pascal launched biting attacks on the Jesuits for their talk of sufficient grace that was not deemed sufficient.[39] Kierkegaard suggested that the leap of faith comes after resignation and in solitude. Rousseau spoke of these impulses as being natural. Nietzsche extolled the artistic, creative, corporeal, Dionysian aspects of human behavior as the authentic reflections of human will, over and against the restrictions imposed by mind, conscience and reason. Nietzsche did not account for the existence of will; Sartre did not explain the origin of human freedom but rather identified it as a fundamental characteristic of the human condition. In short, however much the revolutionary thrust of authentic thought depends upon the rationality of human response to physical and social circumstances, autonomy ultimately requires justification in a world beyond the reaches of reason. An act can be deemed authentic if it stems from impulses that cannot, by analysis, be attributed to some prior terrestrial force. Nonrational invocations or evocations underpin the autonomous choices of authentic thought. And it is also this necessary venture beyond the domain of reason that cements a measure of coherence and community in an otherwise highly particularistic world.

Unicity: Escape from Nihilism

The emphasis on particularity impels authentic thought toward confrontation with frameworks that organize daily life for individuals or societies, toward autonomous choice by sharply individuated persons, toward a diversity of perspectives and outcomes, and, perhaps, toward chaos and anarchy. By abandoning humanist assumptions, the European proponents of authenticity sacrifice the familiar foundations for psychological, social, and political life. Yet their embrace of authenticity implies an acceptance of a truth upon which some reconstruction can begin. By definition, they resist the sirens of nihilism and meaninglessness and embrace a measure of commonality in the human experience that might be termed "unicity." It is much less far-reaching that the essential unity of reason proposed by humanists or by those adherents of religious traditions who see God as the stage director and initiator of all human action. In the authentic view, the fundamental assumption is that such unity is lacking, but the very explanation of human autonomy and particularity requires, in their view, a deeper, more remote and nonetheless decisive oneness that constitutes salvation from nihilism.

For Rousseau and the romantics, nature provided this oneness. It was not that nature could be read like a book for what it revealed about the universe and God's intentions, as European science and the Enlightenment had come to believe. Rousseau contrasted mankind in the state of nature with human efforts to construct societies in a civilized setting. Although he hoped human beings could overcome alienation, he did not imagine they could return to some happier, natural state. But he did suggest that the individual comes to a full understanding of himself or herself through contact with the natural world. It is in the boat on Lake Geneva or in her own garden that Julie has the most trouble suppressing her own, genuinely personal instincts for her lover, St. Preux. Nature helps one to feel oneself beneath the layers of habit and reason that normally govern behavior. And the unicity of nature, of which human beings are not merely observers but form a part, provides assurance of some underlying unity.

For Kierkegaard, the underlying unity is more problematic. Authentic action comes out of solitude, because only an individual can search for truth,[40] and out of resignation, because temporal beings cannot by definition have access to the eternal and cannot therefore know the permanent, unchanging truth. To presume that human beings can know God by reason is to presume that they are not entirely separate things, just as it is contradictory to presume that a philosopher such as Hegel can produce permanent truth about the realm of the evanescent. "The supreme paradox of all thought is the attempt to discover something that thought cannot think."[41] Only God can provide a glimpse of the truth to a person who is prepared to receive it. But if that truth could be rendered permanent in this world and propagated to a group without individual effort and will, then Kierkegaard's initial assumptions would be violated.

Only the existence of God provides some unity to existence; the transcendence of God renders this unity extraordinarily precarious. If human beings cannot know Truth, which is God, they cannot know each other. What they see is difference and unlikeness, which Kierkegaard identifies with sin and error. Only God, who represents likeness, holds the key to overcoming this absolute difference; only God can provide knowledge about such difference, and human success at "understanding" must necessarily be limited to the moments of passion in which an act of faith permits insight. The logic suggests that human bonds depend upon acts of faith rather than reason, and such acts are neither permanent nor comprehensible; they cannot be captured by either a Catholic Church, subordinating Truth to organization, or a Protestant Church, subordinating Truth to reason. Such unicity, if one may call it that, provides scant foundations for social construction.

The question of unicity looms larger for Nietzsche, who proclaimed the "death of God"—the inability of human beings to sustain belief in an ultimate source of truth and goodness, even an inaccessible source, such as the god of which Kierkegaard speaks. For Nietzsche, as for Kierkegaard, temporality constitutes an apparently insuperable barrier for human access to enduring truth. He reminds us that propositions about the preeminence of thought, the self, subjects, and objects have all evolved as part of the historical human experience; to know about them one must use the techniques of genealogy rather than abstract reason, which is itself a product of power and values, according to the genealogical perspective. Yet genealogy constitutes an effort of the mind to get a hold on things: "It does not take sides over what is good or evil so much as it takes sides against every claim that an action is good or evil. But to do so is still to operate within the domain of values and to relate genealogy's allegedly power-conscious commitments to that domain—and that surely makes genealogy normative."[42] For Nietzsche, there is nothing but will to power, which underlies human efforts to make sense of their universe in order to gain mastery over themselves and their condition. To know is thus to exercise the will to power, and knowledge appears to be utterly particularistic, hence perspectival. Yet his embrace of genealogy suggests his commitment to a truthfulness beyond truth. Or perhaps the commitment is, paradoxically, to a truthfulness in which there is no truth.[43]

Nietzsche identified truthfulness with a forthright acceptance of the world of becoming. J. P. Stern wrote: "Authenticity is the deliberate coincidence of what a man is with what he can become."[44] Human beings must accept the impermanence of all that they create, including the most elaborate philosophical systems. They must resign themselves to the "eternal recurrence of the same," a flow of experience and events that constitutes a sort of order in an otherwise chaotic, meaningless world, at least for those enlightened souls who dare to face up to their radical historicity. "The superman is one who can value infinitely what he knows to be valueless."[45] This to say, of course, that one must embrace the irrational for rational reasons: "Willing the eternal return is the supreme will to power because it is the greatest contradiction that man has yet been asked to bear. We must bestow on becoming the absolute value that the ascetic ideal taught us to bestow on being."[46] For Nietzsche, then, impermanence and change constitute the unitary conditions of human experience; grasping these, an authentic human being can escape nihilism by exercising the will to power and creating an authentic self. Such self-determination is a "consummation of the secular searching for values which is central to the recent intellectual and political history of the West,"[47] even though Nietzsche saw himself as undermining the metaphysical foundations of that tradition. Such a straddle, though particularly dramatic in the case of Nietzsche, is endemic to the effort to establish authenticity as a truthfulness beyond truth and beyond radical particularity.

For Nietzsche, being and time were utterly contradictory conceptions, and the result was his rejection of being in favor of becoming as the basis for authentic human action. In his most influential work, *Being and Time,* Heidegger reopened that issue. His very utilization of the term "Being" and his effort to demonstrate how beings and especially the human self, which by Nietzsche's account appears utterly self-determining, may participate in Being. That account, according to Heidegger, appears to leave out the way the human self shares the world with other beings yet remains utterly individual, at least insofar as it responds "authentically" to its own potential for being. That means, first and foremost, responding to its finitude. It is primarily an anxiety in the face of death that lifts the self out of its weary, dreary, everydayness to assume an attitude of resolve and care toward the world: "Man exists authentically when he 'anticipates' and 'resolves upon' this finitude. 'Resolve' establishes our 'freedom-towards-death,' the freedom to face everyday life's impermanence and thereby to face the need to reestablish the world out of which everyday life has grown."[48] Reestablishing the world means looking back toward primordial origins to get beneath reason and everydayness and to undermine politics as usual in favor of some radically different community. Unlike Nietzsche, who suggested that at least the few may be able to impose some sort of order on chaos by facing up to the futility of permanence, Heidegger spoke of a movement backward into "primordial origins"—which at times seem to evoke the "heart of darkness"—that appears to promise a much broader harnessing of the particularistic forces. Yet, as Newell has observed, the exercise may look backward, but the implications are for the future.

> A violent resoluteness to sweep away a world infected with the technological and managerial politics of modern times; the vision of a pure and unified community which will broach no compromise with ordinary political squabbling and interests; the conviction in the signal importance to the West as a whole that Germany lead this revolutionary reencounter with Being: On the basis of these considerations one could begin to examine the openness or vulnerability of Heidegger's philosophy to the kind of political alternative offered by National Socialism.[49]

More generally, Heidegger proposed to reach through his exploration of "fundamental ontology"—the search for Being—"the permanent condition of human impermanence or historicity."[50] And in doing so, he erected a standard for authenticity, a basis for political community, a unitary platform in an otherwise splintered world. The platform necessarily lies beneath tradition and beneath rationality, and it implies the need for revolution against the alienating forces inherent in modernity.

Jean-Paul Sartre attempted to erect a platform on the idea of freedom, which he took to be fundamental to human beings. Again the title of a book, *Being and Nothingness*, suggests how his enterprise differs from that of Heidegger. The threat to Being comes less from time than from facticity and meaninglessness, but the problem for Sartre is not so different: how to establish some linkage among human beings as a basis for ethical action—without recourse to God or universal reason. For Sartre, that linkage lies in the human condition and a shared freedom to utilize consciousness in coping with facticity. The freedom I experience when I understand my condition causes me to accord freedom to another person, and the result is an ethic of authenticity. To deny my freedom is to act in bad faith.[51] Freedom springing from human consciousness constitutes the standard on which an ethic can be erected. Whereas particularity constitutes the fundamental condition of all authentic thought, it is also the principal threat to finding a new truthfulness beyond the truths that can no longer be accepted. Truthfulness requires a standard, and a standard requires an element of commonality in the human experience. If each individual is utterly unique and isolated by virtue of time and facticity, then to make any ethical observation about even a single person, much less a collectivity, is impossible. Meaninglessness, chaos, and anarchy would be the logical consequences. Those who espouse the doctrine of authenticity share a conviction that those consequences can be avoided and a basis for authentic action can be established. Since the demand for authenticity lies in objection to the dictates of universal reason and to the demands of conventionality, the response must lie at some level other than reason or tradition. It must be irrational or arational, and it must be revolutionary. This is why the advocates of authenticity have not been a part of the political mainstream in the West. In fact, a set of political dilemmas emerges naturally from a reading of European thinkers who have wrestled with the question of authenticity.

Authentic thought can enjoy long-term political success only if it demonstrates the ability to harness human autonomy and energy, to organize participation in a body politic by overcoming the particularity of founding groups and their ideas, and to move beyond revolution toward the establishment of permanent institutions. Several forces push in those directions. First is the need for mass action to achieve political objectives. Second is the modern preoccupation with equality as a basis for democracy. Still a third is the eventual need for stability that only institutions can provide. These forces challenge authentic thought to soften itself, without abandoning its basic impulses. Authentic thought must confront the challenges of modernity, group action, democracy, and institutions in the light of fundamental characteristics that seem to point toward a static view of history, radicalism, individualism, elitism, and instability.

Group Action

Authentic thought of all varieties sees history as the product of individual effort. Some Muslim mystics have been content to explore paths toward the authentic as purely personal solutions, but even Nietzsche's Zarathustra finds himself compelled to descend from his mountain re-treat to preach the gospel of liberation. It takes no social scientist to demonstrate that radical ideas become revolutionary only with the sup-port of a group. It may take either religious inspiration or reliable social science, or both, however, to permit authentic thought to move from its base in individual action to the theoretical construction of group action.

Common belief in God does not suffice. For Kierkegaard as for Pascal, God will inspire those who, by their own diligence, strive to understand the meaning of true faith. Genuine autonomy means that human beings must make the effort, and the problem is to show that they will do so as a group, despite their fundamental particularity and without falling back either on universal reason applied to texts (as the Protestant mainstream would suggest) or on tradition and ritual (as utilized by the Catholic Church). An authentic act of faith is unique and incommunicable, accord-ing to Kierkegaard. How one moves from incommunicable individual acts to group action is not self-evident.

Depending upon a neo-Marxian analysis of classes in Latin America, Gutierrez postulated unity of action for those who simultaneously seek the true, revolutionary spirit of Christianity and the revolutionary needs of their countries. Human beings must themselves discover their com-mon purpose in the history they have made, but it is God who helps weld those individual discoveries into a movement capable of effective action. To count on God without sociology would be to deny man's liberty to construct his own world; according to Gutierrez, God acts within history, not beyond it. But sociology without God leaves a group of individuals with similar interests and conclusions incapable of overcoming group in-sularity and reaching their full potential. "The fullness of liberation—a free gift from Christ—is communion with God and with other men," wrote Gutierrez.[52] But he also said that love "is not authentic if it does not take the part of class solidarity and social struggle."[53]

In the absence of God, group action appears even more problematic for the burdens placed upon sociological analysis, which nonetheless cannot be accorded objectivity without compromising free will. Nietzsche seems to assume at some moments in his thinking that the problem will resolve itself as those with greater knowledge, and hence greater will to power, as-sert their natural impulses to rule. Cohesion results from coercion.[54] But for a democrat such as Gramsci, coercion represents acknowledgment of failure in the effort to replace an old hegemony with a new one. For him, intellectuals must serve as intermediaries between a party of the few capable of organizing action and the masses that must ultimately support any successful revolution. On the basis of their analysis, the intellectuals can propose new ideas; the masses dispose on the basis of what they feel. Intellectuals think but do not feel.[55] Such would be a true description of their situation and a true prescription for the remedy. The subjective ratification of the great majority transforms the subjective analysis of the intellectuals into an objective base from which group action is possible. Human beings will undertake such action because they are essentially political and because action aimed at transforming and consciously directing other men completes their humanity, their "human nature."[56] Gramsci put this term in quotation marks because it appears to violate his assertion that human nature is not a constant but a variable, the product of human action. For Gramsci, common consciousness proceeds from common experience. It is not self-evident, then, that individuals, each a product of slightly different historical experience, should feel truth in the same set of propositions or that they should be suddenly capable of feeling, as one such proposition, their inherent human need for group action. The argument establishes plausibility rather than necessity, and thus Gramsci's view of history, as the gradual assertion of man's dominance over nature, similarly remains in the realm of hypothesis rather than certainty. The infirmity of sociology becomes the infirmity of group action and the lameness of history, which defies rigorous sociological understanding.

Equality

Unlike the problem of group action, which may be more acute in the absence of God, the problem of equality appears to pose more critical problems for theistic approaches to authenticity. Both Christianity and Islam contain assertions of the equality of all human beings before God and denunciations of the injustice inherent in existing inequalities. The one attacked the power of Rome, the other assaulted the wealth of Mecca. Moreover, authentic thought of all stripes identifies the inequality of traditional society, whether based in prestige, money, piety, or politics, as a source of inauthenticity. It is passivity in the face of greater power that prevents human beings from realizing their genuine potential. Nietzsche, for example, spoke of the perpetuation of the master-slave relationship as a fixed aspect of the human condition.

Yet the search for authenticity necessarily begins with an individual or a small group and leads most easily to elite domination. For Nietzsche, unencumbered by a transhistoric ethic, elitism represents the only hope for human liberation from the tyranny of a less enlightened, less humane, and more utopian (hence, deluded) elitism. The dominance of superior wills remains the most plausible hypothesis about human behavior. For Gramsci, working from the concept of a human nature in search of fulfillment, the leap may not be long from the need for a political party, together with the recognized fallibility of any political analysis or action, to the acceptance of several parties and some form of liberal democracy, albeit not the liberalism of Croce's dreams. Gramsci's reservations about the capacity of an intellectual class to prescribe for society, lacking either the ability to do objective social science or to feel what is true, as nonintellectuals do, pushed him toward populism. Yet his doubts about the adequacy of spontaneity pulled him back toward "the modern prince"—the political party—which serves both as galvanizing myth and agent of organization. Reworking Machiavelli (in his reference to the prince) and Robert Michels[57] (in his recognition of the need for hierarchy), he anticipated Maurice Duverger[58] (in his discussion of mass parties) and Samuel Huntington[59] (who called political parties the only genuinely modern political invention). In short, Gramsci's response to the problem of political equality, accepting the necessity of elite leadership as well as mass authorization, fits well within the mainstream of the Western liberal debate.[60]

The thrust of all authentic thought is toward the particular and away from the universal. By seeking the true self, it divides rather than unites, distinguishes rather than encompasses. By emphasizing human diversity, it renders difficult the argument for equal treatment for ethnic, religious, political, social, or political minorities. It accepts the fragmentation of the world into groups of disparate identities and purpose without providing much theoretical guidance about the management of such a world.[61]

The more intensely religious versions seem antithetical to the notion of equal sovereignty for weak and strong, yet that idea appears vital to the practical survival of a self-consciously authentic regime, unwilling to depend on a great power for defense. For this reason, the practical problem of maintaining peace at home and normal relations with neighbors dictates compromise, but compromise begins to separate theory from practice and to invite charges of hypocrisy similar to those leveled at an ancien régime. The more a regime seeks legitimacy in piety, the more it is sensitive to such criticism, and the greater the tension it feels with the equalizing, universalizing forces operant internally and externally.

Institutionalization

The contemporary concern for equality derives from the widespread acceptance of development theory as articulated in the West. By contrast, the need for group action stems from the fundamental radicalism of authentic thought as an attempt to restructure society and human beings. That great historian of authenticity movements, Ibn Khaldun, identified group feeling as the critical variable for successful revolution as well as for the durability of the postrevolutionary state. But, as he also observed, group feeling cannot endure. Is the decline of authenticity as inevitable as Ibn Khaldun suggests? Is it as firmly anchored in human instincts as the search for authenticity itself? Every theory of genuine renewal, even if isolated from the pressures of modernity and equality, must confront the problem of institutionalization unless it can, like Ibn Khaldun and Nietzsche, accept the transitory nature of any such endeavor. John Pocock outlined the dilemma this way: "The radical reconstructs the past in order to authorize the future; he historicizes the present in order to deprive it of authority. Both operations may give him a bias in favor of historical explanation, which may detract against his wishes from the very character of his enterprise."[62] One instance of army intervention into politics invites another. One revolution invites another. One invocation of a mythical past invites the search for another, still more hazy, mystical, and authentic.

Rousseau's Julie sought to institutionalize the most genuine part of her being, her love for Saint-Preux, by bringing him and the friends that linked them into her married household. There, her husband, de Wollmar, in his inhumane rationality, left the lovers to discover that the net of social constraints now enmeshing them had, by binding their own consciences, deprived them of the capacity to renew the intense, natural, authentic relationship they had once enjoyed. By taking them to a sacred spot in the woods where Julie and Saint-Preux had first embraced, de Wollmar demonstrated that the lovers could withstand the confrontation with the past; the new institution sustained them. But simultaneously, the past lost its meaning and the new household, designed in part to keep that past alive, also began to lose its fascination for Julie. As her rapport with Saint-Preux gradually lost its irrational power, Julie began to find that part of herself in God. She had, in fact, rediscovered her faith on the day of her wedding to de Wollmar; after the discovery of her inability to institutionalize her love for Saint-Preux, she welcomed death as an escape into authenticity.

Nietzsche recognized the destructive, especially self-destructive, potential of the drive for truthfulness. "I know of no better purpose in life than to be destroyed by that which is great and impossible."[63] Human beings can liberate themselves from their consciences and from God, he thought; they can rescue themselves by dint of will and action from Julie's dilemma, but they still find themselves caught in the web of history, from which there can be no escape. The present constantly loses ground to the past and the future. Institutions may be absolutely critical bits of illusion for the preservation of the human species, reflective of the strongest wills of a particular historical moment, but their very nature—persistence of behavior over time in accord with established rule—seems inconsistent with what Nietzsche meant by the fulfillment of the human potential: autonomy, creativity, courageous action, and acceptance of the radical historicity of existence, of the idea of eternal recurrence.

Not surprisingly, most revolutionary authors emerge somewhat more optimistic. Yet Gramsci rightly chided the Marxist tradition for failure to think carefully about the problem of the "new hegemony," the postrevolutionary culture. His historicism, though less radical than Nietzsche's, prevented him from imagining a utopia beyond yesterday. Human beings must construct an alternative future from elements of the past, cognizant of the need for authority, organization, hierarchy, and the capacity to execute a program as well as the need for a program itself. Gramsci's awareness of the provisional nature of all historical achievement left him receptive to open-ended solutions and skeptical of those that reduce discussion and diminish choice. From nonliberal assumptions, he arrived at a form of liberalism that appears incapable of closing the gap between "good sense" and "common sense," between social realities and cultural hegemony. Without the organization and hierarchy of a political party, action is impossible. With them comes an aggregation of particularities into a common denominator of national program that may well appear inauthentic to those at the bottom.

⌁⌁

Both Westerners and non-Westerners have concerned themselves with the need to discover a mode of truthfulness beyond accepted truth, either because they deem conventional standards of truth unreliable or because they regard those standards as inadequately understood and practiced. The result is a body of thought that is radical in its rejection of tradition and universal reason, particularistic in its understanding of human beings, categoric in its insistence that autonomous human beings shape history, and nonetheless given to belief in a fundamental human bond beyond reason or tradition. That thought challenges modernization theory from within as well as from without and, by doing so, establishes a link between Western thought and the reemergent phenomenon of authenticity movements in the Third World.

Such thought does more. By the persuasiveness of the general argument, it strikes a blow against developmentalism, revealed as one perspective on the human condition that does not enjoy universal support in either the developed or developing worlds—the kind of support that would, by a reasoning similar to Gramsci's, objectify developmentalism in the eyes of many social scientists. Development theory, a product of the Western *ratio*, may be moribund as a consequence, even if policies based on it remain very much in force in most of the Third World. Does authentic thought hold promise as a replacement? The particularity of authentic thinking might seem to negate the philosophical possibility of a general perspective on the human condition derived from that framework, although Europeans such as Heidegger have attempted to find some minimalist framework for the comprehension of mutually exclusive world views. The pressures for equality, the problem of group action, and the need for institutionalization constitute general challenges for which authentic thought as developed in Europe does not offer satisfactory solutions. Have thinkers in the Islamic tradition such as Iqbal, Qutb, Shari'ati, and Arkoun been more successful? That is the question to which this study now turns.

Notes

1. Elie Kedourie, *Nationalism* (London: Hutchinson, 1985), pp. 21–31.

2. Lionel Trilling, *Sincerity and Authenticity* (Cambridge: Harvard University Press, 1972), p. 99.

3. Friedrich Schiller, *On the Aesthetic Education of Man* (New York: Frederick Ungar, 1965), p. 38.

4. Schiller, *Aesthetic Education*, p. 44.

5. Martin Heidegger, *Being and Time*, trans. John Acquarrie and Edward Robinson (New York: Harper, 1962), p. 287.

6. Jean-Paul Sartre, *Réflexions sur la question juive* (Paris: Gallimard, 1954), p. 112.

7. Sartre, *Réflexions*, chap. 4.

8. Mehrzad Boroujerdi, *Iranian Intellectuals and the West: The Tormented Triumph of Nativism* (Syracuse, N.Y.: Syracuse University Press, 1996).

9. Heidegger, *Being and Time*, p. 780.

10. Friedrich Nietzsche, *Beyond Good and Evil*, trans. R. J. Hollingdale (Middlesex: Penguin, 1983), p. 53.

11. John G. A. Pocock, *Politics, Language, and Time: Essays on Political Thought and History* (New York: Atheneum, 1973), p. 234.

12. Pocock, *Politics, Language, and Time*, p. 234. See also Abdallah Laroui, *The Crisis of the Arab Intellectual*, trans. Diarmid Cammell (Berkeley: University of California Press, 1976), for his distinction between tradition as a contemporary social force and tradition as ideology.

13. I owe much to Marshall Berman, *The Politics of Authenticity* (New York: Atheneum, 1970), for my analysis of Montesquieu and Rousseau.

14. Montesquieu, *Lettres persanes* (Paris: Garnier Frères, 1975), pp. 220–223.

15. Jean-Jacques Rousseau, *Julie, ou la nouvelle Héloïse* (Paris: Flammarion 1967), part 1.

16. Rousseau, *Julie*, part 2.

17. Ibid., part 4.

18. Lionel Trilling, *Sincerity and Authenticity* (Cambridge: Harvard University Press, 1972), p. 131.

19. Rousseau, *Julie*, p. 566.

20. Jean-Jacques Rousseau, "Quelle est l'origine de l'inégalité parmi les hommes et si elle est autorisée par la loi naturelle?" in *Du contrat social* (Paris: Garnier, 1962), p. 73.

21. Sören Kierkegaard, *Two Ages: The Age of Revolution and the Present Age*, ed. and trans. Howard V. Hong and Edna H. Hong (Princeton: Princeton University Press, 1978), p. 65.

22. Sören Kierkegaard, *Fear and Trembling: A Dialectical Lyric*, trans. Walter Lowrie (Princeton: Princeton University Press, 1941).

23. Gianni Vattimo, *Il soggetto e la maschera: Nietzsche e il problema della liberazione* (Milano: Bompiani, 1979), part 1.

24. Pocock, *Politics, Language, and Time*, p. 232.

25. Antonio Gramsci, *The Modern Prince and Other Writings* (New York: International Publishers, 1978), p. 60.

26. Vattimo, *Il soggetto e la maschera*, part 2, chap. 3.

27. Ibid., part 3, chap. 4.

28. W. R. Newell, "Heidegger on Freedom and Community: Some Political Implications of His Early Thought," *American Political Science Review*, 78 (1984), p. 781.

29. Fouad Ajami, *The Arab Predicament* (Cambridge: Cambridge University Press, 1981), p. 195.

30. The reasoning is that of Blaise Pascal in *Pensées*, text established by Leon Brunschwigg (Paris: Flammarion, 1976).

31. James Miller, *History and Human Existence: From Marx to Merleau-Ponty* (Berkeley: University of California Press, 1979), p. 72.

32. Gramsci, *Il materialismo storico e la filosofia di Benedetto Croce* (Torino: Edizioni Riuniti, 1975), pp. 115–116.

33. Ibid., p. 3.

34. Ibid., pp. 103–105.

35. Kierkegaard, *Two Ages*, p. 68.

36. Mauro La Spisa, *Fede e Scandolo nei diari di S. A. Kierkegaard* (Firenze: GeG, 1970), p. 77.

37. Stuart Zane Charmé, *Vulgarity and Authenticity: Dimensions of Otherness in the World of Jean-Paul Sartre* (Amherst: University of Massachusetts Press, 1991), p. 40.

38. Charmé, *Vulgarity and Authenticity*.

39. Blaise Pascal, *Lettres écrites à un provincial* (Paris: Flammarion, 1981), pp. 43–51.

40. Kierkegaard, *Philosophical Fragments, or a Fragment of Philosophy*, trans. David F. Swenson and Howard V. Hong (Princeton: Princeton University Press, 1962), pp. 15–16.

41. Ibid., p. 46.

42. S. Kemal, "Some Problems of Genealogy," *Nietzsche-Studien* 19 (1990), p. 36.

43. John Riker, private communication, June 1996.

44. J. P. Stern, *Nietzsche* (Transbridge, England: Harvester, 1978), p. 77.

45. Bernard Yack, *The Longing for Total Revolution: Philosophic Sources of Social Discontent from Rousseau to Marx and Nietzsche* (Princeton: Princeton University Press, 1986), p. 353.

46. Ibid., p. 353.

47. Stern, *Nietzsche*, p. 79.

48. Newell, "Heidegger on Freedom and Community," p. 779.

49. Ibid., p. 782.

50. Ibid., p. 784.

51. See Linda A. Bell, *Sartre's Ethics of Authenticity* (Tuscaloosa: University of Alabama Press, 1989).

52. Gustavo Gutierrez, *A Theology of Liberation* (Maryknoll, N.Y.: Orbis, 1973), p. 36.

53. Ibid., p. 276.

54. Vattimo, *Il soggetto e la maschera*, pp. 349–375.

55. Angelo Broccoli, *Antonio Gramsci e l'educazione come egemonia* (Firenze: La Nuova Italia, 1972), p. 99.

56. Gramsci, *Il materialismo*, pp. 34, 37.

57. Robert Michels, *Political Parties: A Sociological Study of the Oligarchical Tendencies of Modern Democracy*, trans. Eden and Cedar Paul (London: Jarrold and Sons, 1915).

58. Maurice Duverger, *Political Parties: Their Organization and Activity in the Modern State*, 2d rev. ed., trans. Barbara and Robert North (London: Methuen, 1959).

59. Samuel Huntington, *Political Order in Changing Societies* (New Haven: Yale University Press, 1968).

60. See Gramsci, *The Modern Prince*, or for fuller treatment, *Note sul Machiavelli, sulla politica e sullo stato moderno* (Torino: Edizioni Riuniti, 1979).

61. Sartre, for example, saw this diversity as desirable but did not say much about how liberal thought could be modified to accomplish it. Yael Tamir did better in *Liberal Nationalism* (Princeton: Princeton University Press, 1993).

62. Pocock, *Politics, Language, and Time*, p. 261.

63. From *Thoughts out of Season*, quoted by J. P. Stern, *A Study of Nietzsche* (Cambridge: Harvester, 1978), p. 90.

three

Muhammad
Iqbal

THE IDEA OF AUTHENTICITY HELPS ILLUMINATE the thought of Muhammad Iqbal, the Indian Muslim poet-philosopher of the early twentieth century. Inspired by Europe and Islam, Iqbal rejected Europe's conception of progress along with the contemporary pattern of Islamic culture in India. He called upon "true Muslims" to assert themselves against mullahism, mysticism, and monarchy as well as against foreign ways. In a broader sense, he summoned all human beings to rise above acceptance of traditional ways and above the embrace of Western ideas and technology to discover their creative, willful, authentic selves.

One contemporary biographer of Iqbal wrote: "There is no more versatile, prolific and gifted genius in history; and for similar examples of omnicompetence, one has to turn to Michelangelo, Leonardo da Vinci, [Leon Battista] Alberti and [Rabindranath] Tagore."[1] Such comparisons across time and culture are difficult, but there can be little dispute about Iqbal's versatility and competence. Born in the Punjab in 1873 to Muslim parents, Iqbal achieved distinction as a student and a poet before going to Lahore in 1895 to study at Government College. There he studied Islamic culture and Arabic literature with a distinguished British Orientalist, Sir Thomas Arnold. By the turn of the century, he had earned a master's degree in philosophy and started to teach, but he found the academic life restrictive, and the civil service rejected his candidacy on medical grounds. All the while he wrote poetry "in the traditional style, verses on nature and love, of the typical Urdu lyric."[2] His writing reflected his upbringing as a Muslim, his study of Islamic culture, his exposure through his father to Sufism, his awareness of the Islamic revival movement of the era (Sayyid

Ahmad Khan, Jamal al-Din al-Afghani), and a commitment to Indian nationalism based on Muslim-Hindu solidarity.

Iqbal went to study in Europe for three years, first at Cambridge with a neo-Hegelian philosopher, J.M.E. McTaggert, then in Germany at Heidelberg and Munich. He came away with a law degree from England and a doctorate from Germany for a thesis on Persian mysticism. More important, he came away with a deep understanding of European thought, from the theology of Thomas Aquinas to the philosophy of Henri-Louis Bergson and Nietzsche. Wilfred Cantwell Smith wrote:

> Until that trip [to Europe], there was nothing distinctive about Iqbal except his ability. What he had to say, numerous others were saying; only they said it less well. But after three years in England and Germany he returned to India with a new and vibrant message. Not only was it expressed with supreme eloquence; it has been the chief contribution to Indian Islam since that of Sir Sayyid Ahmad.[3]

His message emerged clearly with the publication of *Secrets of the Self* in 1915.

From then on, Iqbal supported himself by working as a barrister but gained recognition as a poet, philosopher, and "prophet" of the new age. Recognition came both from within India and abroad. He was knighted in 1922, selected to the Legislative Council in 1926, appointed president of the annual session of the Muslim League in 1930. In his address to that group, he said he thought India could not paper over differences to become a single, undifferentiated nation. Instead, he called for cooperation between the religious groups. "Perhaps we are unwilling to recognize that each group has a right to free development according to its cultural traditions."[4] The idea become known eventually as the "Pakistan scheme," but Iqbal himself never showed enthusiasm for narrow nationalisms of any sort. Others used his ideas, however, to bolster the emerging case for Muslim separatism, and Iqbal gained general recognition as one of the "fathers" of modern Pakistan. Illness overtook him in 1934, and he died in 1938, almost a decade before India achieved independence and Muslim Pakistan went its separate way.

To appreciate Iqbal's significance to modern writers, one must see him as a theorist of authenticity, seeking to liberate humanity from the clutches of both tradition and modernity, from the mysticism of the East and the reason of the West, from the imperialism of the West and the submissiveness of the East. As he put it in "East and West:"

> *The poppy heard my song and tore her mantle;*
> *The morning breeze is still in search of a garden.*

Ill lodged in Atatürk or Reza Shah,
The Soul of the East is still in search of a body.
The thing I am may merit chastisement;
Only—the world is still in search of a gibbet.[5]

The only standard by which Iqbal might be hung would be a universal one, one that not only did not exist but that, in Iqbal's view, could not emerge from either the reason ("brain-malady") of the West or the mysticism ("heart-malady") of the East.[6] It could only have been the sort of standard that Iqbal himself eventually proposed, a standard of individual truths that turn out to converge. He spoke to all peoples, most especially those of the Third World, in an effort to help them rediscover themselves, their beings, their purposes, their destinies. As Fazlur Rahman has said: "[Iqbal's] main idea was the regeneration of humanity through the unremitting effort of the individual for complete self-realization."[7] Iqbal proposed a general theory of authenticity.

Particularity

Iqbal lamented the erosion of identity not from any commitment to quaint traditions or disregard for the dangers of nationalist fervor but from a conviction, like that of many European writers of the nineteenth and twentieth centuries, that comprehension of reality could only begin with an existential understanding of the self. In a short poem he wrote:

Each atom pants for glory: greed
Of Self-fruition earth's whole creed!
.   .   .   .
Your own heart is your candle, your
Own self is all the light you need;
You are this world's sole truth, all else
Illusion such as sorceries breed.
—These desert thorns prick many a doubt:
Do not complain if bare feet bleed.[8]

Both reason and sense perception can mislead and deceive; only true heart or soul, with its intuitive powers, can be relied upon to discern reality, which is nothing but selves. But if self-fruition is the goal of the self and if the heart is the candle, whence comes the tallow, the wick, and the fire? The reference to desert thorns suggests that the self reflects its past, its environment, and the limitations of the body. Iqbal suggested that neither modern science, obsessed with empirical data, nor mysticism in its escapist forms can provide relief from the concrete circumstances of existence. For a Muslim, the Arabia of Muhammad constitutes the principal defining element of the self—a reality shorn of apparent advantage in the modern era[9] but a hard reality from which Muhammad created a great civilization. The thorns hurt then, too.

The authentic self necessarily reflects the past as part of its present state of being. Its sense of the past comes from the community, which Iqbal called "the link between / What is to come, and what has gone before."[10] For him, the community was the *umma*, the community of believers, which took precedence over ancestral or territorial solidarities. Far from suppressing individualism, the community founded by Muhammad liberated the individual from fear and entrusted human beings with full responsibility for their destinies. Iqbal stressed the finality of Muhammad's prophethood; believers were left to fend for themselves with only the memory of a leader, a book, and a territorial focus to unite them. Formed by their collective experience, Muslims face the world alone, just as they must answer to God alone.

Like Kierkegaard, Iqbal took loneliness to be the primordial human condition. In a poem called "Solitude," he wrote of searching the physical world for anyone or anything that shares his uniqueness; he gets no response except from God, who merely smiles.[11] The smile confirms the individuation, while denying any suggestion that the individual is a part of God or just a reflection of God. Iqbal rejected the mystical view that faith permits obliteration of the individual through absorption into God, although his emphasis on love rather than reason as the essence of faith puts him within the mystic tradition.[12] In fact, it is the suprarational foundation of the self and the highly personal nature of love that impede communication and deepen solitude.[13] When Zinda-Rud begins his tour of the heavens in the *Javid Nama*, he does so alone. And in his opening prayer, he asks: "Where may Adam's son find a kindred spirit?"[14]

Authenticity cannot, however, be equated with the search for solitude in the manner of the ascetic. Iqbal saw asceticism as an escape from the concrete reality of this world and hence as a fleeing from the self in its physical, worldly dimensions. To love God is to exert oneself in the world God created, not to find exit.

> . . . .
> *when the soul's image is perfected in the world,*
> *to behold the commons is to behold God.*
> *Blessed is the man whose single sigh*
> *causes the nine heavens to circle about his dwelling.*[15]

The authentic self is the strong, vigorous, autonomous self. That which enhances strength, vigor, and autonomy augments the quality of the self.

Weakness, passivity, and dependence undermine it by diminishing its particularity.

> *Asking disintegrates the Self*
> *And deprives of illumination the Sinai-bush of the Self.*[16]

Bushes are discrete, unique, concrete, different in the intensity with which they burn and, in the case of the Sinai-bush, self-lighting. The true Muslim lights this world by nurturing his solitude into a fiercely strong, independent self.

Such commitment to the uniqueness of the self put Iqbal into practical and theoretical difficulties. His particularistic understanding of the human condition dictated a position of tolerance toward non-Muslim identities. However, his own position within the Muslim community pushed him toward the espousal of a separate Muslim state, a state committed to the preservation of one identity among others. His particularity thus conditioned his response to the problems of institutions and democracy, but his theoretical problem, common to other exponents of authenticity, was more fundamental. How does the unique self establish contact with other selves and with the world in which it lives? Does not solitude lock the self into a prison of impotence?

Unicity

Iqbal demonstrated that the particularity of the self, properly understood, holds the key to understanding all existence. In fact, he suggested that self is all that is, and in doing so, he denied the significance of dichotomies such as being and becoming, man and God, mind and matter, reason and intuition, science and religion, sacred and profane, subject and object, thinking and action. The self, through self-understanding, frees itself to comprehend the world and to act within it, morally or immorally. The true Muslim reaches this point of understanding by virtue of the concept of *tawḥīd* (oneness of God). Islam is thus not merely the principal defining element of Iqbal's particularity; it is also the religion most consistent with a unitary understanding of reality. Islam, he wrote, "happens to be the only [religion] suitable to my purpose."[17]

Iqbal founded much of his critique of East and West on arguments about false dualism. He reproached the East for abandoning its medieval foray into inductive thinking, which eventually opened the door to the scientific revolution in the West. Muslims wrongly asserted religion as an exclusive mode of understanding, different from science and philosophy, whereas Europe made the opposite error by progressively rejecting religious faith in favor of a supposedly objective truth, that of science. But

Europeans could not prove the superiority of their predilection for science any more than Muslims could demonstrate the superiority of their preference for religion. Both dualisms produced distortions, in Iqbal's view. Europe veered toward dehumanizing materialism, whereas Islamdom lapsed into passivity and mysticism. Europe separated church from state and morality from legality, relegating church and morality to subordinate positions. Islam tolerated an analogous division without authorizing it; temporal power, science, and philosophy all lacked legitimacy. As a result, a degeneration in the material condition of the East paralleled a spiritual degradation in the West.

Iqbal asserted the primordial oneness of the self:

> *It is one*
> *And, being one, brooks no duality;*
> *Grace to its glow I am myself, thou thou.*[18]

The self necessarily recognizes what is not self. Iqbal acknowledged the limitations, demonstrated by Kant, on knowing anything beyond the self but tried to show that knowledge and intuition are merely two modes in which the self apprehends different sorts of reality. By intuition, the self understands itself by understanding God, "the Absolute Ego," and by understanding God, the self gains access to the world He created: nature. Or vice versa, to appreciate nature is to confront God. Iqbal spoke of a chain of being in which entities are distinguished by the degree of their "I-amness."[19] Even the oceans, the mountains, and the stars have their own identities, their own inertias. They, too, are alone in the world,[20] though not isolated; they fashion the being of humans, and humans, by their efforts to understand nature, shape the being of physical space. "It is . . . possible to take thought not as a principle which organizes and integrates its material from the outside but as a potency which is formative of the very being of its material."[21]

The oneness of the human self guarantees the unity of thought and intuition and of thought and being; it also permits oneness with God. Iqbal suggested that the significance of distinctions between spiritual and secular, God and human creatures, break down in the fact that God is a part of the authentic self. The self achieves awareness of existence first through self-consciousness and then through the consciousnesses of others. But only in the communion with God does the self reach full understanding.

> *The God-seeing man sees himself only through God;*
> *Crying One God, he quivers in his own blood.*[22]

Iqbal envisioned God as a mirror in which the self sees its own being more fully; as it develops its own projects and executes them, it does God's will. God has no separate agenda. "In great action alone the self of man becomes united with God without losing its own identity, and transcends the limits of space and time. Action is the highest form of contemplation."[23] To know God is to know oneself in the world that God created.

Like his view of particularity, Iqbal's unitarian perspective coincides with but does not depend upon his vision of Islam. Iqbal traced all his views, and especially his unitarianism, to the Qur'an and Islamic thinkers, especially the mystic Rumi. However, to contend that unity reflected truth because God had decreed it so would vitiate the centrality and destroy the autonomy of the self. He rejected the Sufi doctrine of *waḥdat al-wujūd*, the unity of existence, which was understood to mean the world is only God. Instead, Iqbal sought to show that Islam, with its radical insistence upon God's oneness and upon the finality of Muhammad's prophethood, expresses a truth that is at least equiprimordial with the oneness of self. Ultimately, after criticizing Hallaj out of the mistaken belief that the great mystic espoused this doctrine, he concurred with Hallaj that "the Divine Unity does not result in destroying the personality of the mystic, but makes him more perfect, more sacred, more divine, and makes him its free and living organ."[24] For Iqbal, monotheism constituted both the condition for and the inescapable concomitant of a world of multiple, discrete selves. The prophethood of Muhammad united believers in a concrete social and political organization and provided guarantees against any threat to the unity of the community. In these ways, Islam represented the "unitive principle,"[25] both in theory and practice.

Iqbal regarded Islam as anticlassical in spirit. He interpreted Plato as Nietzsche did, as one who neglected matter for spirit, creativity for logic, and action for thought. The Qur'an bridges, in Iqbal's view, each of these dichotomies. "To Islam matter is spirit realizing itself in space and time," he wrote.[26] Iqbal referred in his poetry to the Qur'anic image of man as a product of both spirit and clay. Islam demands an expression of faith, yet its law reflects reason and justice; it requires inner transformation but, through Muhammad's example, entreats Muslims to transform their world. It sees human beings not as objects of God's wrath or mercy but as the responsible subjects of earthly action. "The Qur'an is a book which emphasizes 'deed' rather than 'idea.'"[27] Since action is "the highest form of contemplation," Islam does not separate temporal from spiritual affairs. Islam prescribes a mode of living in this world. To know God is to know oneself, but the self exists in a world God has made. The true Muslim eschews dichotomies.

Autonomy

In the final lines of Iqbal's *Shikwa and Jawab-i-Shikwa: Complaint and Answer, Iqbal's Dialogue with Allah*, God concludes his reply to a Muslim's lamentation on his condition:

If you are true Muslims your destiny is to grasp what you aspire.
If you break not faith with Muhammad, we shall always
  be with you.
What is this miserable world? To write the world a history pen and
tablet we offer you.[28]

Muslims bear responsibility for their own miseries. It is only they who can turn history to their advantage. Such is the message of *Complaint and Answer*, which formulates the practical, political concern that underlies all of Iqbal's work, the problem of decadence in the East.[29] For Iqbal, human volition produces history, not unseen forces of either spiritual or material origin; fatalism and mechanism deprive the self of its vitality, creativity, and force.

Iqbal regarded the world as a product of human effort. In the *Javid Nama*, Bartari-Hari, an ancient poet of India, tells Zinda-Rud:

> *This world you behold is not the handiwork of God,*
> *the wheel is yours, and the thread spun on your spindle.*
> *Prostrate yourself before the Law of action's reward,*
> *for from action are born Hell, Purgatory and Paradise.*[30]

God has entrusted the world to human beings to make of it what they will, if they will and by their will. They are responsible before themselves and hence before God, mirror of the true self, for their action or inaction.

Success requires effort even in the face of hardship. "Life without prick-lings is no true life; / one must live with a fire under one's feet."[31] In a poem entitled "An Old Baluchi to His Son," Iqbal evoked an image to which he often returned, that of the pearl diver.

> *Fortunes of States through individual prowess*
> *Ripen, each man one star of their ascendant:*
> *Ocean withholds her treasure when the diver*
> *Groping for pearlshells*
> *Clings by land's margin.*[32]

A group can act only if individuals act, and individuals succeed in acting only if they cultivate strength and courage. In *Secrets of the Self*, Iqbal spoke of sheep who try to defang tigers by persuading their enemies that the meek shall inherit the earth.[33] Plato and Christian thinkers lulled the world into passivity, he argued, but Europe then behaved like a tiger, un-abashedly projecting its power on the rest of the globe. He twitted Europe for its hypocrisy in criticizing Islam for its militancy.[34] Iqbal's rhetoric of-ten invokes violence as testimony to the courage and strength of those who seek to shape their world in the face of adversity.

Iqbal took the founding generation of Muslims as evidence that human beings can by force of will transform the world. In the *Javid Nama*, a Martian sage speaks of destiny:

> *Earthlings have gambled away the coin of selfhood,*
> *not comprehending the subtle meaning of destiny;*
> *its subtlety is contained in a single phrase—*
> *"If you transform yourself, it too will be transformed."*[35]

Iqbal's understanding of destiny approached Heidegger's conception of the authentic human potential for Being-in-the-world. In the *Javid Nama*, Hallaj tells Zinda-Rud:

> *The believer true thus petitions God:*
> *"We accord with you, so accord with us."*
> *His resolution is the creator of God's determination*
> *and on the day of battle his arrow is God's arrow.*[36]

Right springs from will, which in turn reflects the reasoned choice of the self, conscious of its own potential through its contact with God. Although the world constrains human options, life nonetheless holds enough freedom for the self to put it beyond the realm of causal necessity.

True Muslims distinguish themselves by the degree to which will dominates necessity. Iqbal posits three stages of advancement for the ego: obedience to the law, which requires limited self-awareness and commitment; self-control (*faqr*), which constitutes "detachment [from] and superiority to one's material possessions,"[37] and divine vice-regency, in which "thought and action, instinct and reason become one."[38] Those who reach divine vice-regency direct, or should direct, earthly affairs. Sharing characteristics of Absolute Ego, such individuals are most fully representative of God because they are the most capable of the "rationally directed creative life," which Iqbal terms the ultimate reality.[39]

Iqbal saw life as movement for both individual and society and thought that the will of the individual constitutes the motive force. Philosophies, religions, and even art must be judged by what they contribute to liveliness. He found Platonism deficient in that regard:

> *Dear is the world of ideas to the dead spirit;*
> *Its gazelles have no grace of movement.*[40]

Neo-Platonic mysticism and the poetry it inspired suffered from the same malady: They induced lethargy. As for Christianity, Iqbal found it oriented more toward death and immortality than toward life and given more to the pursuit of the ascetic ideal than to the improvement of the secular world. In contrast, he regarded Islam as founded in a spirit of movement and change, "melioristic" in its thrust. And this emphasis is for him "the ultimate presupposition and justification of all human effort at scientific discovery and social programs."[41] Islam means submission to God, but discovering God means uncovering one's potential and making the most of it by developing one's spirit, one's energy, and one's will. "A strong will and a strong body is the ethical ideal of Islam."[42] Muhammad's example showed what will and power can accomplish.

Radicalism

Iqbal believed the world of the Indian Muslim in the first decades of this century demanded transformation. But his radicalism ran much deeper than opposition to British rule. Like European theorists of authenticity, Iqbal called for revolt against the pinching movement of tradition and modernity, which squeezed India and the rest of the non-European world. At one moment he expressed fear that the East would lose touch with its inner self by following the lures of material improvement offered by the West, and at the next he bemoaned the power of mysticism, mullahism, and monarchy in the East. In a poem called "Revolution," he repeated his frequent charge: Europe is death for the soul, and Asia is death to the will.[43] He sought salvation for both soul and will through the radical transformation of the human condition. "He was, in effect, a revolutionary."[44]

Iqbal shared Jamal al-Din al-Afghani's revulsion at the state of Islamdom, but he did not admire the European way of life as many of his compatriots did. He wrote:

Thus, wholly overshadowed by the results of his intellectual activity, the modern man has ceased to live soulfully, i.e., from within. In the domain of thought he is living in open conflict with himself; and in the domain of economic and political life he is living in open conflict with others. He finds himself unable to control his ruthless egoism and his infinite gold-hunger which is gradually killing all higher striving in him and bringing him nothing but life-weariness. Absorbed in the "fact," that is to say, the optically present source of sensation, he is entirely cut off from the unplumbed depths of his own being.[45]

In this view, human beings become alienated by virtue of physical separation from their own ideas, which acquire a momentum of their own. They live beholden to the ideologies and institutions spawned by their own imaginations and lose all touch with the creative moment from which they sprang. In a positivistic age, they cherish the data and even see each other as data, but "facts" are static, dead, and distant, whereas life, for Iqbal, is moving and proximate. The inductive method of the Europeans arose not from logic but from creativity. It is that creativity that Iqbal believed modern man had lost. The call for the exploration of the unplumbed depths is the call to authenticity.[46]

The summons to authentic revolution as a remedy for modernity should not be confounded with either a fondness for traditional society as it has evolved or a desire for wholesale resurrection of the past. Iqbal espoused neither. In the *Javid Nama*, the Spirit of India complains that Indians "have estranged themselves from their selfhood; / they have made a prison of ancient customs."[47] Iqbal denounced conventionalism as "self-murder"[48] and said those "who ignore the beaten paths of tradition" are those who genuinely follow in the path of the prophets.[49] As he saw it, the contemporary "traditions" of the East were passivity in the face of imperialism, accommodation of foreign ways, and escapism, all fostered and condoned by the religious and political establishments as well as the Sufi orders. He saved biting irony for the mullahs, the learned men whose rigidity, petty-mindedness, and otherworldliness he found inappropriate to Islam. In the *Javid Nama*, Said Halim Pasha says of the mullah: "Short of vision, blind of taste, an idle gossip, his hair-splitting arguments have fragmented the community."[50] Iqbal said a mullah would find heaven unbearable for the lack of someone to quarrel with over trifles. Although committed to the Sufi preference for heart and love over mind, Iqbal objected to neo-Platonic mysticism for its withdrawal from the world. His objection to monarchy was standard: It violated the principles of Islam and the practice of Islam under Muhammad and his immediate successors.

When Iqbal compared the living tradition of Islam with the Islam of the Qur'an and the Prophet, he found it wanting in daring, in valor, in imagination, and in heroism. That Muslims should have been drawn toward European ways demonstrated the debility of the living tradition. He saw clearly that imperialism had encroached not just upon territory but upon ways of being, and for that he blamed Muslims themselves as much as Europeans. Muslims had become sheep, accepting not just economic and political but psychological dependence.

> *The mind is prisoner to others' thoughts,*
> *Another's music throbs within thy throat,*
> *Thy very speech is borrowed, and thy heart*
> *Dilates with aspirations not thine own.*[51]

The traditional world of the East had become "colonizable," as Albert Memmi and Malek Bennabi would later put it.[52]

The present held no inspiration. "Mosque, school and tavern, all alike are barren."[53] Muslims could only look into the unplumbed depths of their own beings to rediscover the heroic age of Islam. Iqbal viewed

Muhammad as a revolutionary who did not blanch at the use of violence to change the world. "[Iqbal] glorified the early days of Islam because of its revolutionary role in human affairs, but he did not advocate a return to the primitive conditions of those days."[54] It was the spirit of Muhammad and his followers, their creative response to revelation and reality, that he admired.

Iqbal called upon Muslims to recapture that spirit and to act in a similarly revolutionary fashion. In the *Javid Nama*, the Martyr-King says: "Without rebellion the self is unattainable."[55] In the *Javid Nama*, God himself tells Zinda-Rud: "Man of God, be trenchant as a sword, / be yourself your own world's destiny!"[56] Revolution carries a price in human life, and Iqbal clearly believed it had to be paid. His repeated exaltation of strength, power, military prowess, and violence makes that conclusion inescapable.

The revolutionary thrust of Iqbal's thought propelled him into practical politics. His wholehearted espousal of Muslim autonomy in India contributed to the emergence of a new nation-state, Pakistan, yet he also denounced territorial nationalism. He preached tolerance of other faiths but advocated the suppression of Qadianism, which threatened Muslim unity. These positions and others drew charges of inconsistency. Fazlur Rahman has argued that the apparent contradictions reflect an underlying unity of Iqbal's thought. "There seems to us . . . no contradiction in Iqbal's universalistic message on the one hand and in his firm appeals to and unfailing faith in the present Muslim Community."[57] I suggest that it is the nature of the "universalistic message," anchored not in universals but in particularity, that generates the tensions in Iqbal's politics.

Any exponent of authenticity must wrestle with dilemmas generated by potential contradictions among fundamental elements of such thought: its simultaneous emphasis on particularity, unicity, autonomy, and radicalism. For example, the assertion that autonomous human beings shape their own destinies makes apparent the usefulness of group action. Yet the self as ultimate reality, the bedrock of a particularistic view, mitigates against group identification and solidarity. Unicity suggests the possibility of human beings living in consonance with one another and their environment, but the radical denunciation of routine, of everydayness, and of clerical religion makes it difficult to envision any set of institutions by which such consonance could be achieved or maintained. Radicalism predisposes such a system of thought toward adaptation and change, yet the commitment to autonomy sets such a system squarely against the modernist notion of "progress" and moves it toward some seemingly undetermined objective. The particularistic vision of the self favors liberalism and democracy, but the radical rejection of both reason and tradition as adequate bases for decision, as well as the assertion of the need for inspired leadership and iron will, generate reservations about liberal democracy. Insofar as Iqbal sustains an argument for authenticity, he necessarily confronts such dilemmas, magnified or reduced, as the case may be, by his own elaboration of the theory. The significance of Iqbal's contribution depends not on the existence of apparent contradictions but on the fact that he confronts them.

Group Action

Iqbal's *The Mysteries of Selflessness*, coming in the wake of *Secrets of the Self*, constituted his response to the problem of group action. Although in *Secrets of the Self* he had lauded individual autonomy and initiative ("Beware of incurring obligations, beware!"[58] and "Sweet is a little dew gathered by one's own hand"[59]), he demonstrated in *The Mysteries of Selflessness* that the community is a constituent element of the self. As a part of the world and as body as well as spirit, the individual reflects cultural and natural environments. The community reflects the past, and the past is the key to self-understanding; it contains the possibility of authenticity.

> *What thing is history, O self-unaware?*
> *A fable? Or a legendary tale?*
> *Nay, 'tis the thing that maketh thee aware*
> *Of thy true self, alert until the task,*
> *A seasoned traveller; this is the source*
> *Of the soul's ardour, this the nerves that knit*
> *The body of the whole Community.*[60]

A sense of community, built among Muslims on love of the Prophet, thus precedes and conditions any sense of self. A true self knows its path and acquires its impetus from the past, and since the community necessarily mediates historical understanding, what could be more natural than community action?

The solution, however, is not so straightforward. The community from which the Muslim draws strength and inspiration is also the community Iqbal accuses of mullahism, mysticism, and monarchy. It is the community of the *Complaint and Answer*, a community content to blame God for its fate but unwilling to take responsibility for its own destiny. Consequently, when Iqbal felt himself obliged in *The Mysteries of Selflessness* to praise conformity to communal norms, the endorsement came qualified. He entitled the relevant section: "That in Times of Decadence Strict Conformity is Better than Free Speculation."[61] He cited law as the basis of community but elsewhere condemned legalism and the rigidity enforced by the orthodox schools of law. In short, the basis for group action turns out to be the reason for inaction and even an object of Iqbal's revolutionary challenge. Not surprisingly, loneliness outweighs solidarity as a theme of his work, despite *The Mysteries of Selflessness*, which might have been intended to mollify critics as much as to advance Iqbal's central thesis.[62]

The problem of group action becomes one of consciousness-raising. That role falls to great leadership, to someone who can espouse a goal and move people out of their flaccidity. The great leader "reschools them in God's wondrous unity," he said.[63] Even the poet may have a role. Rumi says in the *Javid Nama*: "If the purpose of poetry is the fashioning of men, / poetry is likewise the heir of prophecy."[64] Iqbal saw himself as contributing to the construction of a new community within (but also against) the existing one, and his allies in that task were not self-evident or numerous.

Iqbal's "solution" to the problem of group action partially conceals another difficulty. For Iqbal, faith can be the only genuine basis for group action. He dismisses race and territory as false grounds for solidarity.

> *Our Essence is not bound to any one Place;*
> *The vigor of our wine is not contained*
> *In any bowl.*[65]

Nationalism and racism threaten the unicity of the plurality of selves, which is a central tenet of Iqbal's faith. Faith does divide the contemporary world, but such divisions would melt away if humankind came to accept Iqbal's proposition: To know oneself is to know God, and, conversely, to know God is to know oneself. Since that proposition is the central impulse of Islam, Muslims need not abandon their faith, and non-Muslims need only rally to the proposition to fulfill the promise of unity carried in the assertion of *tawhīd*. *Authentic faith is belief in such a oneness and thus not divisive; enlightened group action can, as a consequence, be reconciled with the universality of understanding to which Iqbal aspires.*

The argument, however consistent, is less than persuasive, because it hinges on the distinction between cultural-religious and ethnic or national sources of identity: "Patriotism is a perfectly natural virtue and has its place in the moral life of man. Yet that which really matters is a man's faith, his culture, his historical tradition. These are the things which in my opinion are worth living for and dying for."[66] His case against nationalism, as an idea of recent origin and relative evanescence—individuals and nations all die but community lives on—stands up much better than the effort to rule out ethnicity as a focal point of identity. Elie Kedourie's demonstrations of the artificiality and perniciousness of territorial nationalism as it has come to grip the modern world buttress Iqbal's contention.[67] But Iqbal's effort to distinguish ethnicity from faith, culture, and historical tradition lacks similar support. To disengage Islam from the culture and history of the Arabs is to ignore the debt of Muhammad to ethnic identity and to diminish the accomplishments of the first century of Islamic history. Muhammad established one community, "the world its parish,"[68] as Iqbal observed, but identity as a Muslim often lies on top of older, ethnic loyalties which, however submerged, have never ceased to underpin culture and historical tradition. If these loyalties cannot be disentangled from a Muslim's identity with Islam, then the possibility of reconciling group action with Iqbal's vision of unity within Islamdom and beyond is diminished.

If Iqbal had been a philosophical idealist, this problem might have been less acute. He might have argued, for instance, that endorsement of Muslim India's cause against a Hindu-dominated state reflected a necessary holding action quite removed from God's ideal of unity, which only He in His Wisdom might one day choose to implement. But Iqbal explicitly rejected a dualistic position. God gave human beings full responsibility for their destiny, Iqbal said. There will be no future prophet to guide them. They must struggle to understand themselves, which means recognizing their origins in community. As they realize their own identities, they will move closer to the Absolute Ego and understand the common ground of being. "All development, creativity and multiplicity must take place with reference to the unitive principle . . . and take place it must."[69] Communalism must be undertaken and understood not just as movement toward universalism but as a projection of it. The tension cannot be relieved by a convenient disjunction of theory and reality. Rather, according to Iqbal, such tension can and must produce creativity.

Creativity evokes individual effort, not group action, however, and the effort to engender rightly guided communal effort thus leads back to the need for poetry, philosophy, and leadership united in one person. That observation appears to be a call for another prophet, but of course it is not; Iqbal repeatedly emphasized the finality of Muhammad's prophethood. Faith may be the basis for community but does not identify those who distinguish the "true Islam" from nationalism and ethnicity and proclaim its universalistic calling. Only enlightened leadership can further the "purpose of Muhammad's mission," which was "to found freedom, equality and brotherhood among all mankind."[70]

Democracy

Freedom, equality, and brotherhood seem to parallel *liberté, egalité,* and *fraternité* and point Iqbal toward liberalism, democracy, and socialism. By freedom, he meant man's autonomy, his capacity to choose either right or wrong. The concept of right conduct depends on the human ability to do otherwise. By equality, he seems to have meant equal dignity. He says

Muhammad was "Impatient with discriminations all, / His soul was pregnant with Equality."[71] Iqbal rejected Nietzsche's contempt for the "herd," recalling that early Islam had drawn its strength from lowly camel herders.[72] By brotherhood, he surely referred not just to the community of believers but to a human species cognizant of its fundamental unity with God and with nature. All three definitions reflect his fundamental principles, but his elaboration of these definitions put him at odds with democratic theory.

In some respects this may seem surprising, since Iqbal prized individuality above all else and said God had put human beings in charge of their own fate. He abhorred distinctions of race, nation, or class. He denounced monarchy, praised the law, and lauded the egalitarianism of early Islam. Yet he was not a social democrat. In a poem entitled "East and West," he wrote:

> *Slavery, slavishness, the root of our*
> *Disease; of theirs, that Demos holds all power;*
> *Heart-malady or brain-malady has oppressed*
> *Man's whole world, sparing neither East nor West.*[73]

He linked democracy with brain-malady via reason and its product, legality. "This is not in itself bad," he wrote, "but unfortunately it tends to displace the purely moral standpoint, and to make the illegal and the wrong identical in meaning."[74] Freedom is responsibility before God for one's actions rather than freedom within the law as made or interpreted by mankind. The separation of secular and religious spheres implied by the concept of positive law is "unthinkable to a Muslim,"[75] he wrote. The religious law, as a set of guidelines offered through Muhammad, enjoys higher status than the positive law, but Iqbal conditioned his appeal for conformity to that law on circumstances of decay. Authenticity comes before the law and especially before the secular law.

His objection to Demos stemmed even more from his understanding of equality than from his notion of freedom. The rule of the majority meant, in the case of Iqbal's India, the domination of Muslims by Hindus. Majority rule would have deprived the Muslims and other minorities of their autonomy. "As far as I can see, there will be no peace in this country until the various peoples that constitute India are given opportunities of free self-development on modern lines without abruptly breaking with their past," he wrote.[76] Since Iqbal saw communities as extensions of the self (and viewed selves as products of communities), he equated their right to self-development with the achievement of selfhood. Communities, not majorities, preserve the equality of human dignity and protect against discrimination.

Moreover, as a radical thinker, Iqbal had to confront the conservative nature of any majority. When he spoke of the slavishness of the East, he was thinking of the majority. When he spoke of conditions in India, he undoubtedly referred not just to the division between Hindus and Muslims but to the unlettered, unambitious, undiscerning characteristics of the great numbers. Radical change of circumstances calls for power and leadership. Minorities have shaped the history of the world, he noted. "Character is the irresistible force which determines the destinies of nations, and an intense character is not possible in a majority."[77]

Iqbal preferred consensus to majority rule as a means of legitimating leadership. "The idea of universal agreement is, in fact, the fundamental principle of Muslim constitutional theory," he said.[78] Consensus gives leadership greater leeway and affirms the unity of the community; it eliminates the problem of minorities by excluding them. Witness Iqbal's attitude toward Qadians and Bahais, who, he said, had put themselves beyond the Islamic community by rejecting the finality of Muhammad's prophethood. Minorities become consensual communities of their own, producing the sort of fragmentation Iqbal feared but accepted as a consequence of the principle of self-determination.

It is perhaps Iqbal's understanding of brotherhood that puts him furthest from liberal, democratic theory and brings him closest to the socialist ideal. For Iqbal, brotherhood is a fact to be understood through a combination of reason and faith. Islam provides such an understanding, though perhaps not the only one, and opens the door to universal brotherhood of the sort socialists also dreamed of. For socialists, fraternity was to emerge as an extension of the natural solidarity of the working class; for Iqbal, it was to be a natural outgrowth of the community of the faith. For him and the socialists, the liberal-democratic propensity to divide the world into peoples with sovereignty over nation-states appeared arbitrary and destructive of universal brotherhood. Equality within those states—the emergence of King Demos—had contributed to imperialistic tendencies, to the subjugation of much of the Third World, and, in particular, to the "slavishness of the East," as he put it. Democracy had produced not brotherhood but alienation.

In this sense, freedom, equality, and brotherhood all conflicted, in Iqbal's view, with liberal democracy as it had been institutionalized in the West and had been proposed as a system of government for an independent Indian state. Certainly, he accepted many of the principles—equal human dignity, for instance—on which democracy is based, and even more important, he accepted the need for the kind of adaptation and change democracy provides. He referred to "spiritual democracy" as the "ultimate aim of Islam,"[79] but he distrusted the idea of democracy, as he distrusted all other ideas divorced from circumstance and the spirit of creation. His call for a return to origins in search of the authentic self took precedence over any and all institutionalized forms of decisionmaking, including the democratic.

Institutions

Institutions represent both the continuity of tradition and the rationality of modernity, but authentic thought rebels against both in the name of innovation, creativity, originality, particularity, autonomy, and truthfulness. In this light, it would be surprising if Iqbal had held a predominantly positive view of institutions.

How Muslims ought to be governed is less clear than how they ought not to be. Although Iqbal praised the dynamism of Mustafa Kemal's Turkey,[80] he vigorously condemned the result as mere imitation of Europe.[81] It contained, he said "no fresh breath," "no design of a new world." He said the secret of Islam was the law, yet he stressed the need for modification more than the need for conformity, except in times of decadence. He lauded the ways of the Prophet, but Iqbal's goal "was never simply to re-create the past in an Islamic State."[82] Rather, he cited the principles of the Islamic "Constitution"—the law of God is supreme and all members enjoy absolute equality[83]—which might presumably be institutionalized differently at various times and places in consonance with what he called the dynamic spirit of Islam.[84] He heaped severities on both the monarchic and the canonical tendencies of Islam for the constraints they placed on that dynamism. Machiavelli received parallel condemnation for his dedication to a dynamic but secular state.[85]

Iqbal did advocate an independent educational system for Muslim India. Complaining that Muslim children learned much more than they needed about Puritanism and Cromwell, he said that British education in India was "not true to our genius as a nation. . . . In order to be truly ourselves, we ought to have our own schools, our own colleges and our own universities."[86] This was clearly a call not for institutional stability but for authenticity and change. Educational institutions, however stodgy, occupy a marginal position in society, reflections of the status quo but producers of innovation and creativity. For one who wishes to transform the consciousness of humankind, they are perhaps indispensable.

That Iqbal understood the value of institutions emerges clearly from *The Mysteries of Selflessness.* In carefully guarded ways, he spends page after page paying homage to the Islamic way. But the main body of his thought cuts against the grain of those arguments and against all known and existing institutions in favor of new, original, authentic solutions. He did not explain how any hypothetical solution could avoid institutionalization or how any society could survive without it. He did say tension and turbulence could produce creativity and seems to have envisioned a changing society with a lower quotient of institutionalization than either traditionalists or some modernists might find acceptable.

Modernity

By its radical rejection of tradition, authentic thought commits itself to a conception of history controlled by human beings. Through a critique of both idealism and materialism, it embraces change as genuine but undetermined. By a denial of duality, it deprives reason of its imperial position and social science of its objective capacity to discern the future. As a consequence of its particularity, authentic thought undermines liberal and Marxist efforts to define development. But what then is the proper direction of change? What is the meaning of history? How does the worldwide infatuation with the idea of development affect one's practical ability to chart another, more authentic course?

Iqbal accepted Ibn Khaldun's perception of life as a phenomenon of continuous movement but rejected all suggestions, including Ibn Khaldun's, that change followed patterns of necessity. Whereas Ibn Khaldun discerned cyclical patterns in human events and traced them to a human nature vacillating from asceticism to hedonism according to the circumstances of the moment, Iqbal believed in the perfectibility of the human species. He spoke of stages of development: (1) obedience to the law, (2) self-control, and (3) divine vice-regency, that level where "thought and action, instinct and reason become one."[87] Although not every person could necessarily achieve divine vice-regency, everyone might aspire to the second level, *faqr*, which signified detachment from one's material possessions.[88] As a consequence, human beings could, contrary to Ibn Khaldun's perspective, rise above their circumstances by surpassing themselves. History as the story of life lies beyond necessity,[89] and Iqbal is certainly an idealist from this perspective.

If human nature itself does not impose limits, neither does God. The Islamic notion of *taqdīr*, destiny, contains no hint of predestination:

> As the Qur'an says: "God created all things and assigned to each its destiny." The destiny of a thing then is not an unrelenting fate working from without like a task master; it is the inward reach of a thing, its realizable possibilities which lie within the depths of its nature, and serially actualize themselves without any feeling of external compulsion.[90]

Human beings possess the possibility of achieving a high degree of selfhood through the absorption of godly qualities. Blessed with self-consciousness, they are capable of looking into themselves, understanding their potential and seeking to realize it. It is they, not God, who determine their own success or failure and qualify, or fail to qualify, for eternal life. That possibility lies within their potential.

To achieve eternal life implies, of course, that humankind can overcome even the ravages of time. Iqbal takes direct issue with Nietzsche on this point. By pushing historicism to its extreme, Nietzsche demonstrated that the passage of time erodes all human effort; just as death takes away the body, changing times and circumstances undercut ideas, even the idea that there is pattern in the events of history. Most human action thus seems predicated on an illusion: that what one is and what one does endures beyond the moment and the circumstance.[91] Can one face the world without such an illusion? The prospect appears overwhelming, but Nietzsche finds relief in eternal recurrence. Although the present is always swept away, it reflects the past and conditions the future, which in turn, both prospectively and retrospectively, refashions history. Permanence is illusion, but so is novelty; continuous creativity works within a circulating stream of human activity. Every evanescent act contributes to the permanence of the human enterprise. Death assures the oneness of life.[92] Such is Nietzsche's hypothesis.

Despite his admiration for some of Nietzsche's thought, especially the critique of idealism, Iqbal found those conclusions unacceptable. Iqbal entertained the possibility of human improvement, which he found consistent with the meliorative outlook of the Qur'an, and he could not accept Nietzsche's arguments about the transience and fragmentation of the self. He sought to reconcile his rejection of philosophical idealism with the possibility of eternal life and to rescue from Nietzschean destruction the prospect of moral improvement—without, of course, falling back into the mechanistic and deterministic traps of Western sociological analysis, which violated his assumptions about human autonomy.

To achieve that purpose, Iqbal posited two sorts of time, serial time and "pure duration"—an idea he adapted from Bergson. God exists in pure duration, whereas the physical world evolves in serial time. But all things with a sense of self also participate in pure duration. Human beings, whose destiny is the realization of their potential for self-consciousness, achieve a sense of self by gathering together their momentary feelings and the sum total of their thoughts and activities into a single being that transcends time; that is what it means to discover the self, to know God and to participate in a phenomenon characteristic of the Absolute Ego, or pure duration. As man moved through the stages of self-consciousness, from obedience to self-control to divine vice-regency, he would be more capable of transcending serial time and experiencing the eternal—pure duration. He could aspire to be the "perfect man" of 'Abd al-Karim al-Jili (d. early fifteenth century). Iqbal said Nietzsche had mistakenly rejected the possibility of "the eternal now," a window of escape toward the health of the individual and the amelioration of the human race. "The perfection of the perfect man, according to Islam, consists in realizing this aspect of time which can be described only as the eternal now. To Nietzsche there is no such thing as the eternal now."[93]

One critic has said: "To [Iqbal], life is perpetual striving in behalf of great and worthy ideals."[94] In an ordinary sense, that is true, but in a more rigorous sense, it is not. The "ideal" he espoused derived not from reason or from God but from suprarational perception of selfhood uniting the disparate images of human activity. The development of the self emerges from the particular via intuition as well as reason. This truth leaves open the course of human striving rather than attaching it to any preordained set of great and worthy ideals, like those so tightly associated with Western notions of development—with this qualification: The self and the community from which it derives its sense of identity stand as primordial values. Their primordiality stems, however, not from reason but from a combination of experience and instinct. For human beings, existence precedes essence, but one facet of human existence is the sense of self, which leads to the discovery of the oneness of the world. Existence leads toward the encounter with essence, which ultimately explains existence. God's essence preconditions existence.

Iqbal's understanding of the human predicament thus combined what he saw as the best elements of East and West. It opened the door to the embrace of technological progress without succumbing to positivism and its irrational attachment to empiricism. It incorporated the mystical insights of the East without accepting quietism as a necessary concomitant. It embraced the dynamic understanding of history without resigning itself either to circularity or meaninglessness. Iqbal opposed Westernization, either by imposition or imitation, without demanding a return to the traditions of the East, which had fallen into disrepair. An authentic response to the human predicament lay, in his view, in the effort to reconcile rationalism and mysticism, permanence and change. "True Islam" does just that, and the intuition of the self authenticates "true Islam."

↵Ↄ

Iqbal's reputation, like that of most great thinkers, does not ride on a single set of accomplishments or a single idea. It does not depend exclusively on the originality of his philosophy, on the quality of his poetry, or on the contemporary usefulness of his political ideas. To focus on his effort to elaborate a general theory of authenticity is not to diminish his other endeavors or even to insist that this project outweighs any other in a long-range perspective. Rather, it is done to elicit the way in which Iqbal was important to writers such as Sayyid Qutb and 'Ali Shari'ati.

His role must be contrasted with that of Muhammad 'Abdu of Egypt, another admirer of Jamal al-Din al-Afghani, who likewise found fault with Islam as it was practiced. 'Abdu labored to reform Islamic doctrine by giving reason its place; he suggested that Islam and reason both reflected God's truth. They could not conflict.[95] But 'Abdu's work inadvertently exposed revelation to the onslaught of reason and legitimated the wholesale infatuation with liberalism and the West that pervaded Egypt in the 1920s. The rapid growth of the Muslim Brotherhood in the 1930s probably reflected a perception that Egypt, influenced by 'Abdu, among others, was losing touch with its own past. Although his name is often associated with Islamic revival and reform, 'Abdu represented one pole of what Iqbal sought to guard against: the tyranny of reason.

The other pole was tradition. Iqbal's conception of Islam prevented him from invoking mere precedent as justification for legal findings. His skepticism of religious scholarship and his outright denunciation of monarchy make it seem dubious he would have seen virtue in the "traditional monarchies" of the Middle East, notwithstanding their efforts at modernization. Iqbal would have been as contemptuous as Abdallah Laroui of those regimes and those movements that utilize "tradition as ideology"— but for entirely different reasons. Laroui demeans them for obstructing the progress of history, whereas Iqbal, denying any such discernible pattern in history, would see tradition as an obstacle to the realization of authenticity. If the principal characteristic of contemporary Islamic "fundamentalism" is the insistence that the Islamic tradition constitutes a political ideology, Iqbal is not a "fundamentalist," although he does plumb the Islamic tradition for inspiration. Laroui claims that the historicism of Marx permits the Arabs to join the West by revolting against it, but Iqbal, one step more radical, would suggest that the revolt cannot be genuinely Eastern if it occurs within a secular, rationalist, historicist, Western perspective.[96]

Does not Iqbal's own thinking lend itself to this criticism? Surely his intense effort to demonstrate Islamic origins for all his ideas reflected sensitivity on that point.[97] Others have sought to show which elements he borrowed from particular European thinkers.[98] Does such borrowing make his thinking about authenticity inauthentic? If Iqbal's fundamental precept is the self as the center of purposive action, it would seem possible for genuinely different people to follow the precept without compromising their originality or their creativity. Rifat Hassan has argued that Iqbal fixed upon this element of his thinking, together with his conviction that spiritual and material worlds cannot be separated, before 1905—before his extensive contact with European thought.[99] And if that precept lurks within Islamic culture as well as within Western culture, as Iqbal claimed, then borrowing is merely a form of substantiation, not of treason.

Whereas Laroui's historicism constitutes a general theory destroying difference, Iqbal's theory of authenticity, though equally general, legitimates particularity, but it also preserves the possibility of solidarity, because the principle itself stems from the nature of the self. Both theories require an act of faith, the one in social science, the other in the self. Iqbal's rings authentic because it is subject to intuitive verification by any reflective person; it is authentically Muslim because it coincides, he argued, with the fundamental impulse of the Islamic faith.

It follows, however, that authenticity does not strictly depend on Islam. The reading of European philosophy seems to have convinced Iqbal that the sense of self lies within human possibilities. Islam represents the best, but perhaps not the only, expression of those possibilities. The truth of his propositions derives from faith, but his faith in the self seems to precede his Islamic faith. Iqbal would contend that the two faiths are mutually reinforcing, but it could be argued that the truth of Islam, as seen by Iqbal, stems from its coincidence with the intuition of the self's potential for being; Islam provides support for that insight and a means for the many to find access to it. The sense of self demands faith in God, but faith in God does not necessarily require an understanding of self; the recent history of Islam stands as testimony to that fact. Like Ibn Khaldun, who argued the philosophers were "wrong when they assume that prophecy exists by necessity,"[100] Iqbal kept his understanding of faith "authentic" by denying the logical necessity of "true Islam" while asserting its centrality to the self-understanding of Muslims. He sought to "save" Islam much as Kierkegaard sought to "save" Christianity from both Platonism and tradition,[101] yet it is still not clear what he preserved. He accepted one precept of modernism—that human beings "are indeed the authors of their own actions"; but he tried to avoid the disastrous consequences of its corollary "that they are fully entitled to act on the basis of their own calculated interests"[102] by showing that genuine individuality reflected an understanding of the common good by virtue of the underlying oneness of being. He left unspecified what that common good would be in the realm of politics. Although he rescued the "true Islam" from the grasp of reason, it is less clear that he saved it from the ravages of autonomy and particularity, which are fundamental to his definition of authenticity.

Notes

1. Syed 'Abdul Vahid, *Iqbal, His Art and Thought* (Lahore: Ashraf, 1944), p. 3.

2. Wilfred Cantwell Smith, *Modern Islam in India: A Social Analysis* (London: Victor Gollancz, 1946), p. 101.

3. Ibid.

4. Vahid, *Iqbal, His Art and Thought*, chap. 1.

5. Muhammad Iqbal, *Poems from Iqbal*, trans. V. G. Kiernan (London: Murray, 1955), p. 72.

6. Ibid., p. 78.

7. Fazl-ur Rahman, "Iqbal and Mysticism," in *Iqbal as a Thinker* (Lahore: Ashraf, 1944), p. 223.

8. Iqbal, "Ghazal No. 13," in *Poems*, p. 31.

9. Iqbal developed this theme in *Shikwa and Jawab-i-Shikwa: Complaint and Answer, Iqbal's Dialogue with Allah*, trans. Khushwant Singh (Delhi: Oxford, 1981).

10. Muhammad Iqbal, *The Mysteries of Selflessness*, trans. Arthur J. Arberry (London: Murray, 1953), p. 5.

11. Iqbal, *Poems*, p. 137.

12. Rahman, "Iqbal and Mysticism," p. 217.

13. Muhammad Iqbal, *The Reconstruction of Religious Thought in Islam* (Lahore: Ashraf, 1982), p. 12.

14. Muhammad Iqbal, *Javid-Nama*, trans. Arthur J. Arberry (London: Allen and Unwin, 1966), p. 21.

15. Ibid., p. 100.

16. Mohammad Iqbal, *Secrets of the Self: A Philosophical Poem*, trans. R. A. Nicholson. (New Delhi: Arnold-Heinemann, 1978), p. 48.

17. Mohamed Iqbal, *Thoughts and Reflections of Iqbal*, ed. Syed Abdul Vahid (Lahore: Ashraf, 1964), sec. 8, p. 99.

18. Iqbal, *Mysteries*, p. 7.

19. Iqbal, *Reconstruction*, p. 31.

20. Iqbal, "Solitude," in *Poems*, pp. 94–95.

21. Iqbal, *Reconstruction*, p. 31.

22. Iqbal, *Javid Nama*, p. 48.

23. Iqbal, *Thoughts*, sec. 9, p. 115.

24. Quoted by Annemarie Schimmel, "Mystic Impact of Hallaj," in *Iqbal: Poet-Philosopher of Pakistan*, ed. Hafeez Malik (New York: Columbia, 1971), p. 314.

25. Fazlur Rahman, "Some Aspects of Iqbal's Political Thought," *Studies in Islam* 5 (1968), p. 162.

26. Iqbal, *Thoughts*, sec. 16, p. 163.

27. Iqbal, *Reconstruction*, preface, p. v.

28. Iqbal, *Complaint and Answer*, p. 96.

29. Vahid, *Iqbal, His Art and Thought*, chap. 2.

30. Iqbal, *Javid Nama*, p. 126.

31. Ibid., p. 94.

32. Iqbal, *Poems*, no. 105, p. 85.

33. Iqbal, *Secrets*, p. 54.

34. Iqbal, *Poems*, no. 61, pp. 62–63.

35. Iqbal, *Javid Nama*, p. 85.

36. Ibid., p. 95.

37. Vahid, *Iqbal, His Art and Thought*, p. 49.

38. Ibid., p. 62.

39. Iqbal, *Reconstruction*, p. 57.

40. Iqbal, *Secrets*, p. 59.

41. Iqbal, *Thoughts*, sec. 3, p. 34.

42. Ibid., p. 41.

43. Iqbal, *Poems*, no. 80, p. 70.

44. Rafiz Zakaria, foreword to *Complaint and Answer*, p. 10.

45. Iqbal, *Reconstruction*, pp. 187–188.

46. See Lionel Trilling, *Sincerity and Authenticity* (Cambridge: Harvard University Press, 1972), pp. 106–110, for an analysis of Conrad's *The Heart of Darkness*.

47. Iqbal, *Javid Nama*, p. 108.

48. Khalifa Abdul Hakim, "Rumi, Nietzsche and Iqbal," in *Iqbal as a Thinker*, p. 169.

49. Ibid., p. 171.

50. Iqbal, *Javid Nama*, p. 65.

51. Iqbal, *Mysteries*, p. 73.

52. Malek Bennabi, *Vocation de l'Islam* (Paris: Seuil, 1954), p. 32, and Albert Memmi, *The Colonizer and the Colonized*, trans. Howard Greenfeld (New York: Orion Press, 1965).

53. Iqbal, *Javid Nama*, p. 70.

54. Zakaria, foreword to *Complaint and Answer*, p. 10.

55. Iqbal, *Javid Nama*, p. 131.

56. Ibid., p. 138.

57. Rahman, "Some Aspects of Iqbal's Political Thought," p. 164.

58. Iqbal, *Secrets*, p. 48.

59. Ibid., p. 50.

60. Iqbal, *Mysteries*, p. 61.

61. Ibid., p. 40.

62. "Iqbal's mind was simply incapable, apparently, of dealing with men in community. He was excellent in thinking about the individual; but he floundered badly when he approached questions of society, the relations of many individuals to one another. He certainly tried to think about such questions and wrote a whole poetical treatise on the subject. But every attempt was a failure; he himself, the poet, knew that he was not at all at home with practical complex affairs." Wilfred Cantwell Smith, *Modern Islam in India*, p. 133.

63. Iqbal, *Mysteries*, p. 9.

64. Iqbal, *Javid Nama*, p. 45.

65. Iqbal, *Mysteries*, p. 29.

66. Iqbal, *Thoughts*, sec. 17, p. 197.

67. Elie Kedourie, *Nationalism* (London: Hutchinson, 1960).

68. Iqbal, *Mysteries*, p. 30.

69. Rahman, "Some Aspects of Iqbal's Political Thought," p. 162.

70. "That the Purpose of Muhammad's Mission Was to Found Freedom, Equality and Brotherhood Among All Mankind" is the title of a section in Iqbal, *Mysteries*, p. 21.

71. Iqbal, *Mysteries*, p. 23.

72. Iqbal, *Thoughts*, sec. 6.

73. Iqbal, *Poems*, sec. 102, p. 78.

74. Iqbal, *Thoughts*, sec. 5, p. 78.

75. Ibid., sec. 16, p. 163.

76. Ibid., p. 189.

77. Ibid., sec. 5, p. 79.

78. Ibid., sec. 4, p. 58.

79. Iqbal, *Reconstruction*, p. 180.

80. Ibid., p. 162.

81. Iqbal, *Javid Nama*, p. 58.

82. Rahman, "Some Aspects of Iqbal's Political Thought", p. 162.

83. Iqbal, *Thoughts*, sec. 3, p. 52.

84. Iqbal, *Reconstruction*, p. 138.

85. Iqbal, *Mysteries*, p. 32.

86. Iqbal, *Thoughts*, sec. 3, p. 44.

87. Vahid, *Iqbal, His Art and Thought*, p. 62.

88. One may nonetheless doubt Vahid's assertion: "Iqbal is not content merely with turning kings into philosophers and philosophers into kings like Plato; he aims at turning every man into a Faqir, and his Faqir is something much more than Plato's Philosopher and King combined." It is true that Iqbal places no limit on man's ability to improve. Vahid, *Iqbal, His Art and Thought*, p. 79.

89. Iqbal, *Reconstruction*, p. 50.

90. Ibid., p. 50.

91. Friedrich Nietzsche, "The Use and Abuse of History," in *Thoughts out of Season*, Part 2 (London: Allen, 1927), p. 12.

92. Nietzsche, *Thus Spoke Zarathustra*, trans. Walter Kauffman (Middlesex: Penguin, 1981), pp. 155–160.

93. Iqbal, *Thoughts*, sec. 22, p. 242.

94. K. G. Saiyidain, "Progressive Trends in Iqbal's Thought," in *Iqbal as a Thinker* (Lahore: Ashraf, 1944), pp. 42–106.

95. Malcolm H. Kerr, *Islamic Reform: The Political and Legal Theories of Muhammad 'Abduh and Rashid Rida* (Berkeley: University of California Press, 1966), p. 109.

96. Abdallah Laroui, *The Crisis of the Arab Intellectual*, trans. Diarmid Cammell (Berkeley: University of California Press, 1976).

97. See A. H. Kamali, "The Heritage of Islamic Thought," in Malik, *Iqbal: Poet-Philosopher of Pakistan*, pp. 211–242, for the best concise discussion of Iqbal's debts to the Islamic tradition.

98. See B. A. Dar, "Inspiration from the West," in Malik, *Iqbal: Poet-Philosopher of Pakistan*, for a succinct discussion.

99. Rifat Hassan, "The Development of Political Philosophy," in Malik, *Iqbal: Poet-Philosopher of Pakistan*, p. 140.

100. Ibn Khaldun, *The Muqaddimah: An Introduction to History*, trans. Franz Rosenthal (Princeton: Princeton University Press, 1967), p. 48.

101. Sören Kierkegaard, *Philosophical Fragments or a Fragment of Philosophy*, trans. David F. Swenson and Howard V. Hong (Princeton: Princeton University Press, 1962).

102. Kerr, *Islamic Reform*, p. 222.

four

✦

Sayyid Qutb

UNLIKE IQBAL, WHO LARDED HIS TEXT with references to Nietzsche, Schopenhauer, and Bergson, Sayyid Qutb studiously avoided such references to learned Europeans, although his literary background suggests he knew something of modern philosophy. Born in Asyut Province in Egypt in 1906 to devout parents, Qutb first studied in Qur'anic schools in his village of Qaha and managed to memorize the Qur'an by the age of ten. At thirteen, with his parents moving to Helwan on the southern outskirts of Cairo, he transferred to secondary school in Cairo, and in 1929, at age sixteen, he entered the Dar al-'Ulum, which ultimately became Cairo University. Studying with Abbas Mahmud al-Aqqad, one of the leading lights of Egyptian liberalism, "he became extremely interested in English literature and read avidly anything he could lay his hands on in translation. Upon graduation he was appointed as inspector of the Ministry of Education, a position he eventually gave up to devote himself exclusively to writing."[1] He wrote poetry, stories, and articles, many of them devoted to the critique of literature. He later said he regretted writing these things.

His decision to abandon literary criticism after World War II represented disillusionment with the West and a renewed interest in Islam. He reacted negatively to British policies during World War II, which he saw as reneging on newly granted Egyptian independence and denying Arabs the right to self-determination in Palestine. During the war, he wrote two books in which he approached the Qur'an as literature, and then in 1948, he finished a book called *Social Justice in Islam*, which was published the following year, while he was on a two-year educational mission to the United States.[2] Upon his return home, he joined the Muslim Brotherhood, a lay movement founded in the 1920s, which by the 1940s had become the single largest political force in Egypt. "His stay in America made a deep impression upon him, and he returned convinced that the materialistic

civilization of the West—Communism being just a logical extreme of it—
is devoid of basic human values and is leading mankind toward spiritual,
social and even physical destruction."[3]

Sayyid Qutb's dedication to the development and propagation of a radical version of Islam from the late 1940s until his death in 1966 put him at
odds not only with occidental imperialism but with the modernist regime
of Gamal 'abd al-Nasir, which came to power in Egypt in 1952. At first
Nasir welcomed the support of the Muslim Brotherhood and liberated its
leaders from prison, but mistrust between the regime and the brotherhood led to a falling out in late 1954, when the brotherhood was banned
and its leaders, including Sayyid Qutb, propagandist and journal editor,
were again jailed. Qutb spent the rest of his life in prison, where he revised thirteen volumes of commentary on the Qur'an and wrote two
other books. Liberated in December 1964 and then rearrested in August
1965, he faced charges based on his claims in a book called *Milestones*,
published during his few months of freedom, that all existing Arab governments (including the Nasir government in Egypt) were un-Islamic. He
was convicted and hung in 1966.

As propagandist for the Muslim Brotherhood in Egypt in the 1950s and
1960s, Sayyid Qutb suffered and died for what Emmanuel Sivan wrongly
calls "a total rejection of modernity, since modernity represents the nega-
tion of God's sovereignty . . . in all fields of life and relegation of religion
to the dustbin of history."[4] The appeal of his thought and the strength of
the radical Islamic groups that have worked from his ideas ("Few Muslim
thinkers have had as significant an impact on the reformulation of contemporary Islamic thought as has Sayyid Qutb"[5]) may depend on a perception that he draws exclusively from an authentic Islamic well. Qutb
himself would have wished to foster that impression, which is nonetheless misleading, if not utterly inaccurate.

Qutb's thought has emerged as a stimulus of radical Sunnism in Egypt
and in the rest of the Arab world, but he does not espouse a return to the
"traditional" world of Islam, whether one places that tradition in the seventh century or the nineteenth. Although Qutb never explicitly called for
violent attack on his own or other governments that he deemed negligent
of Islamic law, his arguments provide a rationale for others to do so. To eschew critique of his thought in terms other than those of the Islamic tradition is to concede a cardinal point the radicals wish to make: that Islamic
radicalism is, by virtue of its basis in faith, different from all other forms of
radicalism and, indeed, from all ideologies. But such a concession, which a
Westerner might make to avoid charges of ethnocentrism, leads directly to
the portrayal of a mystical, inscrutable, militant, and violence-prone Islam.

To analyze the thought of Sayyid Qutb solely within the confines of
Western modernization theory does not make sense either, because his as-

pirations do not fall within its range. Social mobilization, economic growth, political participation—these are not his primary objectives. He cannot be grouped with modernist reformers such as Muhammad 'Abdu, who sought to bring Islam closer to the Western notion of religion, consistent with the rationality of science and the secularism of society. Qutb writes against modernity in a modern way.[6]

Qutb can and must be compared with European and other Third World thinkers because he rejects the dichotomy between Eastern mysticism and Western rationalism. He is modern by virtue of asking what it means to be human, building on the premise used since the eighteenth century by a number of European writers that neither faith nor rationality provides an adequate response. Qutb can be compared with other "authentics" not because he aped European writers, although he was probably more familiar with their work than his references would suggest,[7] but because he posed the same questions. He did not ask "What is authentic Islam?" or, much less, "What is an authentic hadith?" although these are the ways in which he would employ the word "authentic." He asked, rather, "How can human beings act in the world and still be themselves? How can human beings overcome their base instincts in favor of their spiritual qualities in a world of greed, self-interest, materialism, and impersonal rationality? Can spirituality be recovered without retreat from the world, without monasticism?"

Qutb is radical not only because he denounces all existing Muslim governments but because, sounding very much like Rousseau, he speaks of liberating human beings from all that would obstruct the realization of their God-created potential. His thought is evocative of the work of other authentics in its talk of praxis, of Islam as a stream of historical experience rather than as an ideal. He, like Iqbal, argues that autonomous human beings can, by acts of faith and will, shape an authentic Islamic community— in ways that remind one of Pascal and Kierkegaard. And Qutb's ideas, like those of other authentics, hinge on a unitary ideal, common to all versions of Islam but vital to an interpretation that emphasizes the historicity of experience and the decisiveness of human will in historical outcomes. Qutb may be understood as an advocate of authenticity, and his responses to the challenges of modernity, democracy, institutions, and history may be judged against those of others who have shared that perspective.

Radicalism: Liberation of the Self

Qutb's vision of unlimited human potential makes him a radical. He speaks of human beings as capable of achieving peace within themselves, of balancing their most profoundly human instincts with those needs that are fundamentally alien to them, whether biological or social in origin:

"When the soul is at one with its true nature, when its needs and necessities are fulfilled, when its constructive capacities are released, then with ease and without compulsion . . . in natural harmony with life, will it ascend to the lofty summit ordained for it."[8] Such a project requires the understanding of one's "true nature" via faith; it requires the reshaping of individual behavior according to a code consistent with that true nature and the natural harmony of life. For Qutb, the act of submission to God— Islam—is the first act of individual liberation from the domination of other human beings.

That is not enough, for as liberated individuals we cannot, "with ease and without compulsion," achieve our full potential in a society operated according to rules devised by other human beings. We cannot be ourselves because we are still ruled by others. We can only fulfill the promise of our humanity when the society permits us to be at peace with ourselves and with others, when it permits us not just to submit to God but to God alone; we find a home only in a society that is obedient solely to the will of God. Since no such society exists today, human fulfillment thus demands the formation of a revolutionary elite, the overthrow of existing social arrangements, and the construction of a society regulated by divine rules. Like Rousseau, Qutb seeks not a return to the state of nature but a nonalienating reconciliation of human nature with the requirements of civil society.

By starting from the idea of individuals estranged from their "true nature," Qutb places himself in the company of writers who have confronted the problem of alienation in the context of modernity. Like many thinkers, Western and Islamic, he suggests that human beings are two dimensional: One dimension links us to other animal species; the other dimension, to God. From our animal nature comes a set of needs we can scarcely ignore—food, sleep, sex, and so on—and a set of instincts that help satisfy those needs. Our instinct for self-preservation and our love of self drive us beyond necessity toward the fulfillment of "needs" of our own definition. "Man is a passionate self-lover," wrote Qutb. "But he loves only what he imagines to be good for him: wealth, power, and the pleasures of this world."[9] Naturally, human beings associate freedom with the right to pursue these self-centered objectives. Freedom is the freedom to do whatever one wishes.

Human beings are distinguished from animals, however, by their intellect and their spirit. Qutb thus contrasts our human nature with our animal nature, our real needs (i.e., spiritual needs) with physical and imagined needs, the inner being of mind and spirit with the outer person, dominated by the pursuit of comfort and pleasure. "True freedom," he said, is freedom from the domination of the animal side of one's animal existence. It means freedom from the very forces, the gods, that cause humans to seek the freedom to do whatever they wish, to satisfy their whims, however frivolous. Genuine human freedom, based on the noble side of human nature, means freedom for the inner being and control of the base aspects of human character. That, according to Qutb, is the purpose of religion. The Qur'anic revelations opened the way for human beings to abandon their ignorance and barbarism (*jāhilīya*) and to strive toward the achievement of their own potential.

Where Qutb deviates from mainstream Islamic thought and allies himself with Iqbal and modern European philosophy is in his argument that the onset of modernity, even in countries where the Qur'anic revelation is revered, has exacerbated the problem of alienation. In the West, Christianity cultivated the spiritual by rejecting the secular; according to Qutb, the Roman Catholic Church erred in holding to dogmas that put it at odds with science and with the secular world. Religiosity became synonymous with withdrawal from the world, whereas secular thought, including scientific innovation, moved away from religion by choice or necessity. Human beings thus found themselves regarded by empirical science, on the one hand, as creatures driven by economic, political, social, and sexual needs, and by religion, on the other, as sinners capable of overcoming their weaknesses:

> Now, when man's conscience and feelings are governed by a certain law but his actual life and activities are governed by another, and when the two laws emerge from different conceptions, one from human imagination and the other from the inspiration of God, then such an individual must suffer something similar to schizophrenia."[10]

The Western "solution," the compartmentalization of life in which religion occupies one corner of the human consciousness or is banished altogether, as Marxists would have it, separates human beings from their own spirit, the essence of humanity. Modernity of this kind alienates human beings from themselves. That is Qutb's fundamental proposition, and it puts him in the company of other moderns.

For this reason, Qutb found the human predicament more serious than it was more than a millennium ago, before the advent of Islam: "The clouds which weigh over man's nature are thicker and denser than before. The previous ignorance of God was based on a general ignorance, simplicity and primitiveness. That of the present is based on learning, complexity and frivolity."[11] Is it not worse to imagine that one knows the truth about things, about human volition in particular, than not to know? When human beings find themselves enveloped by social institutions ranging from grade schools to governments is not the cure for alienation more difficult than in an unlettered and unfettered Arabia? And is it not easier to persuade human beings to satisfy fundamental needs in different ways than to dissuade them altogether from acknowledging the needs they themselves have created? Alienation afflicts us as individuals, but we find ourselves separated from our own fundamental nature by these clouds—the pollution of the twentieth century—whether we live in the East or the West, or even in a country that calls itself Muslim. Our ability to look back on the successes of the Islamic revolution in overcoming the ignorance and barbarism of the seventh century constitutes our only significant advantage.

If the first *jāhilīya* was general, splintered, and tribal, the modern version is social, organizational, and collective. For that reason, as individuals we can only achieve liberation by freeing ourselves from the clutches of the collectivity, the clutches of other human beings. Collectivities do not budge, however, unless human beings cause them to move. The impulse toward authenticity lies within human nature. Human beings have a natural need for peace within themselves and peace with the universe.[12] They instinctively turn toward religion as a way out of their schizophrenic plight. "Human nature," he wrote, "conforms basically to the norms of being."[13] "Being" connotes permanence, linkage with the world, participation in the world of nature. The "inner man" feels at one with that world; that is the origin of the religious instinct, the reason that seventh-century Arabs saw truth in the message carried by Muhammad and the reason the spirit of contemporary man will eventually seek escape from its imprisonment. To find one's authentic being means making oneself a part of being, submitting to the source of being, giving up one's whole self to God. Islam asserts that every person is capable of that act of faith. For Qutb, that fact guarantees that at least a few will brave the odds and seek to rediscover the essence of human nature by embracing God.

Qutb shares with Iqbal the hope and conviction not just that social inequities can be removed and social institutions renovated but that the human species can transform itself in the direction of its primordial, "upright,"[14] "fairest"[15] nature. He is radical by virtue of his belief in the possibility of overcoming alienation and conflict and of reaching the "lofty summit." Despite the "clouds" overhead, a few people can, by listening to their most fundamental instincts, discover God's path and, by exercising their autonomy, put themselves in tune with their own beings and the universe. It then becomes their duty to help liberate others from the forces of alienation.

Liberation of Society

By engaging in the act of Islam, submitting to God and to God alone, human beings liberate themselves from mortal authority. Freedom, Qutb says, means the freedom to choose submission to God; a few will be able to make that decision even under the most adverse circumstances, but one cannot speak of complete freedom for the individual as long as there exist external constraints on behavior, such as social institutions created by some standard other than God's law, which reflects the natural order of things and is therefore consistent with human nature. Only when rid of all human rulers are individuals free to choose to submit to God and thus to give up their natural freedom to do as they wish, which alienates them from their own true nature and from their fellow human beings. This is a call for "total revolution."[16]

> The true religion is in fact a universal declaration of man's freedom from the servitude to other men and to his own desires which too are a form of servitude. . . . This means that religion is an all-embracing and total revolution against the sovereignty of man in all its types, shapes, systems and states, and completely revolts against every system in which authority may be in the hands of man in any form, or in other words, he may have usurped sovereignty under any shape.[17]

Qutb argued that every prophet had brought the same message; each had been ignored. He denounced rabbinical power in Judaism and the power of the church in Christianity. Qutb also faulted Christianity for its opposition to the development of Western science, which contributed to the bifurcation of society and permitted the emergence of secular political philosophy justifying and rationalizing the exercise of human sovereignty over human affairs.[18] Qutb was no less categoric about the East: "The state of the Muslim community is such that it has forgotten its real 'self'; . . . centuries have elapsed [since] its exit from the stage of history."[19] The creation of a secular monarchy in the seventh century, the interest of the monarchy in creating stability through the elaboration of orthodoxy, the entrusting of orthodoxy to the hands of the ulema, the modern domination of the Islamic world by nation-states committed to nationalism, socialism, and Arabism, and the relegation of Islam to the domain of personal religion—all these facts and others attest to the nonexistence of an Islamic community, one where a person would be free to submit to God and no one else.

The modern *jāhilīya* thus encompasses, according to Qutb, the world that calls itself Muslim[20]—including Nasir's Egypt, where he became a martyr and hero for the Islamic movement. "Our foremost objective is to bring about a revolution in the practical system of the society. The jahiliyy order has to be exterminated root and branch," he wrote.[21] That order includes the Sunni establishment, the ulema, who have since the time of the Umayyads sought to legitimate the claims of secular rulers. Qutb portrayed Islam as a revolutionary movement: "The fundamental Islamic principles are revolutionary. It was a revolution against the deification of men, against injustice, and against political, economic, racial, and religious prejudice."[22] In much the way that Kierkegaard argued that a true Christian must imitate the historical action of Christ, Qutb asked that Muhammad's era be used as inspiration (but not as a model) for an attack on Islam as a living tradition, as a set of inherited dogmas and beliefs, as a community marked for more than one thousand years by a de facto split between secular and religious authority.[23] Severed from its origins, tradition is as dehumanizing as modernity;[24] together they constitute the clouds that prevent human beings from seeing with clarity and choosing the natural path mapped out for them by God.

The cloud metaphor fails, however, to suggest what must be done. No sweet, gentle breeze can disperse the veils of tradition and modernity. Force is required: "But when ... material influences and impediments may be ruling, there is no recourse but to remove them with force, so that when this message may appeal [to] the heart and reason of men, they should be free from all such shackles and bonds to pronounce their verdict open-heartedly."[25] It is perfectly natural, he argued, that Islam should authorize the use of force not for the conversion of souls but in order to clear the terrain of man-made authority so that man may choose to live by the rules of God. It is natural that in an initial period, as when Muhammad recruited a small group of believers in Mecca and sought to understand revelations pertaining to the relationship between man and God, the process of liberation does not require violent struggle.[26] The companions of the Prophet liberated themselves by embracing Islam and, by doing so, set themselves apart from Meccan society, first within the city and eventually by leaving the city for Medina. There, they struck out to defend their right to live by their new beliefs in a hostile environment. Jihad necessarily took a more offensive, more violent turn at that juncture, according to Qutb. Then, only when existing authority had been razed, could a new society be articulated.

Violence is a part of the "natural" process of liberation; to misunderstand that point is to deprive the Islamic community of its chance of escaping the *jāhilīya*, he said,[27] for Islam as a way of life cannot prevail for the great numbers under conditions of external hostility. If it is human nature to be free and if to be free means to live without subordination to others, then it is natural that one should seek to destroy that which obstructs liberation— proof once again that Islam reflects nature, or nature validates "true" Islam.

Qutb did not share Fanon's view on the value of violence in and of itself. He explicitly dissociated himself from the Christian view, emphasized by Kierkegaard, that to live authentically is to share Christ's suffering and to welcome death, which constitutes the ultimate escape from a world of original sin. Quite to the contrary, he spoke of God's path as one of ease for human beings, because it is the natural path and human nature is fundamentally sound.[28] Islam designates the way to eternal life; it guarantees eternal life to those who die on its behalf; a believer welcomes the opportunity to overcome all selfish ambitions and participate in jihad[29] and even to die for the cause.[30] But Islam also reminds men and women that they are accountable for their actions on earth; it provides a code of conduct in this world in preparation for the next, a code designed to provide security against terror and coercion and the general well-being human nature instinctively desires.[31] It eschews forcible conversion. Although violence is a natural part of the process of destroying institutional obstacles to self-discovery, it does not, in Qutb's Islam, constitute a necessary element in the individual's struggle to overcome alienation.[32]

Autonomy

Sayyid Qutb calls for a revolution in which man comes to acknowledge God's absolute sovereignty, but paradoxically, God has left human beings to bring about that state of affairs.[33] They must choose to liberate themselves and their fellow human beings from the worldly situation in which an omnipotent God has put them. Muslims are destined to prevail, but they will only do so if they exert themselves. It is God's will that human effort, offered without coercion or constraint, will carry the day for Islam! Qutb's problem, analogous to that of Gramsci, is to find room for autonomous human action in a deterministic world. To compromise on determinism is to deprive God—or dialectical materialism, in the case of Gramsci—of omnipotence and to deprive history of its meaning; to compromise on human autonomy is to turn revolution into evolution and human beings into puppets. That would scarcely be consistent with what Qutb sees as the ultimate purpose of Islam: "to awaken the 'humanity' of man; to develop it, to invigorate and glorify it and to make it dominant over all other aspects found in human life."[34]

Qutb sought exit from the dilemma by suggesting that God, who might have made puppets, chose instead to fashion autonomous human beings.

He chose to make divine guidance the fruit of exertion and desire for it. . . . He chose, too, to make human nature operate constantly, without being affected or put out of action. . . . He chose that his divinely ordained path for human life should be realized through human exertions, within the limits of human capacities. . . . He chose thereby to raise man to a point of excellence corresponding to the exertions he makes, the abilities he applies, and the patience with which he meets misfortune for the sake of realizing this divinely ordained path, of removing evil from himself and from life around him.[35]

Why God made such a choice is a question Qutb says neither a believer nor an atheist would ask; both see history as a product of human action rather than as repeated divine intervention. The believer would not ask it because faith cannot (despite the convictions of a thinker like 'Abdu) be held responsible to reason; the atheist would not bother to inquire about the motives of a god he or she rejects. But unlike the atheist, the believer regards human autonomy as conditioned by divine creation and divine judgment. The choices available to man are two: whether to submit to God by accepting the conditions and whether to work hard for the realization of God's plan. To submit is to be a Muslim; to work hard on God's behalf is to be a true Muslim and an authentic human being.

Qutb does not agonize over the difficulty of having faith, as did Pascal and Kierkegaard; he writes in a context where "faith," in the sense of professing to be Muslim, could be taken as a given. But he is as emphatic as Iqbal, or as Kierkegaard, for that matter, in stating that human beings do not fulfill their destinies by mouthing truths or by being born in a predominantly Muslim (Christian) region of the globe. For Qutb, in reading Sura 98, the "and" is critical: "Those who believe *and* do righteous deeds are the best of all creatures" [emphasis mine].[36] The words "effort," "exertion," "work," "struggle" (jihad) are as fundamental to Qutb's vocabulary as they are to Iqbal's. The possible rewards are the overcoming of individual alienation, the achievement of greater individual comfort, the reduction of human affliction and injustice through the advancement of God's cause on earth, and, most important, eternal life.

Despite the similarity between Kierkegaard and Qutb in their insistence that a faith must be lived, not just professed, and that living a faith requires deep commitment, they differ profoundly on the possibility of human self-improvement. Kierkegaard despaired of escaping torment within this world of original sin; living the faith meant sacrifice, self-denial, asceticism, and death. For Qutb, quite to the contrary, human beings need not repress natural desires but need only, through extraordinary effort, bring them under the dominion of self-control.[37] He wrote of the voluntary and involuntary "quarters" of human existence and of the need for balance between them. Self-control means not rejection of the natural laws to which the body is subject but choosing and striving to prevent one's life from being governed exclusively by the involuntary. By working to implement God's plan, one harnesses voluntary exertion to the divinely provided wagon, which only moves in a predetermined direction. Man can thus pull himself, so to speak, from the schizophrenia of life without departing the earth. Kierkegaard's pessimism confirms what Qutb saw as a fundamental difference between Islam and Christianity: Islam offers reward in this world as well as the next; Christianity promises eternal reward in return for suffering in the here and now.

The individual has a right to expect material as well as spiritual compensation for effort dispensed in the pursuit of the proper objectives. Qutb, like Iqbal, notes that God helps those who help themselves. "He chose thereby to raise man to a point of excellence corresponding to the exertions he has made, the abilities he has applied."[38] Moreover, the individual who achieves wealth by dint of honest effort need feel no pangs of guilt, provided that person obeys Islamic prescriptions for charity. Although Islam reflects a strong impulse toward equality, Qutb emphasizes equal human dignity rather than equality of result, which would clash with the natural diversity of the human species.

The more general benefit of exertion comes from the enlargement and preservation of the Islamic community. By laboring to establish a new community, the Prophet and his companions improved the condition of their lives. By carrying the fight to all of Arabia, they brought peace where there had been war, equal treatment where there had been discrimination, a single standard of law and justice where there had prevailed a mosaic of petty sheikhdoms. Qutb asked himself whether this early generation was cut from some different cloth, and his answer was no; they believed, and they struggled. They showed that the human will can triumph over "beliefs and ideas, circumstances and tradition."[39] Consequently, similar efforts would produce an analogous improvement in the human condition, though not a definitive one.

Qutb did not delude himself about the possibility of perfection on earth. Not everyone can be expected to join the struggle; not everyone can be expected to achieve self-control. Human beings cannot entirely escape the affliction into which they are born[40] except in the hereafter, but to earn eternal reward they must strive to do righteous deeds: "Positiveness and activity have a moral aspect in the path of Islam. Idleness and negativism are immoral, since they contradict the purpose of human existence, . . . namely the vice-regency of God on earth, and the use of all that God has subordinated to man for the purpose of constructive activity."[41] Human beings must act and then take responsibility for those acts on the day of judgment.[42] They can and must try to change their lives and their world in conformity with the divine plan. This is the driving force of revolution and, at the same time, the mechanism by which God retains control of history. For "it is ultimately God's will which is decisive, and without which man by himself will attain nothing."[43]

The paradox opens a greater space for human volition than most other thought, Islamic or European. For example, by stressing action rather than belief or ritual, Qutb distanced himself from many versions of Sufism as well as from folk Islam. By demanding willful change, he challenged the establishmentarian defense of the secular and religious order. By insisting upon the miraculous power of God, necessary to the achieve-

ment of any human purpose, he differed from Ibn Khaldun, whose discovery of sociological laws made him pessimistic about the possibility of
permanent human improvement;[44] he differed as well from the moderns,
who see human beings trapped in a web of class conflict, a struggle for individual betterment, or a stampede for worldwide modernization. Qutb's
"mystical"[45] faith in the power of God liberates the human will from the
constructions of its own reason.

Particularity

Sayyid Qutb spoke of the universal applicability of the Qur'anic message.
Its timeless validity cuts across national, ethnic, and ideological boundaries. He lauded Islamic principles as logical and ridiculed the Roman
Catholic Church for its medieval opposition to scientific discovery. He
saw no geographical limits for the revolution he solicited. Yet, his fundamental concern with human alienation and his search for what it means
to be "truly human" led him to postulate a reconciliation between the "inner" and the "outer" person, between what individuals feel in the deep-
est recesses of being and what they are driven to think and do by virtue of
their own physical needs and the demands of the society. Reconciliation
occurs when at least one individual decides to live differently from others
by following deeply embedded instincts to embrace the true Islam. Only
a person exposed to the culture of Islam can have such instincts. Revolution means practical action, not abstraction; it means setting oneself apart
from general beliefs; it means acting out one's particularity against what
is taken to be rational and universal; it means acting at a given moment
within a specific historical context. The thrust of Qutbian thought is particularistic in its attention to identity, practicality, circumstance, time, and
mystical communication.

With Iqbal, as with European romantics, to be human was first and
foremost to be a genuine individual. With Qutb, one cannot speak of a
theory of individuation. Those who assert themselves as individuals become Muslims to overcome their alienation; they sacrifice their individuality to God in order to recover their natural humanity. Qutb did not need
to labor, as had Iqbal, to demonstrate that the authentic self would unite
with other authentic selves to achieve common purpose. But, for him, the
individual and the group necessarily set themselves apart from society by
virtue of their faith, their goals, and their methods. The act of submission
makes individual authenticity virtually synonymous with participation
in the group.

For Qutb, Islam contains the only appropriate response to the question
of what it means to be "truly human." A non-Muslim is unlikely to find
the answer.[46] However, unlike other modern thinkers such as Muham-

mad 'Abdu and Rashid Rida, Qutb concerned himself less with the doctrine of Islam per se than with how one must live to be a true Muslim. In his understanding of Islam as a set of revelations, as a collection of authenticated hadith, and as a set of universal values emergent from those sources, Qutb had little quarrel with the establishment. In these ways, his ideas fall within the realm of orthodoxy,[47] but he warns repeatedly that Islam is not a set of abstractions. Islam is not just another set of ideals different from but parallel to those expounded in the West:

> For idealism is dreams and will continue to be dreams because it looks at a world that is not seen and whose realization is not sought after, because it cannot be realized on this earth. As for Islam, it is a creative force for the actualization of a particular vision of life which is capable of being brought into being, when one is influenced by it in a positive way, [and] which is not satisfied with emotions and feelings.[48]

Islam calls upon human beings to realize their potential by living a particular kind of life; they do so by responding in some mystical, highly personal way to the instincts buried within their own sense of themselves, instincts that draw them toward nature and toward God—the true God. They do so by acting as individuals in geographical and cultural space as well as in time. What they create is a society different not only by virtue of its values but by the circumstances of its existence.

Qutb suggests that the Qur'an contains two levels of meaning, one abstract and general, conveying universal values, and the other specific in its advice to a group or a generation. But since the call to practical action constitutes a part of the universal message, the first level cannot be skimmed without reference to the second. The Qur'an is a book of practical advice to be studied afresh in every age and in every setting. A Muslim of the first generation distinguished himself by listening to recitations of the Qur'an "to find out what the Almighty had prescribed for his individual life and for the group."[49] The companions of Muhammad sought to translate prescription into action, "while the later generations were brought up by the method of instruction for academic research and enjoyment."[50] If the Meccan companions and the Medinan helpers were better Muslims than their successors, it was by virtue of their concrete accomplishments as human beings. Within the limits of their capacities and their environment, they tried to live in a way worthy of God's creatures.

Although Qutb's writing conveys admiration for the early achievements of Islam, he suffers under no illusion that those achievements could be translated into Egypt in the twentieth century. He did suggest that the task of the early leaders of Islam was more difficult for lack of a previous example, but the human material they had to work with—the

Arabs of the seventh century—may have been more receptive to the message as a result of their closeness to nature and to their own instincts. The modern *jāhilīya* makes it more difficult for human beings to discover themselves beneath superficiality. Even so, modern revolutionaries can benefit from all earlier experience. Qutb took inspiration from the founding generation's commitment to the realization of a new and different way of life but never yearned to recapture the specific ways of the Medina state.

The principles of Islam are timeless; they have only been realized at certain junctures in history. Qutb thought in terms of stages of realization. The revelations received in Mecca entreated Muhammad and his followers to reconsider their relationship to the universe; at a second stage, in Medina, God pushed them to organize a community, to establish institutions, to strike out for the liberation of other human beings. The community achieved enormous successes, before monarchy replaced divine sovereignty. The monarchical phase, emergent from the early successes, produced decadence but also pointed the way toward revival. In each phase, the Islamic achievements reflected not just the will and actions of individual Muslims but also the limits of human capability and of physical and historical circumstances.[51] When Qutb referred to the "particular method" of Islam, he meant the progressive realization of the Islamic idea in history—one step at a time. He thought of history as the long voyage of humanity toward the realization of its potential, a voyage marked by achievement, decay, and revival. Islam provides "signposts on the road."[52]

Being human means to live in the world; the truth about what it means to be human emerges as human action in this world, as history conditioned by previous history. Truth-in-the-world stems from the evolution of history and even from its darker moments. The *jāhilīya* shaped early Islam; the modern jāhilīya pushes human beings toward truth by making them feel alienated from themselves. Qutb accepted Ibn Khaldun's dynamic but without cyclical necessity; Qutb embraced a sort of historical movement toward truth reminiscent of Hegel or Heidegger, without enunciating a formal dialectic. It is not at all certain that Qutb envisioned progress as an inevitable result.[53]

The consequences of his views are at least two. First, breakthroughs toward truth are partial, temporary, approximate, and cumulative. The condition for a definitive breakthrough would be a thorough transformation of human nature such that the sons and daughters of true Muslims, born into an Islamic society, without feeling alienation and adversity, would dedicate themselves with the energy of their parents to the maintenance and expansion of the Islamic order. Qutb doubted that humanity could ever be so perfect that history as the history of struggle toward truth would come to an end. The attainment of the humane life cannot, in his view, attain permanence and universality, even though Islam is permanent and universal. To be human is to be finite and particular.

Second, contemporary Islam benefits from its location in geography and history. A religion primarily of the Third World, it builds from a degree of alienation not experienced in the West, an alienation produced by Western domination as well as by the deterioration of Islamic civilization. It benefits from the experience of the early Muslims and the accomplishments of science and reason since the seventh century. Qutb regretted that Muslims had failed to pursue their endeavors in empirical science beyond the Middle Ages, permitting the construction of a scientific edifice in Europe divorced from the Islamic context in which it had developed, an edifice that challenged religion for the control of life.[54] But Qutb did not lament the development of science per se, challenge the utility of reason, or demand the destruction of technology. These factors merely change the historical bases for Islamic revival.

For Qutb, reason and science fall within history, which is itself a process by which human beings, following their God-given instincts, struggle toward the realization of truth. Reason cannot, as a consequence, be invoked to prove or disprove the fundamental insights that give meaning and direction to the flow of events. Faith drives human beings to use reason in understanding Islamic revelation, which is for the most part logical; unlike Christianity, it contains few riddles and no mysticism in Qutb's view. Yet he spoke of a special language in which human beings commune with nature and with themselves: "This language is part of human nature. It is a language which does not use sounds and articulation. It is a communication to the heart and an inspiration to the souls which come alive whenever man looks up to the universe for an inspiring touch or a cheerful sight."[55] They submit to God because, deep within themselves, they feel it is the natural thing to do. Reason is necessarily subordinate to these primordial, mystical instincts; it cannot reduce the truth value of either these instincts toward God or revelations of God's will. Faith is prior to reason in the struggle toward truth.[56] A truth that is lived, conditioned by a particular act of faith, does not presuppose the universality that reason might convey to it.

None of these considerations detracts from the universal applicability of Islamic revelation, but Islam has not carried the day either by its principles or by its appeal to universal reason. In fact, for Qutb, Islam's dilemma is that it has become a sort of intellectual common denominator, a mere theory, "diverting Islam from its natural function of infusing life and resplendent faith into the veins and arteries of a living society and enlightening the body of an organized movement."[57] The universal applicability of Islam must not obscure the imperative for concrete realization: "Qutb identified three levels of particularity in Islam: Thus the particular system of thought of this religion, its particular ideology and its dynamic movement of a peculiar nature are not three different things, separate from each other, but are fulfilled simultaneously."[58] What makes Islam unique is not its value system, which is universal, but its call for the realization of those values, the liberation of man from domination by other men; for him, both Judaism and Christianity had lost sight of this objective, although their revelations also contained it. The ideology, as a set of ideas linking thought to action, is distinct from its practical orientation. It offers precise instruction for the implementation of God's will and depends upon human effort for achievement. The "dynamic movement of a peculiar nature" would seem to be the historicity of the Islamic vision. If the goal is liberation of human beings within this world, the advice must be geared to this world, and the methods must be appropriate to circumstance. The revelations of Mecca were different from those of Medina; jihad, irrelevant in Mecca, became the method of Medina. In short, the radicalism of the fundamental impulse, the ideological emphasis on human autonomy, and the particularity of the method are all "petals" of the same flower—a particular living, natural thing.

Unicity

Unicity is the other face of particularity. The monotheism of Islam gives it a single focus. The doctrine of *tawḥīd* asserts the oneness of existence under God. But these ideas, however standard to Islam, acquire additional significance in Qutb's thought as a counterweight to the concreteness of Islam. If Islam is not merely a set of beliefs but a way of life—and not even a way of life but several of them, separate in time and space, fashioned according to God's instructions by distinctly human endeavor— then the unity of Islam, much less the unity of existence, is not self-evident.[59] If human beings determine their own history, what ties this life to a life beyond? What links one individual to another and one society to another? What permits human beings to understand their worldly reality in order to shape it? What permits human beings to overcome their selfishness and to work on behalf of common goals? Qutb's response, like Iqbal's and Ibn Khaldun's, hinges on an understanding of human nature as a reflection of *tawḥīd*.

The universe is one, because God created it that way. Human beings are part of that universe by virtue of their chemical composition and their physical location within it. They can understand that world and move within it as a result of their similarity to other living things and inanimate objects; mind, composed of matter, operates on the world from a position well within it, and it thinks about the self from a position within as well, foreclosing any possibility of division between mind and body. The natural condition of the universe is thus one of peace and harmony of humans with nature, humans with other humans, humans with their own beings.

What distinguishes human beings from other creatures is their ability to intuit this central, indivisible truth.[60] The intuition comes from the soul, located somewhere deep within human nature beyond the reaches of human reason. Qutb said the human physique, animals, and nature as a whole serve as constant reminders of this truth, but even when society manages to obscure the unity of being with a variety of projects and goals, the human spirit can penetrate the obscurity and sense the truth, which is not something separate—nor is the spirit something separate—from the universe but is the whole of it. The spirit, sensing the wholeness of things, reaches out toward the One God, source of the wholeness; recognizing that it possesses no separate avenue of truth, it submits to God and follows the path of submission, mapped out in Islamic revelation, reflecting the oneness of all things and leading toward oneness with God in eternal life. For this reason, authentic actions, however peculiar to place and circumstance and however reflective of individual will, contribute to the unity of existence because they derive their legitimacy from it.

Conflict and discord arise when human beings ignore this fundamental truth buried within themselves and attempt to fashion "the law of life from the code of [their] desires instead of the Divine code."[61] Human beings generate philosophies in which mind takes precedence over body or body over mind; they develop images of themselves as engaged in a struggle with nature and picture society as a battlefield where classes and ethnic groups strive for superiority; and they conveniently posit no correlation between comportment in the City of Man and access to the City of God. These ideas foster physical conflict among human beings and accentuate estrangement within the individual, who cannot fully ignore the primordial sense of oneness. Human beings, endowed with access to that truth, instinctively know that peace is the natural condition for an individual, a society, and the universe as a whole. They seek peace through truth, and truth lies with Islam. Islam must eventually prevail.

Understood in this way as a product of the fundamental human impulse toward truth, Islam cannot be partial. It cannot be confined to one sphere of human behavior called "religion," as distinguished from the political or economic domains; it cannot be limited to the individual's personal life, as distinguished from public life: "Islam encourages the individual to use his mind and body and does not substitute ritual for rules to govern behavior. It does not cater for the individual and neglect his role in society. It does not concern itself with his private life to the detriment of his political role in society nor ignore the relationship of his state to other states."[62] Islam speaks to the whole person, the whole society, the whole of mankind, not by choice but by the necessity born of conformity with truth, which is one.

Qutb's critique of the modern *jāhilīya* stems from his identification of Islam with the dynamic unity of the universe as much as it does from his assertions of the particularistic and autonomous character of human actions. Islam is not passivity or retreat into mystical solitude; it is not merely a set of abstract principles, enlightened scriptures, and inspiring historical examples; it is not a religious establishment that dedicates itself to erudite scholarship while political leaders, declaiming their piety, lead their countries without reference to God's order. True Muslims are not those who proclaim: "I am a planner; I am a Muslim. And what does the one have to do with the other?"[63] The Qutbian revolution is total in that it demands the total elimination of obstacles to human fulfillment and total human submission to a God, whose domain is, by the very definition of God, the totality of the human activity—indeed of the universe.

Does that make Qutb an advocate of "neo-Islamic totalitarianism?"[64] What sort of institutions could characterize a "true" Islamic society without compromising the absolute sovereignty of God? How would such a society respond to the worldwide pressures for greater entitlement to goods and services? Rejecting the materialistic and rationalistic premises of modernity, how would it confront the fact of modernization? How would it treat the pressures for greater participation engendered by social mobilization in Egypt, as elsewhere?

The Muslim Brotherhood found its early strength in young people with Western-style, technical education; the more radical descendants of the brotherhood continued to recruit from this category in the 1970s.[65] These groups reflect the alienation produced by modernization. Successful in liberating fellow Muslims from human domination in any form, including liberal democracy, would they paradoxically restrict political participation by snuffing out modernization or repressing its effects? Sayyid Qutb's version of Islamic authenticity supplies relatively clear responses to the questions about modernity and group action but provides much less precise ideas about institutions and participation.

Modernity

Qutb deplored many aspects of modern society and modern thought. He criticized not just the behavior of the sexes in the West or the conduct of Western banking, both of which he found contrary to Islamic law, but also the prevalence of concern for material goods in both socialist and capitalist countries. He attributed a decline of morality to the relegation of religion to Sunday (or Friday or Saturday) ritual, the fragmentation of the individual into economic, political, social, and ethical roles in circumstances where the ethical could not prevail. In thoroughly Western fashion, he attacked advertising for cultivating artificial needs that further magnify the domination of the animalistic instincts of human beings and further estrange them from their spiritual natures.

Qutb faulted Western thought for its willingness to separate religious and secular concerns and for its overweening attachment to rationalism. Actually, he blamed the church as much as philosophy for the relationship of distance and hostility that developed between science and theology, church and state, achievement and salvation in the West. In the triumph of the Enlightenment and the modern political economy, he saw the enslavement of human beings to sociological laws. Beneath the theory of liberal democracy, he found a rationale for the domination of some human beings over others, and in Marxism he detected deterministic denigration of the human role in creating history.[66] He rejected the idea of human confinement within parameters of behavior established by human reason or, worse, by biological and psychological instincts such as those defined by Darwin and Freud.

If Qutb can be called antimodern for these reasons, he appears more modern in his attachment to the idea of change, if not progress. He wrote:

> Islam is a continuous movement for the progress of life; it does not accept the prevalent condition at a time or of a generation, nor does it justify it or beautify it because it is existent. Its primary mission is to change that condition and make it better, to continuously suggest the creative, creating movement for the newer forms of life.[67]

However much his ideas may be anchored in scripture—ideas he insists are impervious to change—his model of history projects continuous evolution spurred by human effort along the path charted by revelation. Qutb took issue with Marx and Darwin about the role of necessity in history and about the standard by which progress should be measured, but not about history as evolution in an identifiable direction.[68] The purpose of Islam is progressive fulfillment of the human potential of human beings; since spirit separates man from animals, progress must thus be measured by spiritual as well as material standards. Material prosperity must be derivative rather than primary in the evolution of society. "Islam is not opposed to material advancement and material means, and does not belittle their importance, but regards the material progress acquired under the shade of the Divine system as a benediction and blessing from God, Most High."[69] Qutb would seem to embrace material progress but regard long-term moral improvement as anything but guaranteed. He paints a picture of "potential historical progress, rooted in the Islamic idea of successive prophetic missions."[70] Islam had brought improvement to Arabia, but the extensiveness of the *jāhilīya* prevented enduring global improvement, and evolving material conditions actually produced moral decline. Islam could offer the promise of regeneration but could not guarantee enduring commitment from human beings, whose faith and effort Qutb clearly deemed essential to long-term moral improvement.

On the Parsonian scale, Qutb appears quite modern as well. Erected on a consummatory foundation rather than on reason, his ideas nonetheless emerge in a logical fabric. William Shepard refers to "a process of 'rationalization' not unlike what Weber ascribes to the Calvinists, who probably even more than Sayyid Qutb ascribed everything to God, and yet contributed to the secularization of modern thought."[71] Moreover, he insisted that Islam is eminently comprehensible and reasonable in its demands on human nature. Although his thought is particularistic, it conforms more to "scripturalist unitarian puritanism" than to a saint-dominated, superstition-ridden, popularistic Islam.[72] He did not evince any interest in a throwback to simple, tribal society where role allocation would be diffuse. His orientation toward achievement rather than ascription should be abundantly clear from his embrace of autonomous human action. In short, although Qutb disdained the standards of Western social science and the efforts of sociology to predict human behavior, his ideas appear more modern than traditional by social scientific standards. More important, he acknowledged the usefulness of science and technology and endorsed the vision of history upon which all Western developmentalism is based.

From a vantage point amid industrialization and bourgeoisification, Qutb took a postindustrial, postbourgeois stance. Without minimizing the importance of economic growth and the satisfaction of "genuine" human needs, he preached the transcendence of modernism in the pursuit of human fulfillment. For Qutb, Islam permits capitalist enterprise to flourish and grow but throws a safety net under society to minimize hardship, acknowledges legitimate gain but prohibits fraud and corruption, including usury, and concerns itself with both social productivity and social justice.[73] Qutb's antimodernism is distinctly postbourgeois and postmodern in its rational mistrust of universal reason, premodern in its embrace of faith and fundamental values.

This is intent. Could it be argued that Qutb's Islam, which he insists is practical rather than theoretical, would, once in power, be obliged to slow the processes of industrialization? Laroui has accused Islamic revivalists of magnifying the "retardation" of the Arab world by fixing their gaze on moments of a glorious past.[74] In his view, all contemporary Arab regimes err by acknowledging Islam as a part, albeit small, of their working ideologies, giving comfort to the forces of superstition, reaction, and conservatism. Such regimes compromise their abilities to escape Third World status. Qutb, quite to the contrary, condemned those same regimes for their unwillingness to embrace Islam as ideology and criticized all contemporary religious establishments for their pliability in the face of secular demands. He did reinforce traditional views on the status of women in society,[75] but it is difficult to portray him as a defender of landlords, Sufi sheikhs, rural saints, or the ulema.

Qutb's thoroughgoing scripturalism and less thoroughgoing historicism permit him to abandon the past as easily as Laroui. By separating the word of God from the use human beings make of it, he liberates the Qur'an from any single reading and the *shari'a* (Islamic law) from any single body of *fiqh* (legal interpretation). Every Qur'anic verse has two meanings, he said: one to be grasped by any given generation, the other absolute and general. Within the limits imposed by the permanent, ahistorical principles, Islam must necessarily evolve. Yet values escape relativism by their firm anchoring in the ahistorical word of God; only the mode of their expression varies with time. Such a moderate version of historicism fits easily with Qutb's general perspective; he emphasizes human inability to understand truth. The full, unchanging, permanent truth of the Qur'an always lies slightly beyond human understanding, as does the fact that there exists such a truth. Laroui's historicism is similarly limited by his faith in the truth of the historical process; within Laroui's own rationalist system, the veracity of that truth is impossible to defend.

The weakness in Qutb's modernity lies in his relative inattention to the question of how one gets there from here. What would be, for example, a Qutbian policy of economic development that would take account of Islamic values? To what extent must there be economic growth to satisfy basic human needs and what, exactly, are those secondary, nonessential needs that may be ignored? More fundamentally, by what sort of institutions ought such decisions to be made? Qutb described Islam as a unique religion with a unique, step-by-step method. Hence, questions about institutions and policy cannot be posed until there exists a genuine Islamic entity ready to face them. In the interim, true Muslims must proceed to organize themselves for the assault on the *jāhilīya*.

Group Action

Qutb distinguished himself from Iqbal by his focus on the group as prime historical mover. For Iqbal, who began his analysis with *Secrets of the Self* and whose masterwork, the *Javid Nama*, portrayed a single individual in search of the truth, group action remained hypothetical, even though necessary and desirable. For Qutb, however, the starting point is not the self but "human nature," commonality rather than individuation. By their very nature, human beings can commune with the universe in a "secret language" that permits them to understand the oneness of nature, the oneness of God. Unarticulated though it may be, that language would seem to be universal, permitting human beings to be drawn toward the same God in the same way. It is natural that those who understand the secret language and commit themselves to the path of God should form a single group.

Qutb's preoccupation with community equals or surpasses Iqbal's commitment to the individual. Iqbal's affirmations of community often seem to be afterthoughts designed to stifle criticism. Qutb's repeated references to individual responsibility on the day of judgment, individual achievement, and individual reward seem similarly perfunctory. The duty of individuals is to submit to God, to join the community of believers, to give up their own, individual freedom to do whatever they might wish in order to do God's bidding. Qutb saw the group as the secret to Muhammad's success and the key to any contemporary effort to follow God's way. Realization of the divine plan would occur not by individual preaching or by divine enforcement, he said. Rather,

> it is brought into being by a group of people undertaking the task, believing in it completely and conforming to it as closely as possible, trying to bring it into being in the hearts and lives of others, too, striving to this end with all they possess. They struggle against human weakness and human passion within themselves; they struggle against those whom weakness and passion impel to resist divine guidance.[76]

In this concentration on the group Qutb again reveals his modernity.

The Islamic method, derived from the career of the Prophet and propounded by Qutb as a "program for moving society from a state of *jāhilīya* to a state of Islam,"[77] turns out to be a formula for group action: (1) recruitment of a vanguard elite, (2) solidification of group consciousness, (3) segregation of the group from society, (4) enlargement of the group, (5) seizure of power, and (6) establishment of the new society. Each step requires appropriate advice and action. For example, the Meccan verses of the Qur'an focus on the place of human beings in the universe and their relationship to the sovereign God; they offer little in the way of practical advice about organizing or governing a community; they do not advocate jihad, as do the later verses that were revealed to Muhammad at Medina. Weak in the early stages, the group would need protection within an established body politic. Once stronger in intensity and numbers, it could strike out on its own, build its own organization and carry the campaign to others. Qutb viewed the Qur'an as a guidebook for the vanguard, providing advice tailored to the needs of the movement as it developed from a tiny nucleus surrounding Muhammad into an Islamic state whose dominance in Arabia had been established.

By his emphasis on the early stages, Qutb urged patience on his contemporaries and subordination of the individual to the group. Clearly, he identified the position of the Muslim Brotherhood in Egypt in the 1950s and 1960s with the companions of the Prophet in the years before the *hijra*. For lack of strength, they were forced to live in the *jāhilīya*, to cooperate in some measure with the authorities, and to concentrate on understanding "true Islam" and reinforcing group solidarity. Being steadfast is a virtue, he wrote, but to counsel others to be steadfast is even more important. Likewise, to urge others to be merciful is more important than being merciful.[78] The objective for those who would establish a true Islamic party or Islamic society must be creation of a "movement which is dynamic, active and organized, whose members are closely knit, mutually cooperative and marked by cohesion and unity."[79] Qutb saw himself working at that task even from his confinement in Nasir's prisons.

For Qutb, the group makes possible the realization of community, and in community lies the cure for individual alienation. In that sense, group action takes precedence over both individual and community. Qutb speaks of the uniqueness of Islam and the uniqueness of its method. The uniqueness of Islam lies in the wholeness of its vision, in its penetration of every aspect of human life, in its concept of community, and, especially, in its insistence that the vision must be realized. The uniqueness of method is its one-step-at-a-time approach; a group must act in a way appropriate for the time period and cultural setting according to a series of directions God has set down in the Qur'an. A genuine Islamic society emerges from such group action; it does not emerge from the abstract contemplation of the Medina state (622–660), from speculation about how an ideal Islamic community might be structured, or from misguided loyalty to an existing community where God does not reign sovereign: "The Muslim Society comes into existence only when individuals or groups of people turn from service of something other than God, whether along with or apart from Him, to service of God alone with no associate and when these groups decide to organize their life on the basis of this service."[80] Islam aims at the restoration of individual wholeness; the establishment of an Islamic community, in which external expectations of the individual conform to his or her internal instincts, is indispensable to that end. But the group constitutes a dynamic intermediary, the only possible bridge between individual aspiration and general achievement. When Qutb said that Islam cannot be separated from its method, he meant that Islam demands realization, realization requires method, and the method is group activity according to the conditions of time and place along a path outlined by God. The path and the method, both permanent and unchanging, produce a concrete community that is historically unique. The realization of community, tantamount to the general reduction of individual alienation, depends upon group action. It is not inevitable.

Attention to the group as a historical actor makes Qutb's thought highly useful to contemporary revolutionaries. Qutb is to Ibn Khaldun in somewhat the same way Lenin is to Marx. Unlike Ibn Khaldun, who thought group feeling had, ultimately, to be based in blood ties, Qutb insists that faith can be sufficient; a group is not necessarily born of social circumstances but is constructed by human volition. Like Ibn Khaldun, he saw history as a product of group action but did not embrace Ibn Khaldun's perception of a cyclical and apparently deterministic mechanism that causes societies to decline once they have arisen. Qutb shares with Ibn Khaldun a strong sense that a social achievement will not endure once the volition from which it arose disappears. The vanguard represents the will to build and the will to persevere. When that will disappears, institutions may serve to mask the reality but are in fact hollow. Time will topple them. Qutb seems to endorse the modern idea of dialectic.[81]

How is it then possible to think in Qutbian terms about a stable Islamic society? What becomes of the vanguard once a true Islamic state has been formed? How is it possible for human beings to govern a society without infringing upon the sovereignty of God? What is the role of the individual who has exercised his freedom by submitting himself to God, whose will rules the society? And what is the place of minorities who do not submit?

Institutions

Sayyid Qutb avoided most questions about institutions by asserting that they must emerge from an already constituted Islamic society. In his *Social Justice in Islam*, he wrote extensively of the values articulated in the Qur'an that would inform an Islamic society and shape the institutions. He wrote of the need for social order and the need for specific codes of law, inspired by the *shari'a*, which could command obedience. He wrote of the need for responsible leadership and of the duties of rulers and ruled, but unlike Sayyid Abu al-A'la Mawdudi, the Pakistani whom he admired and followed on so many matters, Qutb refrained from suggesting the forms Islamic government might take. The fact is more disconcerting in Qutb than it is with Iqbal: Qutb's orientation toward the group, in contrast with Iqbal's individualistic stance, renders revolution more plausible and the need for substitute institutions more pressing.

Qutb rejects any importation of institutions from other times or other places. In *Social Justice* he had already deplored the tendency in the Muslim world to "cast aside our own fundamental principles and doctrines and . . . bring in those of democracy, socialism or communism."[82] He said he would rely on Islamic "principles and doctrines," which are permanent, but not on institutions erected on those foundations in other historical moments. To the contrary, consistent with his rebellion against the establishment, he distinguished between the *shari'a*, the eternal principles of law rooted in the Qur'an and the hadith, and the body of law called *fiqh*, extracted from those principles by legal experts. As a set of human decisions and actions, *fiqh* must be renewed with every age; those who are fighting for the new order must make a new *fiqh* on the basis of the permanent values. Qutb would never have suggested that the institutions of the Medina state be revived some thirteen centuries later; it is only the principles of those institutions, enunciated in the *shari'a*, that can be invoked. As William Shepard has argued, Qutb's definition of Islam as a system by which solutions can be produced "justifies the refusal to spell out details of that system at present."[83] Only the system properly implemented can generate specific proposals.

The fundamental principle is that of a pact between ruler and ruled, a *bay'a*, similar to the pact between man and God. By submitting to God, man liberates himself from the domination of other men, but since all men can never be expected to submit, social order requires that Muslims obey God's deputy on earth—be he Prophet, caliph, or imam—provided he rules by the Book, the eternal principles laid down by God. The pact between rulers and ruled is thus conditional on behavior; Qutb made creative use of Ibn Taymiyya on that point to oppose the mainstream of the Sunni tradition.[84]

Along with the right to revolt, Muslims also retain the right to consultation, the *shura*. Qutb referred to collaboration but said "no specific method of administering it has . . . been laid down."[85] Later in his commentary on the Qur'an, he suggested that the *shura*, though inspired by Muhammad's use of it, would take some entirely unprecedented form and in an unspecified way would affect the selection of the imam from among the virtuous. Only a newly established Islamic society could determine the exact form such consultation might take.[86] But it would not, in Qutb's view, take the form of European parliamentary democracy, born of other social circumstances, built on individualism, and designed to protect individual interest rather than the general welfare.[87] Such an adoption of foreign ways would be unnatural; it could not arise from within the Islamic framework, although many other solutions presumably could, one after the other, each validated by a temporary set of social circumstances. Institutions thus provide no enduring base for individual rights or social stability.

Olivier Carré[88] speaks of Qutb's political mysticism. Somehow an imam must emerge to keep social order and help implement God's will on earth. He must exercise power without infringing upon God's sovereignty and thereby violating the human right to freedom from domination by other human beings. He must establish institutions and laws that reflect the eternal code and the specific needs of time and place in the knowledge that

such efforts cannot be lasting. His efforts, profiting from the previous experience of Islam, will advance the human cause and prepare the way for
yet another wave of human exertion but cannot themselves reach perfection. Not even a prophet, not even the last of the prophets, Muhammad,
could do that. Qutb sketched the shape of an ideal Islamic society, which
contrasts with existing conditions, and called for revolution in the name of
that vision. But he offered little suggestion about how the vision might be
achieved or even little hope that modest improvements might endure. He
proposed a journey into the mists with the Qur'an specifying only the direction of travel but not rest stops or even the destination. Such a journey
requires strong leadership, an enlightened despot, an imam commanding
absolute, even fanatical obedience.[89]

Nonetheless, Qutb thought the scriptures pose limits. Islam secures
man from injustice, emancipates him from "enslavement" to man-made
law, guarantees him "all his social rights, his honor and his wealth," assures him the sanctity of home and assures him sustenance.[90] Subjects
have a right to expect social justice from their rulers,[91] and the premises of
social justice are "an absolute freedom of conscience, a complete equality
of all mankind, and a permanent mutual responsibility in society."[92] Mutual responsibility would seem to refer to the duty of subjects to obey
rulers whose authority derives from the conformity of their actions with
the law of God. A ruler, he said, has no privileges. "If he upholds the law
and sees that religious duties are observed, then he has reached the limit
of his powers."[93]

True to both his scripturalism and his historicism, Qutb formulated not
a theory of neo-Islamic totalitarianism but one of tension, contradiction,
and evolution. Eternal law is the basis of the community, eliminating any
need for human intervention; such is the permanent truth. But historical
circumstance necessitates adaptation under strong, even autocratic leadership, which is bound to overstep the narrow boundaries of legitimate
action, exposing itself to complaint, protest, and even revolution. This is
the dynamic of Islamic history. Qutb sought a prolongation of that history, not an escape from it via ahistorical (i.e., prophetic) leadership or institutional permanence, both of which violate the premises of his argument: The only permanent truth lies in revelation, and God has left
people to cope with that truth as best they can. But who, then, can cope?
Who is entitled to participate in the new Islamic society?

Participation

Qutb, member and ideologue of a mass movement, and Iqbal, the poet-
philosopher, took predictable—"where you stand depends on where you
sit"—positions on the issue of participation. On the one hand, Iqbal, with
his emphasis on the ego, envisioned renewal beginning with a person of

superior insight and understanding, one who could by understanding the self penetrate to the heart of the universe and arrive at an understanding of God in the Islamic manner. Such a person need not be a Muslim. On the other hand, Qutb, who was both more egalitarian and less universal in his vision, thought any person possesses an instinct for the truth of things, but non-Muslims, more thoroughly alienated, cannot break out of the modern *jāhilīya*. Any Muslim, but only a Muslim, can lead the world out of its schizophrenia.

By such an argument, Qutb seemingly hoped to avoid Iqbal's predicament; in "saving" Islam from itself and tying the "true Islam" to the nature of the universe, Iqbal opened the door to other versions of the "natural" faith. In *Islam: The Religion of the Future*, Qutb devoted several pages to expositions of the views of Alexis Carrel and John Foster Dulles; he also mentioned Bertrand Russell as someone who had understood the "schizophrenia" of the West. Carrel had seen the inadequacy of science as a basis for truth but failed, according to Qutb, to see that the problem lay with reason itself—the basis of science—rather than with the manner in which the West was doing science.[94] Dulles had deplored the decline of spirituality in the West and had called for a return to Christianity, but he did not understand, according to Qutb, that Christianity had lost its capacity to dominate Western consciousness and reinvigorate the whole of life.[95] None of the three could see the truth from their position as "white men" inside a white man's culture. "It is we alone, the champions of this Islamic system, who can perform the great leap from the cage of decadent Western civilization."[96]

The argument, which reserves to contemporary Muslims the role of leadership, fits uneasily with Qutb's emphasis on human autonomy and his analysis of Muslim society. It underscores his belief in particularity. In combating determinism in any shape or form, he extolled the capacity of human beings to triumph over environment, society, and history itself. Moreover, he noted that Muhammad had brought the same message as previous prophets, a message neglected or distorted by the Jews and the Christians, but Muslims had lost sight of that message. "What is required," he wrote,

> is a system that does not differentiate between faith and words. A system that rejects the allegation that it is impossible to have social justice without adopting atheism and materialism, or the allegation that materialism must be the prime factor, or that slavery and despotism can be lawful means for securing abundance of material production, or that freedom of thought must be suppressed for the sake of maintaining affluence. What is required is a system that does not enjoin the cessation of scientific progress in the name of religion, nor confine the practice of religion to the suppression of science and knowledge. Finally, what is needed is a system whereby worship [practices] evolve until work becomes one of the aspects of that worship.[97]

For Qutb, that describes Islam (though surely not the Islam he criticizes for its passivity, its subservience to political authority, and its unwillingness to challenge materialism). Having undergone less distortion than Christianity and Judaism and with a more recent prophet as its guide, Islam can serve as a basis for renewal. Only Muslims have the capacity to become true human beings and lead others toward the triumph of human nature.

What Muslims can do for non-Muslims is to free them from the social contexts that restrict their ability to choose Islam. Having founded a true Islamic society, Muslims can carry the battle to other states and liberate non-Muslims from the external conditions of their alienation. Such non-Muslims then have the option of choosing Islam or living under the protection of the Islamic state. Only by becoming Muslims can they become full participants in the society.

Qutb echoes standard Islamic arguments against the political relevance of ethnicity, language, or nationality. Believers must be regarded as equals with respect to rights and duties; they have a right to a government of laws and not of men. Yet the responsibility for the creation of such a government lies with a vanguard of "true Muslims," determined not just to believe but to live their beliefs. They participate by giving up their right to individual decision in favor of the will of God, represented by Holy Law as interpreted by the community. But whence comes that interpretation? Who leads the jihad? Who decides when jihad is appropriate? What is the role of Muslims and "true Muslims" in those decisions? If leadership there must be in the form of an imam, then what is the role of believers and "true believers" in that selection? Qutb merely suggests that answers to these questions must come from a true Islamic society, once constituted.

To call this a recipe for either "neo-Islamic totalitarianism" or liberal democracy would seem unwarranted. The need for scriptural sanction weakens the prerogative of leadership; the Qur'anic "constitution" stands for freedom to choose and practice one's religion, protection of one's honor and dignity, sanctity of the home, and even sustenance of the individual, according to Qutb. Most important, the scriptural basis of the society guarantees a government of general rules rather than arbitrary decision. But the liberty of the individual does not extend beyond the right to be consulted on political decisions, and it is not clear that everyone, rather than just a vanguard, or a vanguard of the vanguard, should have that right. In any case, no individual or group could make a decision that conflicted with the general rules. If "social justice" is the objective, as suggested by the title of Qutb's book, then equality need not be a part of either the process or the outcome. The trouble is that justice implies an authority and social order—Qutb recognized the need—that would be difficult to defend against the sort of attack Qutb launches against the contemporary Islamic world. How is it that human beings, without prophetic help or divine intervention, can convert scripture into institutions without imparting any human quality to their work and alienating themselves as well as others? Rousseau's *volonté générale* (general will) comes to mind not as a solution but as an evocation of the sort of ambiguities inherent in the Qutbian view.

✍

All efforts to characterize Sayyid Qutb as either traditional or modern, reactionary or progressive, socialist or capitalist, liberal or authoritarian, fail in one way or another. He is traditional in his appeal to the Qur'an, in his demand that Muslims look to scripture for their guidance, but he is modern in his effort to put the accomplishments of Muhammad and his contemporaries in a context of space and time. He is reactionary by current standards in his stance on the position of women but progressive in his suggestion that *fiqh* must constantly adapt to fresh circumstances. He sounds socialist in his concern for the welfare of all and capitalist in his discovery of the "Protestant ethic" in Islam. Like a liberal, he dreamed of a society of laws not of men, but like a Rousseauist democrat he voiced great optimism about human nature ("upright" and "fair") and great distrust of social institutions.

To put him in the Islamic context is only somewhat easier. Surely, he represents a cycle of puritanical revolt against the adaptive, compromising ways of Islam, but he represents not the force of the nomads sweeping in from the desert but a product of the city attacking the city from within. Although the pattern of religious revival aimed at political and social revolution is familiar, the dynamic is new, conditioned by the twentieth century in thought and action. Unlike 'Abdu and Rida, he rejected the idea of reconciling Islamic doctrine with European thought; he sounds "normativist" by comparison. But from a seemingly orthodox perspective based in the permanent and unchanging, he derived a formula for revolution against current Islamic practice not in the hope of resurrecting the past but with the promise of an open-ended future. Qutb reached back to Ibn Taymiyya to justify his distinction between Muslims and "true Muslims" and the need for jihad within the Islamic community; he sought to shield innovation with tradition in a pattern familiar to Islamic history. For that reason, some would put him with 'Abdu and Rida in the "neo-normativist,"[98] reformist line, even though he rejected their brand of rationalism.

To see Qutb as but the leader of the nth puritanical revival movement in the history of Islam, although accurate, is to miss what makes the contemporary revival unique: its confrontation with modernity and modern thought as internal to the Muslim condition. Iqbal and Qutb both addressed aspects of the same question: How can I live in such a way as to be at peace with myself and that world? That is the issue of authenticity. Both Iqbal and Qutb argued that the solution required the transformation of the self and the society. Iqbal concentrated on the first part of the problem, the rediscovery of the self beneath passivity, stagnation, ritual, and foreign domination. Qutb worked on the problem of transition from individual rediscovery to dominance in a society; he sought to galvanize a group into action and explicate a rationale for its revolt against an existing society. He left to others, those who would achieve power, the design of new institutions.[99]

The nature of the task pushed Qutb away from the philosophical language of Iqbal as well as removing him from the more specific, institutional reflections of Mawdudi. One does not recruit Egyptians to the Muslim Brotherhood with complicated poetry and esoteric references to Nietzsche and Bergson à la Iqbal. And one does not build group solidarity against a secular regime by initiating speculation, and hence quarrels, about the nature of institutions a future Islamic society might choose to build. Rather, one works within the orthodox language of Islam but imparts to that language a revolutionary spin. The key to Qutb's success is the apparent orthodoxy of his appeal,[101] but the orthodoxy of the language does not make Qutb any less modern than Qutb or Mawdudi in his understanding of the problem or in his objectives.[102]

In his effort to save the self, Iqbal found Islam ideally suited to his purposes but not, perhaps, rigorously necessary; for him, one discovered God through the self. Qutb reversed the procedure, and by doing so, he restored Islam to necessary status and laid the base for Muslim solidarity. Rather than understanding the ego, an ordinary person need only be sensitive to the totality of nature to feel the religious instinct. All human beings understand the secret language. But only Muslims, less alienated than Christians or Jews by the secularization of society, are able to respond and join the vanguard in its struggle to realize the full potential of humanity. Such is Qutb's call to action, which is more narrowly Islamic than Iqbal's and more broadly appealing.

Individuation is the principal casualty. In his insistence on a uniform human nature and an equal ability to feel the oneness of nature, Qutb posits human beings who will respond alike by giving up their own volition in order to follow the will of God. Although circumstances might render humans diverse, such diversity could never be regarded as fundamental. It could not threaten solidarity. Would it be sufficient to gain the respect of society and to be worthy of defense? Individuals would be free from the oppression of other human beings; would they also be free to be themselves? Qutb's answer is that true human beings give back to God the freedom they have been granted. Self-serving action is by definition unworthy and unnatural; mankind is essentially good, fair, and one. Unity overwhelms. Let scoundrels beware.

The principles of Islamic law remain as the bulwark of liberty, as they have (or have not been) for centuries. Would those principles be safer if radically separated from the concrete interpretations accorded them by generations of ulema? Would the individual be safer and less alienated in a society without human governance? Or would the new moralism become yet another cover for secularist behavior, preparing society for the next wave of puritanism? Qutb might well acquiesce in that judgment, for he refrains from suggesting that any revival can be the definitive one. But if that is the case and if decline follows revival and alienation follows wholeness, then any effort at change is futile. Qutb's historicism, fundamental to his revolutionary interpretation of Islam, leaves Muslims with nothing permanent to cling to but the values contained in a set of scriptures whose full meaning they can as mere human beings never understand. Such a situation may appear exhilarating, but it may also seem frightening and hopeless. It might take a good deal of consciousness-raising and coercion to convince Egyptians, much less a larger group of Sunnis, to embark on the Qutbian adventure.

Notes

1. Yvonne Y. Haddad, "Sayyid Qutb: Ideologue of Islamic Revival," in *Voices of Resurgent Islam*, ed. John Esposito (New York: Oxford University Press, 1983), p. 69.

2. William Shepard, "The Development of the Thought of Sayyid Qutb as Reflected in Earlier and Later Editions of 'Social Justice in Islam,'" in *Die Welt des Islams* (32, 2 (1992), p. 198. Shepard mentions claims that friends helped Qutb leave Egypt to escape arrest, although several accounts say that the Ministry of Education sponsored his trip.

3. M. M. Siddiqui, "An Outline of Sayyed Qutb's Life," in Sayyid Qutb, *Islam and Universal Peace* (Indianapolis, Ind.: American Trust Publications, 1993), p. xii.

4. Emmanuel Sivan, *Radical Islam: Medieval Theology and Modern Politics* (New Haven: Yale University Press, 1985), p. 27.

5. Haddad, "Sayyid Qutb: Ideologue," p. 67.

6. Yvonne Yazbeck Haddad goes to the point of suggesting a comparison of Qutb's thinking with other ideologies of liberation but then backs off. See her "The Qur'anic Justification for an Islamic Revolution: The View of Sayyid Qutb," in *Middle East Journal* 37, 1, p. 28.

7. William Shepard thinks not. "Despite more than two years in the U.S., I have doubts as to how well he ever learned English. In fact, I think one would find that radical Islamism tends to appeal to people who, while influenced by the Western, do not know a Western language well and thus do not have firsthand access to the sources of Western culture." Comment in correspondence, February 3, 1994.

8. Sayyid Qutb, *This Religion of Islam* (Delhi: Markazi Maktaba Islami, 1974), p. 27.

9. Sayyid Qutb, *In the Shade of the Qur'an*, trans. M. Adil Salahi and Ashur A. Shamis (London: MWH, 1979), p. 261.

10. Sayyid Qutb, *Islam: The Religion of the Future* (Delhi: Markazi Maktaba Islami, 1974), p. 23.

11. Qutb, *This Religion of Islam*, p. 87.

12. Syed Qutb, *Milestones* (Karachi: International Islamic, 1981), p. 167.

13. Qutb, *This Religion of Islam*, p. 23.

14. Qutb, *In the Shade of the Qur'an*, p. 212.

15. Qutb, *This Religion of Islam*, p. 30.

16. Qutb's use of the term "total revolution" seems similar to its usage by Bernard Yack, *The Longing for Total Revolution: Philosophic Sources of Social Discontent from Rousseau to Marx and Nietzsche* (Princeton: Princeton University Press, 1986).

17. Qutb, *Milestones*, p. 114.

18. See Qutb, *The Religion of the Future*, pp. 51ff.

19. Qutb, *Milestones*, p. 47.

20. Ibid., p. 152.

21. Ibid., p. 63.

22. Ibid., p. 72.

23. I agree with Bruno Etienne that Qutb cannot be called a fundamentalist or an integralist. He is not calling for personal confrontation with the text or even challenging much of the standard interpretation. Nor is he demanding a return to abandoned ritual. See Etienne's *L'islamisme radical* (Paris: Hachette, 1987), pp. 167–168.

24. Hence, any utilization of the word "traditional" with regard to Qutb, as in the title of Haddad's chapter about Qutb's views on history ("The Traditional Response" in Haddad's *Contemporary Islam and the Challenge of History* [Albany: SUNY Press, 1982]), is perhaps misleading.

25. Qutb, *Milestones*, p. 5.

26. Ibid., pp. 126ff.

27. See Ibid., p. 138.

28. Qutb, *In the Shade of the Qur'an*, p. 141.

29. Qutb, *Milestones*, p. 136.

30. Ibid., p. 263.

31. Qutb, *Islam and Universal Peace*, p. 12.

32. Qutb denied that Islam is bloodthirsty. See *Milestones*, p. 143.

33. William Shepard has written: "I think it fair to say that Sayyid Qutb shares to some extent, and in his own way, in that modern sense of the remoteness of the divine which, in more extreme forms in the West, has been labelled 'The Eclipse of God' of even 'The Death of God.'" From "Islam as a 'System' in the Later Writings of Sayyid Qutb," *Middle Eastern Studies* 25, 1 (January 1989), p. 42.

34. Qutb, *Milestones*, p. 122.

35. Qutb, *This Religion of Islam*, pp. 3–4.

36. Qutb, *In the Shade of the Qur'an*, p. 249.

37. Ibid., pp. 104–105.

38. Qutb, *This Religion of Islam*, pp. 3–4.

39. Ibid., p. 59.

40. Qutb, *In the Shade of the Qur'an*, p. 176.

41. Qutb, *This Religion of Islam*, p. 30.

42. Qutb underscores the role of human volition in his discussion of Sura 84, especially in one line: "Oh man! You labour hard unto your Lord, and you shall meet him." From *In the Shade of the Qur'an*, p. 104.

43. Qutb, *This Religion of Islam*, p. 12.

44. Olivier Carré, *Mystique et politique: Lecture révolutionnaire du Coran par Sayyid Qutb, frère musulman radical* (Paris: Editions du Cerf, 1984), p. 137.

45. The term is Carré's; it must be used with care, for Qutb himself took care to dissociate himself, just as had Iqbal, from mysticism and its tendency toward passivism. He is a mystic in the sense that he calls for belief even and especially in that which cannot be defended by reason. He does, however, insist that Islam is inherently reasonable in its demands and in its structure, which coincides with nature.

46. See discussion of John Foster Dulles and Alexis Carrel in Qutb, *Islam: The Religion of the Future*, pp. 83–124.

47. Etienne, *L'islamisme radical*, p. 253.

48. Sayyid Qutb, "History as the Interpretation of Events," in Haddad, *Contemporary Islam and the Challenge of History*, p. 165.

49. Qutb, *Milestones*, p. 56.

50. Ibid., p. 59.

51. See William Shepard, "The Development of the Thought of Sayyid Qutb," *Die Welt des Islams* 32 (1992), p. 203, for a discussion of changes in the text of Qutb's *Social Justice in Islam* from the first edition to the last on the question of consultation in the choice of the "Rightly Guided caliphs." In the last edition, Qutb wrote: "Practical circumstances determined who should be consulted in each period so clearly that there was no uncertainty about it" [Shepard's translation].

52. This is the title of his book, *Maalim fi al-Tariq*, which might be translated as "signposts" rather than "milestones."

53. "My most recent research has convinced me that by the end of his life, SQ had divested himself of the idea of progress, except in relation to material technology." William Shepard, personal correspondence, February 3, 1994.

54. Qutb, *Milestones*, p. 201.

55. Qutb, *In the Shade of the Qur'an*, p. 184.

56. See William Shepard, "The Development of the Thought of Sayyid Qutb," p. 204, for a clear analysis of *Milestones* on this point.

57. Qutb, *Milestones*, p. 88.

58. Ibid., p. 90.

59. See Shepard, "Islam as a 'System.'"

60. Qutb, *Milestones*, p. 167.

61. Ibid., p. 169.

62. Qutb, *Islam and Universal Peace*, p. 3.

63. Interview with Egyptian planner, 1981.

64. The term is Manfred Halpern's in *Social Change in the Middle East and North Africa* (Princeton: Princeton University Press, 1963).

65. See Richard P. Mitchell, *The Society of Muslim Brothers* (London: Oxford University Press, 1969); see also Sivan, *Radical Islam*, and Etienne, *L'islamisme radical*.

66. Qutb, *Religion of the Future*, p. 71.

67. Qutb, "History as the Interpretation of Events," p. 163.

68. Qutb, *Milestones*, p. 185.

69. Ibid., p. 185.

70. Shepard, "Islam as a 'System,'" p. 43.

71. Ibid.

72. The terms are Ernest Gellner's in *Muslim Society* (Cambridge: Cambridge University Press, 1981).

73. Sayed Kotb [Qutb], *Social Justice in Islam*, trans. John B. Hardie (New York: Octagon, 1953).

74. Abdallah Laroui, *The Crisis of the Arab Intellectual*, trans. Diarmid Cammell (Berkeley: University of California Press, 1976).

75. See Carré, *Mystique et politique*, chap. 2; also Sylvia G. Haim, "Sayyid Qutb," *Asian and African Studies* 16 (1982), pp. 151–153.

76. Qutb, *This Religion of Islam*, p. 6.

77. Shepard, "Islam as a 'System,'" p. 41.

78. Qutb, *In the Shade of the Qur'an*, p. 179.

79. Qutb, *Milestones*, p. 101.

80. Qutb, "No God but God—The Program for Life," in *Milestones*, chap. 5, trans. William Shepard, p. 3 (typescript).

81. Shepard, "Islam as a 'System,'" p. 44.

82. Kotb [Qutb], *Social Justice*, chap. 1.

83. Shepard, "Islam as a 'System,'" p. 39.

84. "The genius of Qutb consisted in his grounding his argument in the thought of a prominent medieval thinker, Ibn Taymiyya (1268–1328), and of some of his votaries, through an act of 'creative interpretation.'" Sivan, *Radical Islam*, p. 94.

85. Kotb [Qutb], *Social Justice*, p. 95.

86. Carré, *Mystique et politique*, p. 197.

87. Ibid., p. 196.

88. Carré, *Mystique et politique*.

89. Ibid., p. 213.

90. Qutb, *Islam and Universal Peace*, pp. 27–29.

91. Kotb [Qutb], *Social Justice*, p. 97.

92. Ibid., pp. 62–63.

93. Ibid., p. 97.

94. Qutb, *The Religion of the Future*, pp. 94, 108.

95. Ibid., pp. 101, 111.

96. Ibid., p. 121.

97. Ibid., p. 103.

98. Haddad, "The Qur'anic Justification," pp. 15–19.

99. Sayyid Abu al-A'la Mawdudi, who influenced Qutb, had worked on that problem more thoroughly as Pakistan achieved independence. See Mawdudi, *The Islamic Law and Constitution*, trans. Khurshid Ahmad, 3d ed. (Lahore: Islamic Publications, 1967.)

101. Etienne, *L'islamisme radical*, p. 253.

102. Sivan has said Mawdudi showed some "residual modernism" in advocating democracy. Presumably, he would see Mawdudi as already having backed away from the modernism of Iqbal. The problem with all such observations about "modernism," including my own, is the multiple meanings of that term. In some ways Qutb is more "modern" than Iqbal; in others, he is not. See Sivan, *Radical Islam*, p. 73.

five

◈

'Ali Shari'ati

DOES THE PURSUIT OF CULTURAL AUTHENTICITY conflict with political order? If one begins from a proposition about fundamental human difference,
is it possible to reconstruct a common ground for the foundation of political
cooperation? Or must the search for authenticity necessarily foment conflict between East and West, Sunni and Shi'i, Serb and Bosnian, Kurd and
Turk? Does the construction of an Islamic republic necessarily entail a state
seeking either to convert its neighbors or conquer them, a state caught between its pursuit of difference and its need to function in a larger world?

The writings and oratory of 'Ali Shari'ati helped generate a revolutionary atmosphere in the final decade of the late shah's reign in Iran. About
Shari'ati's influence there appears to be little dispute. One student of the
period says, "It is an undeniable fact that, next to Khomeini, he is the
most influential figure in the Islamic movement that led to the revolution
of 1979."[1] But little else about this man is beyond contention. Critics
charge him with inadequate knowledge of Islam and a superficial understanding of the West.[2] Shari'ati is said by some to have sacrificed logical
rigor and a dedication to truth for political influence,[3] and by others he is
said to have been a marginal political force, much more interested in
ideas than in action.[4] He advocated a return to Islam but in ways that
challenged both the religious establishment and the maverick Ruhollah
Khomeini's revolutionary ideas, and he both embraced and rejected
Western ideas in similar, and seemingly inconsistent, fashion.[5] He is portrayed as primarily interested in the reform of Islam in the tradition of
Muhammad 'Abdu[6] and, quite to the contrary, as prepared to use and
abuse Islam for political purposes, in the manner of Jamal al-Din al-
Afghani, that is, as more a revolutionary than a theologian or philosopher.[7] Ajami wrote of Shari'ati as a liberal, despite Shari'ati's apparent
preference for equality over liberty and his endorsement of populism.[8]

117

The problem in assessing Shari'ati lies in deciding upon which standards to apply. Evaluated from the perspective of mainstream Western philosophy from Plato to Kant, Shari'ati's ideas appear to vacillate between idealism and empiricism without fixing themselves firmly in either camp. Seen instead in the tradition of what Arkoun has called "Islamic Reason,"[9] itself reinforced by Greek thought, Shari'ati's arguments look undisciplined, ill supported, and even heretical. He helps himself to those aspects of the Shi'i tradition he finds useful, just as he helps himself to elements of Marxism or liberalism, without committing himself to the principles from which those aspects or elements arise. From either of these perspectives, Shari'ati has created a hodgepodge of half-baked ideas that need not be taken seriously, however great his prerevolutionary influence in Iran may have been.[10]

Shari'ati might better be evaluated for his contributions to an analysis of authenticity. What makes a human being unique? How can identity be preserved under the onslaught of modernity? To what extent can the products of universal reason be embraced without compromising what is unique about a person or a culture? To what extent must reason be rejected? These are the questions that drive Shari'ati and that define the search for authenticity. Like other advocates of authenticity, Shari'ati is suspect among secularists for a lack of complete commitment to rationality and is suspect in the eyes of religious establishments for lack of faith in a dogmatic tradition. Mysticism permeates his work as it does the work of Iqbal and Qutb, empowering them all with popular followings and making them dubious members of the academic community. In short, Shari'ati participates in the confusions, ambiguities, and contradictions common to other advocates of authenticity. To assess his enterprise against that backdrop reveals a coherence not otherwise apparent and helps one see that shortcomings reflect not just Shari'ati's personal weaknesses but the grave difficulty of his enterprise.

Within the universe of authentics, Shari'ati should be regarded as an internationalist, one whose work can be read as a plea for rediscovering common human bonds through the exploration of distinctive cultural roots. Although he exhorts intellectuals to explore their cultural roots, especially their Islamic, Shi'i heritage, as a basis for understanding themselves and the foundations of mass action, his aim and objective remains the liberation not of the Shi'a or Muslims in general but of human beings of all sorts, cultures, and faiths.[11] However imperfectly and inadequately, he sketches a U-shaped path from an externally imposed universality associated with the West through cultural rediscovery and back toward a common human bond based not in reason but "authenticity." In doing that, he lays a possible ground for escape from the ravages of self-determination.

A Theory of Authenticity

Shari'ati called for revolt against both modernity and tradition in the name of authenticity. Colonialism had sought to propagate a single, foreign, universal culture in order to generate a single, uniform set of consumers. Traditionalism had deteriorated into a routinized, ritualized "fossilized" means of insulating Iran from the forces of history. But Islam and modernity also represented the cure, for in his view Islam in general and Shi'ism in particular contained the potential for inciting revolt and enabling Iran to save itself from modernity through modern revolution. Modernity and tradition constituted the essence of the problem and also the solution.

Shari'ati grew up on the margin of East and West. Born in 1933 near Mashad in the northeastern province of Iran, he lived at a distance from the secularizing, modernizing force of Reza Shah and from the cosmopolitanism of Tehran. His father had founded a Center for the Propagation of Islamic Truths in Mashad. Yet Shari'ati began his own career by teaching in a secular public school, and even later, when his criticism of the religious establishment struck raw nerves, he resisted formal religious training at the hands of the ulema. He studied Western sociological and political philosophy as well as Islamology in Paris, but he returned to Iran in 1964 as an established opponent of the Westernizing, modernizing, authoritarian rule of Muhammad Reza Pahlavi. His Western education drew him toward opponents of colonialism, such as Jacques Berque and Frantz Fanon.[12] His study of Islam pulled him into conflict with the religious hierarchy in Iran. Between 1966 and 1970, he lectured first at the Ferdowsi University of Mashad and then at the Husayniyeh Irshad in Tehran, where, as a founding member of the institute, he became the leading light. To silence him, the regime closed the institute in 1973 and arrested his father. 'Ali Shari'ati then gave himself up and served eighteen months in prison. (He had already served eight months in 1957 and six months on his return to Iran in 1964, always on political charges.) Exiled to his hometown after liberation from prison, Shari'ati "managed to continue writing and even participating in semipublic gatherings." But then he left for Europe, "finding life in Iran unbearable."[13] He died in London on June 9, 1977.

The British authorities ruled that he had died of a massive heart attack; his supporters accused the shah's secret police. After all, Shari'ati belongs to a tradition which for fourteen centuries has believed that its leaders have either been killed by the sword of an oppressor or by the poison of a conspirator.[14]

Radicalism

Shari'ati was never systematically anti-Western. In an essay on art, he wrote that Iranians erred not in imitating the West but in failing to do so. Iranians are neither Eastern nor Western, he said in effect.[15] He meant, I think, that Iranian intellectuals had failed to imitate the West in creating a new culture from their own resources, in criticizing the eighteenth century dogmas of universal truth upon which colonialism had been constructed, and in rejecting positivistic attitudes toward religion. "There is no universal prototype of being 'enlightened,'" he wrote.[16] What he rejected was not Western thought as a whole but what he termed the central impulse of modernity: "All human beings must become 'consumer animals' and all nations must be stripped of their authenticity."[17] More precisely, he reproached Iranians for not understanding, as many Europeans had come to argue, that this absolutist definition of modernity lacked any but relative authority.

Shari'ati treats Marxist thought as another effort—not unlike what he refers to as biologism, sociologism, naturalism, and liberalism—to portray limited truth as universal. Several aspects of Marxism appealed to Shari'ati: its emphasis on social reality, its attention to history as a source of truth, its analysis of capitalism and imperialism, its call for revolution. But far from liberating man, he argued, Marxism presupposed a humankind subject to a history it could not control. "In short, humanity turns out to be the product of the mode of material production."[18] Shari'ati revolted against such materialist assertions as well as against the liberal prescriptions for humankind.

An authentic response to these alienating forces, hence to any genuine revolt, could only come from the inside, from the spirit, according to Shari'ati. "Spiritual knowledge alone can raise the existential value of man to a degree that protects him against any feeling of inferiority toward Occidental greatness."[19] Since religion tends the spirit and since religion in Iran means Islam, the burden of revolution lies with Islam. But Islam in Iran, far from positioning itself at the cutting edge, had been subverted into a force for conservation. "It is common knowledge that the true Islam was turned into the mockery we have today, not by the philosophical or military opponents of Islam, but by its supporters, the traditionalists . . . judges . . . Muslim jurisconsults, speculative theologians, interpreters of the Qur'an, religious judges, rulers, preachers, theosophists, and the caliphs."[20] Whereas the thrust of modernity comes from the outside, the strength of tradition lies within. Perhaps that explains the edge of bitterness in Shari'ati's assault on tradition that is not to be found in his analysis of modernity.

Shari'ati sounds much like Iqbal and Qutb, though also like Rousseau, Montesquieu, and Kierkegaard, when he describes the alienating impact of tradition: "History is a long cemetery, silent and sad, empty and cold, black and deathly, generation after generation. Everything is repetition, imitation. Lives, thoughts, hopes are only tradition and inheritance. Culture, civilization, art and faith are only so many dead stones."[21] The past, then, immobilizes human beings by subordinating individuality and spirit to an overriding pattern of legitimate action. However, human beings would be utterly incapacitated without a past from which to draw a sense of self. "It is absolutely impossible for an individual who has no past to have a future," wrote Shari'ati.[22] How does one imagine, create, project, and expect without reference to the past? The well-being of the spirit depends upon one's understanding of the past.

Shari'ati sees regime and clergy, perhaps moved on occasion by outsiders, as the manipulators of the Iranian past and the architects of tradition as a prison. The late shah evoked not religion but the unchanging place of monarchy in Iran, whereas the men of the cloth emphasized the unchanging role of Islam.

> The tragedy [in Iran] is that, on the one hand, those who have controlled our religion over the past two centuries have transformed it into its present static form and, on the other hand, our enlightened people who understand the present age and the needs of our generation and time, do not understand religion. . . . Meanwhile, true Islam remains unknown and incarcerated in the depths of history.[23]

For Shari'ati, "true" Islam is revolutionary, and "true" Shi'ism is a particularly revolutionary brand of Islam.[24] In Iran, the "red Shi'ism" of 'Ali ('Alī ibn abī tālib), cousin and son-in-law of the Prophet, had become the "black Shi'ism" of the Safavis and the spiritual and temporal revolution begun by Muhammad and turned into a defense of ceremony, sayings, and rituals.[25]

The battle shapes up as Islam versus "true Islam," "narcotic" religion versus "true" religion, religion against religion, Islam versus Islam. Shari'ati calls upon Islamologists to lead an intellectual revolution in the discovery of that distinction. It takes people who know both Islam and the contemporary world, he said, to see that "true Islam" is revolutionary. "It is a question of an Islam that comes forward as a revolutionary ideology, generating an ideal capable of transforming the system, the environment and social relations."[26]

The debate turns on methodology. For Shari'ati, knowledge of the "true Islam" would appear to depend upon at least four methods: the history of Islam, and especially the early days of Islam; study of the contemporary world and its needs; familiarity with Islamic scripture, and receptivity to the most mystical elements of religion. Traditional scholarship emphasized scripture with grudging, unofficial room for the mystical. In the *madrasa,* the traditional secondary school, students worked through rhetoric, logic, the Arabic language, the Qur'an, compilations of hadith, and the law as compiled and interpreted by learned men over the centuries. Islamic history meant history as seen through scripture, not the history of scripture itself in its spatial and temporal context. For Shari'ati, Islamology required an examination of the situation in which Islam had emerged and the impact of Islam on that situation. It meant seeing, for example, how the Prophet retained the form, or container, of many a custom of pre-Islamic Arabia, how he "change[d] the container, the contents, spirit, direction, and practical application of this custom in a revolutionary, decisive and immediate manner."[27] For example, Islam adopted the traditional point of religious pilgrimage in Mecca, the Kaaba, but imparted to it a new significance. The advent of Islam brought a moderate change in customs but a radical change in the meaning of those customs.

Shari'ati speaks of this as the "method" of Muhammad, not the method of God, and he speaks of prophets as those who combine mysticism and intellectual acuity with a sharp sense of what the masses of people need and want. The "true Islam" must be discovered not in scripture but in the activity of exemplary Muslims, Muhammad foremost among them. As a Shi'i Muslim, Shari'ati puts 'Ali and his wife, Fatima, daughter of the Prophet, close behind Muhammad in importance and bemoans insufficient historical knowledge of them. What passes for such knowledge is a formalized, abstract, wart-free portrait derived from scripture. Knowledge of scripture preempts the understanding of Islamic practice.

Islam is revolutionary because the prophet Muhammad acted in a revolutionary manner to transform life in Medina, then in Mecca, and finally in Arabia as a whole. When Shari'ati calls for a revolution that would start from *"table rase* and rebuild everything,"[28] he does so out of conviction that this was the essence of Muhammad's activity. When he says that the Shi'a "do not accept the path chosen by history," he means that the early followers of 'Ali, the most illustrious proponents of the Shi'i school of thought, revolted against their destiny as had Muhammad before them.[29] Of Shi'ism he wrote:

> The awakened call and the possibilities of learning of this school are based upon the twin principles of imamate and justice. It produces revolutionary cries of 'Ashura and the aggressive mobilization of the masses against the existing conditions. It invites people to await the hidden Imam who is in occultation. . . . It keeps alive the hope of "redemption after martyrdom." It promotes the idea of revenge and revolt, faith in the ultimate downfall of tyrants and the decrees of destiny against the ruling powers who spread justice by the sword.[30]

The legitimacy of Shi'ism flows from continuation of the revolutionary tradition begun by Muhammad but nipped in the bud by the Umayyads.

The partisans of 'Ali resisted the drift toward standardization, bureaucratization, codification, authoritarianism, and inauthenticity, in Shari'ati's view, by continuing to espouse a personalistic vision of Islamic leadership. In Iran, they succumbed to the transformation of "red Shi'ism" into "black Shi'ism" only after the year 1500 and under Safavi rule.

Such analysis of Shari'ati's position suggests why he resisted the rather insistent proposal of some ulema that he withhold his critique and spend a few years in the study of Islam. That would have meant study of the scriptural tradition, which he regarded as a cause of Islamic distress rather than as a cure for its emphasis on continuity. Such study was unlikely to improve his knowledge of actual Islamic history, contemporary needs, or the mysticism necessary to sustain a sense of authentic identity. His rejection of such study makes it difficult to call Shari'ati a "reformer" in the sense that Muhammad 'Abdu sought reform of the traditional Islamic understanding of scripture. Shari'ati rejected the idea of reform; rather than reform of doctrine, he sought to undermine dogma and doctrine as the basis of the religion. And in this regard he resembles Iqbal, Qutb, and Arkoun more than he does 'Abdu.

Nonetheless, Shari'ati's proclamation of revolutionary Islam and revolutionary Shi'ism seems no more secure than the nature of the times in which it was proclaimed. By insisting that an interpreter of Islam must know contemporary social conditions as well as Islamic history, he would seem to imply that social conditions might sometimes dictate a conservative Islam, not revolution. Might not Muhammad then be properly understood as a builder of stable institutions and of an enduring system of justice? Shari'ati's definition of the "true Islam" ultimately lies in the pres-ent; logical consistency requires that he locate his own thinking and actions as squarely within history as he puts those of Muhammad, 'Ali, and Fatima. Although Shari'ati also speaks of Islam as commitment to "enduring ideals," it is difficult to imagine he would include revolution among them, for he explains Islamic revolution not as an ideal but as a necessity of circumstance. Does this approach liberate human beings from their history or enslave them?

Autonomy

Shari'ati meant to liberate human beings from history and from God by making them conscious of their capacities. Family, social circumstances, customs, historical context, economic and physical needs—all these factors shape human beings but do not determine their responses. Rather, by virtue of their humanity, by virtue of God's gift of volition, human beings can say yes or no at every juncture. Will emerges in Shari'ati's thought, as it does for other authentics, as the defining characteristic of what it means to be human, and the search for the source of will leads deep into the mystical recesses of the human spirit. To realize their authentic personalities, human beings must respond not merely to external cues but to the mystical, spiritual qualities within, which put them closer to a remote, unknowable God, the unifying force of the universe.

Shahrough Akhavi sees a pair of related contradictions in Shari'ati's position. First, he wonders how Shari'ati can insist both upon an autonomous human being, apparently free to choose conduct of which God would not approve, as the prime generator of human history and upon God as an "absolute hidden being," ultimate guardian of the universe.[31] Second, he observes that Shari'ati, apparently a phenomenologist, believes that human beings cannot themselves penetrate to the truth of things; they must look at both material objects and ideas as signs or indications of truth but must not confuse these signs (readings of the Qur'an, for example) with truth itself. Can one regard human beings as fully autonomous if in fact their "autonomous" choices reflect only the "appearances of reality?"[32] Might not their ability to choose be mere illusion, itself fostered by manipulative forces they do not understand?

Both objections carry weight but would apply to much authentic thought, surely to the work of Iqbal and Qutb as well as to that of a European Christian existentialist such as Kierkegaard. Shari'ati seems to have opted for the Iqbalian solution, with all its defects. The common starting point, which simultaneously opens the way to criticism and resolves the problem, is that logic and rationality are neither necessary nor sufficient avenues to truth. Human beings may come closest to truth and God through inward reflection and the creativity that springs from it. Poetry for Iqbal and art in general for Shari'ati express those inner strivings for truth. The existence of God and the oneness of the universe are intuitive rather than demonstrated but are consequently no less "true." What can be demonstrated by modern methods is the impact of human action. The prophets, especially Muhammad, reshaped the world by force of will. Western technology and imperialism have altered the basis of choice in the Third World. But it cannot be demonstrated, even by the standards of logic, that this success represents Truth in some larger sense.

For Shari'ati, then, authentic human behavior depends upon both the rational and the irrational and hence upon worldly and otherworldly orientations. Human autonomy depends upon submission to one's innermost being, one's spiritual being, which leads toward God. If there is some hidden manipulation of the universe via this spiritual communication, it would be by definition unknowable by logic and rationality. What Shari'ati argues with conviction and persuasiveness is the lack of proof for verifiable determinism of any sort, material or ideal. Similarly, the insufficiency of human reason does not, even by logical standards, preclude the possibility of human access to spiritual truth and, as a result, to genuine autonomy.

Such considerations do not negate the logic of Akhavi's objections. They merely underscore two somewhat contradictory assertions of authentic thought: that human beings make their own world but that a part of what makes a human beings unique and authentic is a mystical, otherworldly quality. Without that mystical quality, human beings lack the will to affect their world in a positive, purposeful, fully human way. To be human is to have a solid footing in two worlds, one historical and amenable to reason, the other beyond the confines of Western logic. Such thought will always come up short by the standards of reason alone.

Like Qutb, Shari'ati speaks of an awakening for human beings who otherwise slumber through history. Gabriel descended to rescue the Prophet from passivity, isolation, and individualism by giving him a mission, pushing him into battle. Although Muhammad was the final prophet, every person is "heir of the prophets."[33] Man is "always moving, searching, struggling, working and wanting. He will not be satisfied."[34] "True" Islam, unlike the "narcotic religion" propagated to render human beings submissive to the authority of past and present, provides an example and a doctrine for the exercise of such initiative and energy. According to Shari'ati, the principal lesson brought by Muhammad is that human beings as individuals inspired by God can wrest their fate from the grip of "nature, history, society and the self,"[35] which can be but the involuntary product of external forces. The mystical awakening opens the way for the voluntary reconstruction (Iqbal's term) of self and society. And as Qutb observes, Islam entreats believers to undertake jihad—effort, striving, struggle—toward these ends, which are human ends. Muslims undertake jihad in the name of God to fashion their own personalities and make their own history, escaping the determinant conceptions of religion, history, and self that have imprisoned them.

Particularity

Shari'ati's radicalism leads him to reject tradition and modernity, both hostile to the authentic understanding of self. Human beings must choose their personalities and shape their own lives, but on what basis must they choose? What is the link between their choices and something Shari'ati calls their "primordial being?" Why would one suppose that Iranians, faced with choices stemming from the clash of tradition and modernity, would proceed any differently from Europeans? What is the foundation for authentic revolt and choice? For Shari'ati, that foundation is culture.

He defines culture as the "totality of material and spiritual savings of a particular race and society," as opposed to what he calls "civilization," which is the "totality of material and spiritual accumulations of humanity."[36] Technology constitutes an aspect of civilization, because it is universal, he says, but culture distinguishes one ethnic group, race, or nation from another. He calls culture the "inherent attribute of a society" and the "spiritual essence of a race or a nation."[37] Culture divides, whereas civilization unites, and although it lies within the power of human beings to modify the culture they have produced, Shari'ati is not clear on whether one could imagine cultures dissolving themselves into an undifferentiated world civilization. At times, he speaks of "human nature" as if it floated above culture, as when he speaks of "human values" as "sacred ideals, which, although their applicability may vary, are eternal and absolute and may change only as the human species changes or disappears"[38] or when he speaks of mysticism "as a manifestation of the primordial nature of man."[39] But even then he argues that values will be applied differently in each culture, and the mystical instinct may merely help explain the drive for religion, generator of a variety of cultures rather than a single civilization. For Shari'ati, the particular preempts and conditions the universal.

Shari'ati's essay on Fatima, daughter of the Prophet and wife of 'Ali, turns on this point. He seeks to portray her not as a model of female liberation, leadership, subordination, activity, or passivity. Rather, he argues that Fatima's greatness stemmed from her ability to play a whole series of roles dictated by her particular circumstances. The title of the essay and the final line is "Fatima is Fatima." She asserted her influence on Islamic history not by following a script or imitating a model but by being herself. By virtue of her success, she has become a part of Shi'i myth and legend, serving with 'Ali as an example for the present. But the problem, says Shari'ati, is the paucity of what is known and written about them as concrete historical personalities. Instead, they are portrayed as reflecting universal Islamic values, unchanging models, and a static culture. The details of reality and history have become obscured by retrospective idealism.

Ideologies reshape cultures and civilization. They arise from "particular human self-consciousness" generated in concrete social circumstances. They are effective if they express the needs and aspirations of a given society. "Any school [of thought] which is not based upon the cultural foundations of a society looks like a good book in a library which is used only by a small group of students and professors . . . If a free-thinker separates himself from his society, no matter where he goes or what he does, his society will remain in everlasting corruption."[40] Prophets succeed precisely because they emerge from the masses and speak a language that is generally accessible. They make universal claims, but their success in remaking culture stems from their understanding of the circumstances in which they lived and worked. Whatever the truth of their claims, "a valid and true statement expressed at an improper time and place will be futile."[41]

Shari'ati proposes a universal definition of "enlightenment" and argues that there is no universal prototype for being "enlightened." Francis Bacon was enlightened for his time and place, Sartre for his. "The enlightened soul is a person who is self-conscious of his 'human condition' in his time and historical and social setting, and whose awareness inevitably and necessarily gives him a sense of social responsibility."[42] The form of enlightenment seems to be unchanging, but its content must vary, as must the educational system designed to produce enlightenment. To be sure, science is universal, and a scientist may learn the same things the world over, but scientific learning, the quintessence of enlightenment in one set of circumstances, may not be apt in another. Enlightenment must begin with knowledge of context.

For an Iranian, that context is the "totality of things which have been accumulated as the Iranian culture: Islamic principles, story, myth, art, philosophy, oration, and theosophy comprise our culture."[43] It is not the truth of Islamic principles from which an intellectual must begin but rather their existence in Iranian culture. Better understanding of context would require not a more thorough training in exegesis but rather an understanding of how principles, stories, and myths emerged from historical circumstance and what they have come to mean, hence Shari'ati's insistence, given the predominance of Shi'ism in Iran, on the vital necessity of research on the historical figures of 'Ali and Fatima, whose lives have generated a plethora of stories and myths taken to be fundamental to Shi'ism. Shari'ati would not challenge the "sacred truth" of Islamic principles, but as he put it with regard to a somewhat different issue, "the questions I am raising here are . . . by whom, for what purpose, and at what time this sacred truth is being utilized."[44] Enlightenment thus begins with knowledge of the concrete interaction of ideas, and consciousness arises from physical surroundings and historical developments. Abstract, ideological understandings can only be useful and meaningful if they reflect such familiarity.

Mysticism is the other pillar of particularity. "Mysticism follows love," wrote Shari'ati. "Love is the extra-material energy that is the source and active cause of human behavior."[45] Mysticism saves one's thoughts and actions from the erosion of history, either by authorizing indifference and passivity toward ongoing historical developments, an attitude Shari'ati and other authentics deplore, or by becoming the basis for individual will and action. By reaching beyond the rational, one may believe in the efficaciousness of human activity while nonetheless engaging in the sort of cold-blooded, myth-destroying analysis that undermines the absoluteness of all principles, even one's own. Through mysticism one feels at "home" in the world, spiritually comfortable, thoroughly oneself, despite physical separation and alienation from physical objects and historical process. Strangely—and this is perhaps the essence of mysticism—this particularistic, personalistic spiritual endeavor both solidifies individuality and relinks the individual, otherwise alienated, to a larger world.

Shari'ati's treatment of the pilgrimage to Mecca, in an essay called *Hajj*, illustrates the links between particularity, mysticism, and universalism.[46] By writing about pilgrimage, Shari'ati distances himself from those who see Islam as a set of abstract principles.[47] By going on pilgrimage, a Muslim seeks to experience faith as the early Muslims did, to walk where they walked and pray where they prayed. It is a return to origins[48] for human beings who divest themselves of their daily routine, the clothes that symbolize culture and materialism, the petty purposes for which one lives, all those things that come to overlay the self and alienate human beings from their spiritual, inner selves. Pilgrims must be prepared to die before they leave; debts must be paid, a will drawn, anger and hostilities dropped.[49] "He witnesses his own dead body and visits his own grave. Man is reminded of the final goal of his life. He experiences death at Miqat and resurrection after which he must continue his mission in the desert between Miqat and Miad."[50] The theme echoes one frequently expressed in authentic thought, whether in Rousseau or Heidegger, Iqbal or Qutb: Only at death does one experience one's authentic being. Only death is utterly personal. Only at death does one see the full scope of one's life in all its particularity.

From that initial preparation for death, the pilgrim then moves toward God. Shari'ati wrote not so much about the ritual or the rules as about what the pilgrims feel. The surroundings, the masses of similarly clad pilgrims, the Kaaba, the heat and dryness—all produce sensation, helping the pilgrim to recreate the feelings and faith of Abraham, Hagar, and Muhammad. One feels drawn away from the self into a mass of human beings being swept along. One feels the excitement as one approaches the Kaaba. The sense of self dissolves, only to return again as one steps out of the Tawaf circling crowds at the point of entering. "After denying and killing all of the previous and false egos, you will discover your 'authentic ego.'"[51] Later, in Mashar, the pilgrim feels utterly alone, despite the presence of a mass of people spending the night there. As one moves on to Mina, one feels the power of love behind individual and collective action.

For Shari'ati, what matters about the hajj is the intent with which a pilgrim performs the ritual and the feelings derived from the observance. Like Kierkegaard, he focuses upon Abraham's decision to sacrifice a son (Ishmael in the Islamic tradition) as something a pilgrim must confront: What is this person's Ishmael? Is one free to make the proper choice? Can one act from faith even without explanation, as did Abraham? Scripture entreats faith and even pilgrimage, but Shari'ati, like Kierkegaard, asks that the pilgrim be prepared to make Ibrahim's "leap of faith," not because it is required, for then there is no genuine choice, but because it can and must be freely chosen. Rather than returning home content with having fulfilled one of the duties of a Muslim and confident of a good life beyond death, the pilgrims must assume responsibility as did Abraham for the state of the faith and the state of their people. Abraham and Ishmael built the Kaaba together, and the pilgrim must return to build a "house for the people."[52]

By undertaking the hajj, a pilgrim moves closer to God, but this means the fulfillment of the authentic self, liberated from the ordinary routines, obligations, and duties of life and freed to think about the past and responsibilities for the future. By confronting the historicity of Islam, one must come to grips with the needs of the present. By reflecting upon the exemplary actions of early believers, one moves toward an understanding of what must be done in the present. By sensing the unchanging and eternal, one sees that genuine faith, such as that of Abraham, calls for responsibility on earth. Islam is not a religion of pious forms leading toward eternal life but an invitation to individuals to take stock of themselves and the world in which they live in order to follow the lead of their ancestors in making that world a better place. For Shari'ati, authentic faith requires appropriate action from responsible individuals fully conscious of their particular backgrounds in concrete circumstances.

Another, somewhat contradictory message also runs through Shari'ati's discussion of the pilgrimage. The pilgrim grasps individuality and at the same time melts into the masses of pilgrims who circumambulate the Kaaba and follow the rest of the timeworn route. Although Shari'ati regards faith as a personal matter and views the hajj as important for the consciousness it instills, he also argues that the faith leads toward a realization of the oneness of humanity and, even beyond that, of the universe. From an understanding of particularity and historicity emerges a sense of unity and oneness (tawḥīd) that is critical to Shar'iati's general argument, as it is to those of other authentics. Uniformity produced by routine, ritual, and tradition stand in the way of an authentic, choice-driven life, but a world of individual choice promises chaos, unless there is some fundamental unity beneath or beyond choice. Shari'ati's vision of a better world, and certainly his hopes for getting there, presuppose that such unity exists, despite the particularistic nature of the phenomenal world he entreats us to confront.

Unicity

No theme runs more insistently through Shari'ati's work than tawḥīd, a Qur'anic idea rescued, rejuvenated, and reinvigorated to mean much more than the oneness of God. As Shari'ati uses it, however, this highly traditional term begins to sound radical in Jacobin, socialist, idealist, transhistoric ways. He brandishes tawḥīd as a sword to combat religious division, the partition of knowledge, the separation of God and man, and the meaninglessness of discrete historical events. If he does not brandish it

energetically and successfully, he risks a world caught in cultural particularities, speaking different languages, worshipping different gods; but if
he wields it too viciously, he threatens the particularity that distinguishes
human beings from other creatures and anchors the concept of individual
authenticity. He also fuels the arguments of the traditionalists about a single, unchanging Islam and those of the idealists about a single concept of
modernity. The line he attempts to walk is thin and perhaps nonexistent.

For Shari'ati, the unicity of the universe is a matter of instinct and faith.
It cannot be a product of empirical proof, for inspection of the phenomenal world leads him to conclusions about particularity and multiplicity.
The world abounds with contradictions and distinctions, which empiricism can seek to contain but not overcome. Logic may be helpful but cannot suffice, for logic cannot demonstrate the sufficiency of logic. Moreover, a part of what Shari'ati means by unity is the unity of feeling and
knowledge, of love and truth, which cannot, of course, be demonstrated
definitively in the realm of knowledge alone.[53]

Shari'ati invokes logic but then acknowledges its inadequacy as a proof.
Reflecting and modifying existentialist refrains, he says there can be no
meaning in human beings, who are a part of the universe, unless there is
meaning in the universe. It is not possible for human beings to have choice
and responsibility in a world without the existence of conscience, will, direction, and intelligence. Human beings participate in Being; if Being is absurd, all is absurd.[54] But human reason, as only one element in Being, cannot examine itself from the outside and verify this proposition. In fact, all
efforts to do so lead to breakdowns of moral and social consensus, to division rather than unity. Hence, like Iqbal, Shari'ati relies on poetry and
mysticism to demonstrate the oneness of the universe.

In a bit of poetry, he muses about the role of one and zero in a number
composed of one and an infinity of zeros.

> They do not exist but they do
> They are zero
> That is, they are hollow
> They are nothing
> They are absurd
> They are meaningless
> They are not really numbers either
> They are not
> Because only one is really a number
> And it is a unit.[55]

At first blush, the poem appears to suggest that the particularity and
multiplicity of the world, which Shari'ati has taken pains to establish as

the only starting point for authentic existence, constitute illusions generated from a base of unity. Because the metaphor is abstract, Shari'ati also
appears to deviate from his distrust of logic detached from social context.
Probably, though, he intends to argue by indirection that multiplicity and
particularity depend upon unity. The zeros in the number "1,000,000"
lack meaning only if there is no number one (or other digit) preceding
them. Standing alone, they are absurd, meaningless. Thus, many individuals living together as mere bits of matter similarly lack meaning and
purpose. Their great number makes it easy to forget that they are first
units, individuals, and authentic individuals, not mere numbers. They are
something rather than nothing, because they share in the property of
unity, that *tawhīd* of which Shari'ati speaks. This is one reason that self-
knowledge, the introspection of the particular self, turns out to be knowledge of God, the root of the oneness of things.

Embedded in a poem, the metaphor of "One Followed by an Eternity of
Zeroes," persuades more by its mystical than its logical qualities. In fact,
Sufi-like, Shari'ati suggests that the human capacity for love serves to ce-
ment the individual into the universe.

> [Love] has an unknowable source and can inflame and melt all of my exis-
> tence; it even impels me to self-denial. Love grants me values higher and
> more sublime than expediency; and no physical, material or biochemical ac-
> count can comprehend it. If love were taken away from man, he would be-
> come an isolated, stagnant being, useful only to the systems of production.[56]

The effect of love cannot be verified, only felt, and the resulting hypothetical fusion of God, nature, and man does not lend itself, either, to the test
of rationality. But the failure of Shari'ati's thought to pass the test of rationality in its insistence on unicity offers eloquent testimony that he belongs among the advocates of authenticity.

Islam, and especially Shi'ism, contributes to the sense of unity but
seems nonessential. Islam emphasizes *tawhīd* in its scriptures and in its
practices, such as the hajj, which draws Muslims out of themselves and
into that communion with God and universe that Shari'ati tries to portray
in his essay on the pilgrimage. But Shari'ati also describes Islam as the religion of humanity. "To adore God is to adore the values of man and consequently to become divine in constantly moving closer to God."[57] Presumably non-Muslims might also move toward God by embracing the
proper human values embedded in a number of religions.

'Ali offers to Shi'i Muslims an example of the love and truth united in a
single nature. Iranians still mourn the family of 'Ali. The family evokes a
love that lifts Iranians out of themselves and toward the sort of mystical
unity of which Shari'ati speaks. Non-Shi'a or non-Muslims could participate in this overarching sense of oneness. In fact, Shari'ati says Islam en-

dorses "one giant human society (ummah) on the face of the earth which
is based on economic and humane equality and on lofty and divine
ideals."[58] That society would not necessarily be Shi'i or even Muslim. In
fact, for it to be Muslim in the way much of the world is currently Muslim
would mean a perpetuation of splintering. Only the "true Islam," extracted from its accidental circumstances, and "true Shi'ism," separated
from ritual and myth, draw people beyond their particularistic understandings and toward the radical unity Shari'ati envisioned.

Shari'ati fashioned this delicate balance between unity and diversity under the same sort of pressures felt by other authentics. On the one hand, he
saw a need to defend the self against the other, to defend one's culture
against universalizing theories of modernization, to combat the passivity
of Muslims who would separate religious belief and practice from the concrete condition of Muslims in the twentieth century, to start toward revolution not by hypothesizing what the masses ought to believe but, like
Gramsci, by acknowledging the hegemony of particularistic belief. On the
other hand, he saw a natural human aspiration to overcome the gap between self and other, the need for peoples of diverse cultures to live together, the need for unity in the name of revolution and equality, and, perhaps most important, the heightened need for transcendent meaning in a
world increasingly conscious of its estrangement. These pressures drove
him toward a delicate balance similar to those crafted by Iqbal and Qutb,
though his balance was different in its assumption of Shi'ism as a starting
point but like theirs in the ambivalence of its practical applications.
Shari'ati resembles Iqbal and Qutb in that he, too, believed the mystical
energy of Muslims would tip that delicate balance away from particularity
toward harmony, yet he is currently remembered as a thinker whose ideas
contributed to a culture-bound revolution, as Qutb continues to be remembered as an ideologue of Egyptian revolution and Iqbal cannot escape
his ultimate endorsement of Pakistani separatism.

Shari'ati generated a Shi'i theory of authenticity and contributed to the
Iranian Revolution, which has thus far remained nationalistic and xeno-
phobic. Although it is easy to see in retrospect that he would not have ap-
proved the institutionalization based on clerical rule, it is perhaps less obvious that his ideas do not necessarily sustain Shi'i nationalism, Iranian
nationalism, or even a permanent restoration of the Islamic *umma*. Rather,
Shari'ati appears extraordinarily conscious of the political pitfalls of authentic thought, wary of its potentially divisive consequences, and devoted
to seeking a cure. In his view, unicity will necessarily emerge from the pro-
liferation of particularities. Internationalism will triumph over nationalism.

This commitment stems from the expression Shari'ati gave to the authentic impulses of autonomy and unicity, which seem to triumph over the bet-
ter-known trademarks of his and other authentic thought: radicalism and

particularity. Politics must begin from a particularistic cultural base, which is the only possible meeting point for elites and masses, but autonomy means that human beings ultimately make and control their culture. They must do so with the tools at their disposition at a given moment. Tomorrow's circumstances may differ from today's; the cultural politics of today may prove inappropriate tomorrow in the light of the ongoing, revolutionary discovery of the oneness of human beings that lies beneath the cultural veneer. Nothing prevents human beings, fully in control of their destiny, from fashioning a political structure on this increasingly unified framework. In fact, evolving circumstances may require it.

Autonomy Revisited

Shari'ati's debts to existentialism reveal themselves in his conception of human beings as self-conscious, creative choosers.[59] As generators of their own cultures, histories, and personalities, they have imposed constraints on their own choices. The development of material society represents human choice and then comes to dictate choice. Technology arrives to liberate human beings from natural necessities only to shackle them in another era. Freely chosen religion deteriorates into ritual and dogma that restrict choice and diminish moral responsibility. What is chosen in one generation is inherited as a constraint in the next.

From this perspective, humankind has split into ethnicities, races, classes, language groups, and religions by virtue of a set of choices that perpetuate themselves and determine behavior. In the face of such diversity, European imperialism took two approaches. In the case of Africa, Europe sought to demean native cultures, languages, and religions and to replace them with European versions; the recovery of African cultures in a nationalistic vein thus constituted a necessary phase in African liberation, in Shari'ati's view. In the case of the Muslim world, however, Europe reified Islam and the cultural mosaic of Middle Eastern societies through both scholarship and policy, contributing to the stultification of tradition. As a result, the mere reassertion of culture would only contribute to subservience rather than liberation, as would the wholesale adoption of European values. Progress thus requires liberation both from ossified tradition and from the externally imposed sameness of modernity. In both Africa and the Muslim world, liberation requires cultural choice; it requires the modification of the cultural constraints upon behavior rather than passive acknowledgment or mere reproduction.

Shari'ati expresses admiration for Camus's definition of becoming: "I revolt, therefore I am." It is the role of "free thinkers" to rebel against constraints and thereby generate options for themselves and for others. To break out of the "prisons" in which human beings find themselves,

whether naturalistic, historicist, or technological, they must study and explore. To liberate oneself from historical determinism, one studies history.
To liberate oneself from the clutches of naturalism, one studies science; to
liberate oneself from technology, one studies the philosophy of technology; and to liberate oneself from the constraints of religious tradition, free
thinkers must engage themselves in religious studies. Shari'ati mapped
an extensive program of Islamic studies for the Husayniyeh Irshad[60] with
a view toward opening up choices through research on the evolution of
culture in concrete historical conditions. He saw culture as a vast grab bag
of possibilities, as yet little explored and exploited by the Shi'a of Iran.
Historical, literary, philosophical, linguistic, and artistic research could
transform culture from constraint into empowerment.

Shari'ati's writing emphasizes the Islamic heritage, especially the Shi'i
tradition, of Iran to the virtual exclusion of other moments in its history. His
reasons for doing so would appear to be thoroughly political: For one, the
shah had sought to resurrect memories of ancient Iranian greatness to bolster the glory of the Peacock Throne; for another, surely more important, he
believed the great masses of Iranians felt thoroughly a part of Islamic culture. The success of the revolution confirmed his point. Any effort to lead
the Iranian people out of their alienation would require work from within
the constraints imposed by popular perceptions of Islam, especially if the
intent was to change rather than to reinforce those perceptions and further
rigidify tradition. The gap between elites and masses had first to be diminished, in Shari'ati's view, so that elites could articulate options generated
from within a culture recognized as having general validity. Only research—only "Islamology" as he called it—could uncover those options.
"An enlightened person in an Islamic society, regardless of his own ideological convictions, must, of necessity, be an Islamologist."[61]

The shah invoked ancient Iranian culture in an attempt to stabilize and
rigidify, albeit unsuccessfully; Shari'ati invokes culture in the hope of
bringing together elites and masses in a common understanding of the
choices lurking in their common historical experience. He pushes for the
detailed exploration of particularity, not to reinforce but to escape it. The
shah sought to utilize the trappings of ancient Iran in a thoroughly modern, utterly different context. Shari'ati encourages a thorough investigation of the changing circumstances in which Islam and Shi'ism evolved,
as well as a thorough understanding of the modern context in which
choices must be made.

> We must accurately understand the world, modern civilization, Western cul-
> ture, the colonial powers, and the apparent and hidden relationships be-
> tween the East and the West. In particular, we must understand the specific
> aims of Islam—as a religion, as a culture, and as a history that affects a large

segment of human society. We must discuss all intellectual issues, schools of thought and ideologies which constitute the prevailing trends of the word, ideologies which whether we like it or not influence our own thoughts and feelings, and particularly those of our intellectuals. We must also comprehend the objective international realities, factors and powers involved, the available resources and the existing conditions.[62]

Such realism never seems to have troubled the shah in his search for "authenticity." For Shari'ati, authenticity lies with a set of choices emerging from the self within its cultural matrix; authenticity is a state of becoming, not a state of being, and for that reason it does not necessarily point to a specific political configuration appropriate to any time or place.

In fact, the more Shari'ati probes the Islamic tradition in its greatest specificity, the more he finds human behavior rather than Shi'i or Islamic behavior. For example, his essays on Fatima seek to demonstrate that she fills no stereotype. No one had mapped a role for her. No revelation specified her behavior. He portrays her as an unique person, who responded to her circumstances and fashioned an extraordinary place for herself in Islamic history. She was a daughter, a wife, a Muslim, a woman, but first and foremost a human being. She followed the "be yourself" motto dear to advocates of authenticity.

Similarly, Shari'ati's impressive treatment of the hajj consistently emphasizes the ways in which rituals drive pilgrims to peel off layer after layer of nonessentials and to feel, in community with each other, their primordial humanity before their Creator. Distinctive clothes give way to simple, common dress. Differences of class, race, gender, age, and origin disappear. Egos melt in the sea of humanity. Selfishness evaporates with the example of Ibrahim in submission to God. By rediscovering the love of God, the pilgrims liberate themselves from human instincts. "It may be concluded that you can free yourself from the fourth jail [the first three are nature, history, and society] through 'love'! This knowledge endows you with such a degree of consciousness and creativity that allows you to build yourself up to the will of Allah and not to be merely a servant of nature."[63] For Shari'ati, then, the hajj permits a voyage of the individual toward God and, hence, toward the discovery of the human essence. The hajj, though culturally specific, broadens the horizons of a pilgrim to encompass history and humanity.

Shari'ati returns to a favorite theme, the zero and the one, to illustrate the nature of choice available to human beings.

Man is a creature who descended upon this earth and was left alone. Therefore, you are only an existing phenomenon and must construct your own nature. You are a Zero or a nothing who may become everything! You are a "doubt" or a "possibility" who may acquire the shape of a man. If you choose to be human and consciously discover your nature (faith), you will be able to liberate yourself. You will be able to find the fate of history and realize that history is the fate of man through the ages as well as an evolution from zero toward Allah. From one nothing you begin to know man and his values and so you adopt humanity.[64]

In what is perhaps the ultimate expression of belief in human autonomy, he wrote: "The text of your fate will be written by others if you 'do not know'; but you will write it if you 'know.'"[65] Knowing means understanding nature, history, society, and the self, and knowing the self requires not just logic but a faith in God that draws one out of the self, narrowly conceived, and toward the rest of humanity. Shari'ati develops the argument with references to the Qur'an and careful extrapolations from the ritual of pilgrimage, but he argues unambiguously that the search for authenticity in an Islamic context carries one not just toward what it means to be a Muslim but toward what it means to be authentically human, to escape alienation by understanding one's circumstances and exercising choice.

Particularity thus appears to be an accidental result of thousands of years of misguided human choice. Autonomy precedes particularity but also supersedes it, for culture can be both created and modified. Particularity marks the world as we know it; the great cultural gaps that divide us and set East against West, rich against poor, and Sunni against Shi'i constitute an undeniable aspect of reality, which one ignores at the risk of alienation. For the great masses of humanity, these particularities appear immutable. But the struggle for authenticity, although rooted in the recognition of particularity, draws the enlightened toward an understanding of the human capacity for choice and, as a result, toward the capacity to escape the "prisons" of particularity. Authenticity rides on the triumph of autonomy over particularity. In political terms, authenticity does not appear to require Shi'ism, the nation-state, the Islamic *umma*, or any particular political configuration in the long run. In the short run, however, the authority of an imam may be useful, the nation-state may serve to combat colonialism, class consciousness may serve to promote equality, and ethnic solidarity may contribute to the struggle for justice. But these human choices reflect constantly changing circumstances; the larger reality is the oneness of history, dominated by God.

Unicity Revisited

Shari'ati describes history as combat between monotheism and polytheism, with monotheism both the starting point and the ultimate objective. He paints a state of nature that echoes Rousseau: "Long ago, people lived as a brotherhood. Forests and rivers were their commonwealth. They all had their share sitting at the free table of nature. Fishing and hunting was a means for acquiring food for survival. God was the only owner and all peoples were considered equal."[66] Then came quarrels between Cain and Abel, which initiated the era of polytheism. The "old" polytheism meant belief in a plurality of divinities; the new polytheism embraces a host of idols, which may be ideologies (fascism, socialism), instincts (love, power), heroes (political), or lifestyles (materialism). These are the modern enemies of "monotheism," according to Shari'ati.

Such polytheism must ultimately give way to unicity, in Shari'ati's estimation, and that is the case for someone such as Qutb, for that matter. For Qutb, though, the reasoning is rather simple; the world must rally to the "true" Islam. Since the world does not now share a single faith, Qutb's assertion that a single faith will prevail does not seem plausible. Shari'ati, by contrast, seems to suggest that the search for authenticity must necessarily be conducted in every cultural context. His recipe for the search does not presuppose Islam. He argues that there is no single, universal recipe for enlightenment. The search for the self must be conducted according to the cultural milieu and the historical period. Obviously, it cannot begin with Islam in a non-Islamic culture. Shari'ati wrote:

> A return to self means a return to that particular human self which has been formed throughout history, has given us spiritual personality and cultural identity, and has shaped our intellectual direction. I mean that continuous true spirit which, although buried under historical debris, events, scenes and incidents and although covered with the burden of the past and the troubles of the present, has an "uninterrupted motion" that reaches contemporaries. I mean that reality which carries with it our essential humanity, our sublime moral or ideological spirit and our spiritual resources and facilities. . . . The self that I have in mind is an "eternal man." It is an old person who embodies and personifies those millions of human beings who have lived in many centuries and have experienced changes, revolutions, various cultures, and ideologies. At the present we are that person.[67]

The image differs from Plato's Allegory of the Cave; rather than peering at shadows on the wall, human beings must comprehend, recognize, and shed all the layers of history and culture that define their identities but obscure their essential humanity. One finds Truth not by leaving the cave for the sunlight and a painful encounter with the Form of the Good but by peeling away the layers of human history and culture. There is nonetheless to be found in Shari'ati a firm belief in "human nature."

> It is based on nature that Allah created all of mankind, that is, human nature and not the nature of those who rely on Eastern or Western empires and favor one ruler or class over another. It is a nature that considers humanity to

be Allah's representative and guardian of the earth. It is a nature that gives mankind sovereignty over the world and freedom from being a hostage.[68]

Although he rejects European humanism for its association with imperialism, he nonetheless observes, "The oneness of the human race is a sacred truth."[69] It need not be demonstrated.

Such a position puts Shari'ati's commitment to particularity in jeopardy and the distance he takes from European universalism in some doubt. From his preoccupation with the world of "becoming," he ends up by asserting the importance of "being." While rejecting the necessity of modernization theory and Marxism, he retains the teleology of Marxism, Islam, and Christianity. History, marked by extraordinary vicissitudes and diversity of cultures, is nonetheless sweeping humanity closer together, toward a discovery of its essential oneness. But this great onrush occurs not from faith alone or from mechanisms of society but from the multiple, self-discovering pursuit of cultural authenticity; the pursuit of difference leads back toward commonality. Islam is but one of the streams for the enactment of the process.

$$ \text{ﻟﺪ} $$

Shari'ati was thoroughly liberal in the American sense of one committed to societal change in the name of progress. Surely he was not a liberal in the classic sense of one committed to individual human rights even at the expense of human equality. Although he was a radical in his rejection of both tradition and modernity, his vision depended more on a notion of continuing, incremental, partial changes than on one great cataclysmic struggle to right all evil and enact the truth. He followed Marx in the hope that the eventual victory over human alienation would produce a great coming together. Unlike liberals such as Locke or Rousseau, who presuppose the existence of something called a "people" and unlike most Islamists, who take the *umma* as the political building block, Shari'ati's logic and faith drove him to embrace a thoroughgoing internationalism, almost Marxist in its fervor. He praised nationalism as a "progressive" force in opposing colonialism, but he could not embrace it in an absolute sense any more than he could justify, from his principles, the defense of any arbitrary set of political arrangements. Such arrangements and associations fall into the domain of human choice, which necessarily shifts with the historical and cultural terrain.

The commitment to unicity runs through all authentic thought. For the romantics, the pursuit of the self leads one closer and closer to nature. Death is the ultimate realization of selfhood and also the reunion with the natural world. For Nietzsche, the campaign leads to the discovery of the notion of eternal recurrence, the great flow of experience in which differences dissolve into sameness. For many Islamists, such as Qutb, faith and struggle pull people together into a group and then a community. What distinguishes Shari'ati's thought is its position between a Nietzschean mysticism and Qutb's commitment to practical politics. His is a gently utopian vision that welcomes all political tools at appropriate moments but leaves open the future for the gradual breakdown of particularities; it is a commitment to authenticity that attempts to eschew the dangers of commitment to heroic figures, formulas dredged up from the past, or groups proclaiming themselves to be purveyors of Truth. To dismiss him as a mere "ideologue of the Iranian Revolution" and an exponent of Shi'i authenticity would be to miss what may be his greatest contribution—his suggestions about the possible reconciliation of sharpening cultural differences with the increasing need for political unification.

The contradictions in Shari'ati's thought result from the intractability of this dilemma. Political success still seems to lie with those who embrace one or the other extreme, either the universality of culture and norms, as in the Western world (albeit applied to particular, arbitrarily mapped entities), or difference even at the cost of civil war and genocide. Shari'ati, who is often said to be more concerned with politics than philosophy, charts a political course integrating these strands from within the Islamic context. Because neither Western universalism nor an arbitrary and intolerant particularity is any longer viable as a basis for political construction, Shari'ati deserves a fresh hearing.

Notes

1. Houchang Esfandiar Chehabi, "Modernist Shi'ism and Politics: The Liberation Movement of Iran," Ph.D. diss., Yale University, 1986, p. 355.

2. See Abdulaziz Sachedina, "'Ali Shariati: Ideologue of the Iranian Revolution," in *Voices of Resurgent Islam*, ed. John L. Esposito (New York: Oxford University Press, 1983).

3. Shahrough Akhavi, "Shariati's Social Thought," in *Religion and Politics in Iran*, ed. Nikki R. Keddie (New Haven: Yale University Press, 1983).

4. See Abbas Navabi, "Reform and Revolution in Shi'i Islam: The Thought of Ali Shariati," Ph.D. diss., Indiana University, 1988.

5. Navabi wrote in "Reform and Revolution," p. 188: "Shariati's own view of Shi'ism as revolutionary ideology shares some of Shi'i elitism and authoritarianism. But that only means that Shariati was confused and inconsistent. He was still in search of an 'orientation' and was not quite sure how to integrate the many ideas that influenced him." Yann Richard has written: "Shariati thus takes the traditional theory of ijtihad, mixing it with democratic principles, but makes no historical or theological analysis, so that it is hard to know his precise position. This lack of precision does not keep young Iranian intellectuals and others from rally-

ing to Shariati." See Richard's section, "Contemporary Shi'i Thought," in Nikki Keddie, *Roots of Revolution* (New Haven: Yale, 1981), p. 225.

6. That is Navabi's general conclusion. Fouad Ajami took a similar position in "The Impossible Life of Moslem Liberalism: The Doctrines of Ali Shariati and Their Defeat," *New Republic*, June 2, 1986.

7. This is the thrust of Akhavi's critique in "Shariati's Social Thought."

8. See Ajami, "The Impossible Life of Moslem Liberalism."

9. Mohammed Arkoun, *Pour une critique de la raison islamique* (Paris: Maisonneuve and Larose, 1984); in English, see his *Rethinking Islam*, trans. and ed. Robert D. Lee (Boulder: Westview, 1994.)

10. Ajami, "The Impossible Life of Moslem Liberalism," painted him as a failure; the Islamic Revolution overwhelmed his brand of liberal modernism.

11. Navabi, in "Reform and Revolution," supported this general argument, although his principal objective was to assess Shariati's thought on the spectrum of reform-revolution. He wrote (p. 184): "Shariati with all his genuine and justified opposition to cultural imperialism and cultural alienation considered himself, like Abduh and Iqbal before him, as an Islamic member of 'a world cultural community' rather than as a medieval representative in the modern world."

12. Chehabi said Shari'ati didn't have much personal contact with either Sartre, whom he met once in a café, or Fanon, with whom he corresponded for a "short time." He did attend lectures by the French sociologist Georges Gurvitch. For a careful discussion of Shariati's life and his influence on Iranian politics, see Chehabi, "Modernist Shi'ism and Politics," chap. 7.

13. Mehbi Abedi, "Ali Shariati: The Architect of the 1979 Islamic Revolution of Iran," *Iranian Studies* 19 (1986), p. 232.

14. Ibid.

15. Ali Shariati, *Art Awaiting the Saviour*, trans. Homa Fardjadi (Houston: Free Islamic Literatures, 1980), p. 6.

16. Ali Shari'ati, *What Is to Be Done*, ed. Farhang Rajaee (Houston: Institute for Research and Islamic Studies, 1986), p. 10.

17. Ibid., p. 29.

18. Ali Shari'ati, *Marxism and Other Western Fallacies: An Islamic Critique*, trans. R. Campbell (Berkeley: Mizan, 1980), p. 35.

19. Ali Shariati, *Histoire et destinée*, trans. F. Hamèd and N. Yavari-d'Hellencourt (Paris: Sindbad, 1982), p. 29.

20. Shari'ati, *What Is to Be Done*, p. 38.

21. Shariati, *Histoire*, p. 26.

22. Ali Shariati, *Man and Islam*, trans. Fatollah Marjani (Houston: Free Islamic Literature, 1981), p. 40.

23. Shari'ati, *What Is to Be Done*, p. 21.

24. See Roger M. Savory, "Orthodoxy and Aberrancy in the Ithnā 'Asharī Shī'ī Tradition," in *Islamic Studies Presented to C. J. Adams*, ed. Wael B. Hallaq (Leiden: Brill, 1991), pp. 169–181.

25. See Ali Shariati, *Red Shi'ism*, trans. Habib Shirazi (Houston: Free Islamic Literatures, 1980).

26. Shariati, *Histoire et destinée*, p. 36.

27. Ali Shariati, *Fatima Is Fatima*, trans. Laleh Bakhtiar (Tehran: Shariati Foundation, c. 1980), p. 65.

28. Shariati, *Histoire et destinée*, p. 36.

29. Shariati, *Red Shi'ism*, p. 8.

30. Ibid., p. 12.

31. Akhavi, "Shariati's Social Thought," p. 135.

32. Ibid., p. 131.

33. Shariati, *Histoire et destinée*, p. 28.

34. Shariati, *Art Awaiting the Saviour*, p. 13.

35. Ibid., p. 13.

36. Ali Shariati, *Culture and Ideology*, trans. Fatollah Marjani (Houston: Free Islamic Literatures, 1980), p. 6.

37. Ibid., p. 11.

38. Shari'ati, *Marxism*, p. 30.

39. Ibid., p. 101.

40. Sharati, *Man and Islam*, p. 106.

41. Shari'ati, *What Is to Be Done*, p. 15.

42. Ibid., p. 4.

43. Shariati, *Culture and Ideology*, p. 11.

44. Shari'ati, *What Is to Be Done*, p. 16.

45. Shari'ati, *Marxism*, p. 114.

46. See Steven R. Benson, "Islam and Social Change in the Writings of 'Alī Sharī'atī: His *Hajj* as a Mystical Handbook for Revolutionaries," *Muslim World* 81 (1991), pp. 9–26, for an excellent analysis of the mystical themes in Shariati's little book on the pilgrimage.

47. Steven Runciman has observed that Augustine, whose main thrust was to integrate Christianity with Greek philosophy, to universalize its teachings, saw pilgrimage as irrelevant to Christianity. See his *A History of the Crusades*, vol. 1 (Cambridge: Cambridge University Press, 1951), p. 40.

48. Ali Shariati, *Hajj*, trans. Ali A. Behzadnia and Najla Denny (Houston: Free Islamic Literatures, 1980), p. 7.

49. Ibid., p. 6.

50. Ibid., p. 10.

51. Ibid., p. 35.

52. Ibid., p. 150.

53. See the discussion of wisdom and love in Shariati, *Fatima Is Fatima*, p. 33.

54. Shariati, *Histoire et destinée*, chap. 20.

55. Ali Shariati, *One Followed by an Eternity of Zeroes*, trans. Ali Asghar Ghassemy (Houston: Free Islamic Literatures, 1980), p. 18.

56. Shari'ati, *Marxism*, p. 112.

57. Shariati, *Histoire et Destinée*, p. 100.

58. Shari'ati, *What Is to Be Done*, p. 55.

59. Ali Shariati, "Modern Man and His Prisons," in *Man and Islam*, p. 49.

60. See "What Is to Be Done: A Practical Plan for Husayniah Irshād," in Shari'ati, *What Is to Be Done*.

61. Shari'ati, *What Is to Be Done*, p. 27.

62. Ibid., p. 64.

63. Shariati, *Hajj,* p. 79.

64. Ibid., p. 79.

65. Ibid., pp. 79–80. In the translated edition, this sentence appears in all caps, with three exclamation points as final punctuation.

66. Shariati, *Hajj,* p. 125.

67. Shari'ati, *What Is to Be Done,* note 22, p. 69.

68. Ibid., p. 96.

69. Ibid., p. 16.

six

※

Mohammed
Arkoun

THE PSYCHOLOGICAL DISTANCE from Sayyid Qutb to Mohammed Arkoun is greater than the geographical span between Cairo, where Qutb lived and died, and Paris, where Arkoun taught for most of his academic career; greater than the contrast in physical circumstances represented by Qutb's cell in Nasir's prisons and Arkoun's university chair.[1] Historian, critic, and skeptic, Arkoun overwhelms his reader with sophisticated methodologies selected from the realms of contemporary semiotics, linguistics, anthropology, sociology, and philosophy. Qutb mentions few sources besides the Qur'an and the hadith; he seems enmeshed in the Islamic Reason that Arkoun rejects as part of a medieval mentality the Arabs must abandon if they are to come to terms with the present. In fact, Arkoun dismisses the "fundamentalist," "integralist," "authentic" movements within Islam as hopelessly ahistorical, idealistic, unscientific, exclusivist, and intolerant—as wedded to formulas and rhetoric that serve to mask ugly realities and exacerbate tensions in the Islamic world. It is unlikely that Qutb would have been any more sympathetic to Arkoun's brand of social science than Arkoun is to Qutb's formula for Islamic revolution.

Notwithstanding this apparent contrast, Arkoun is himself an exponent of Islamic authenticity, one step more radical than Iqbal, Shari'ati, and Qutb in a theoretical sense and, perhaps, two or three steps less radical than Qutb on a practical level. They all confront the same questions: How can Muslims act truthfully and effectively in an age when neither abstract reason nor mere faith seems sufficient as a guide? How can Muslims escape the frontal collision of tradition and modernity without losing their own sense of self-worth or their ability to compete in a world dominated by Western technology? Like the other writers considered in this study, Arkoun confronts the problem of authenticity, although he would prefer not to call it that.

For Arkoun, "authenticity" in the context of Arab-Islamic thought translates as 'aṣāla in Arabic, a word linked to the Islamic revival movement. The root, 'sl, is also the root of 'uṣūl, as in 'uṣūl al-fiqh or 'uṣūl al-dīn, meaning foundations of jurisprudence or foundations of religion;[2] a call to 'aṣāla suggests a return to the framework of orthodoxy bolstered by Islamic Reason, an apparent reinvocation of the transcendent ideas Arkoun takes to be a cause of alienation in the Arab world. Yet the 'aṣāla movement reflects social conditions of the period since World War II: the tensions between developed and underdeveloped worlds, rich and poor, literate and illiterate, bearers of traditional culture and those who paste together fragments of revolutionary ideology, Western culture, and the Arab-Islamic heritage.

> The discourse of 'aṣāla expresses indirectly all these gaps together with all the individual and collective anguish, the living sickness [mal de vivre] they bring. In effect, in place of brutally making dramatic diagnoses—which would have the effect of demobilizing energy in a crucial phase—it espouses the quiet, recognized way of exorcising an illness, the affirmation of self, as a way of rising above obvious difficulties. For that reason, the discourse of 'aṣāla is structurally better adapted than other [forms of discourse] to the sociocultural framework of understanding and historic action in the contemporary Maghrib.[3]

In short, the call to authenticity reflects contemporary realities (though "indirectly"), but it is escapist in its invocation of orthodoxy as a route to rediscovering the self. Such is Arkoun's view.

For Arkoun, the 'aṣāla movement asserts an exclusive claim to the truth without confronting the problem of truth itself and the historical conditions under which Islamic truth emerged. The movement's claim is "sociologically true, epistemologically unacceptable."[4] He dissociates himself from the term "'aṣāla," or authenticity, for that reason. Arkoun, however, wrestles with the same problem of finding a standard of truthfulness from which the Islamic world can take its bearings in a world of chaotic change, the problem of locating firm ground which Muslims take to be genuinely theirs and which simultaneously serves them as a link with the world around them. Arkoun describes himself as driven "(1) to understand the Arab-Muslim personality claimed by the nationalist movement, and (2) to determine the extent to which the modern civilization represented by the colonial power should be considered a universal civilization."[5] Finding both these standards based in myth, he searches for a kind of truthfulness to which he can commit himself.

Arkoun aspires to authenticity defined as the "sentiment of being,"[6] as a way of "being in the world" in a truthful manner,[7] as the capacity to work, think, and feel from "inner necessity," from "deep personal choice," and with "joy,"[8] as the opposite of externally defined virtue, as creativity and willfulness as opposed to roteness, everydayness, and repetition. Writing about development in the Maghrib, Arkoun asked:

> How can one cure this painful feeling that a large part of what is written or said about the personality of the Maghrib never penetrates the real country [*reste extérieur au pays réel*] and is inadequate or straight out false in the light of the various sorts of testimony groups would provide about themselves if a confining ideology did not limit their creativity, their routes toward intellectual and cultural achievement?[9]

Truth must thus be concrete, lived, felt, particular. Ideologies, deduced from abstract universals, whether those of the Qur'an or those of Plato, cannot reflect such truth and in fact prevent its emergence. They alienate.

> Why does one encounter in so many citizens of the Maghrib that irrepressible nostalgia for possibilities that are deeply felt but always put off, pushed back and put down: the possibility of a consciousness coinciding with the immediate circumstances of a territory, an environment, a history, a social order, a language.[10]

The radical hope of overcoming alienation lies deep within human nature, obscured by false consciousness. To be at home in the world, to be at one with others and with one's surroundings, one must presumably resist those who "put off, push back and put down . . . the possibility of a national culture liberated from conventional abstract models (music, poetry, decorative arts, architecture) from the imitation of genres and imported works, from the ideas and tastes of an Arabized or Westernized intelligentsia."[11] This thought could be lifted from nineteenth-century German historicist writing; genuine culture springs from within; if culture shapes consciousness, how can consciousness be genuine, if culture is not? Or conversely, how can culture be genuine if consciousness is not? It is not clear which must come first. Arkoun went on to discuss

> the possibility of an integrated sociocultural life, capable of attenuating the sort of internal and external exile that inspires so much literature and popular music and of avoiding the brutal substitution of Saharan and peasant values with those of the industrial world, and of overcoming the long-standing opposition between enlightened, managing elites and the masses attracted by "counter-revolution.[12]

The emergence of a new consciousness promises fraternity, and in unity lies the potential for human control over the seemingly inexorable march of modernity. The route to a reassertion of human autonomy depends on a comprehension and transformation of human consciousness in the context of the world to be managed. This transformation makes possible a mode of thought "finally free to attack, working from the Maghribi example, all the problems we have enumerated à propos of Islam, the Qur'an, the Prophet, and so on."[13]

The underlying assumption is that modern thought, freed of dependence on universals, can diminish alienation by synchronizing consciousness with social reality.

The themes of authentic thought are all there: insistence that truth must emerge from the particular; radical dissatisfaction with conventional wisdom, both traditional and modern; assertion of the need to liberate human volition from the constraints of ideology and the passivity bred of disuse; and an assertion about the oneness of existence, the condition for the overcoming of divergences between internal and external realities.

Arkoun's position on ethnic, geographical, and methodological frontiers gives his work special interest. His Berber origins make him sensitive to the oppressive potential of Arab-Islamic orthodoxy. He was born in 1928 at Taourirt-Mimoun in the Kabylia region of Algeria; Berber is his mother tongue, French his second language, and Arabic his third. As a student of Islam who grew up in French schools and made his way to the top of the French university system, he relishes his position on the line dividing the Orient from Orientalism and identifies with both and with neither. He empathizes with the complaint of the East about Western scholarship but reproaches both Orient and Orientalism for the same sins: attachment to universals, identification of truth with essences, and neglect of history.[14] A Muslim historian, he pleads for the help of non-Muslims and nonhistorians in reassessing the relationship of Islamic thought to text, to language, to groups, to power, to time, and to place, in order to discover those "positivities" that could underpin an "objective" understanding of the "totality" of the Islamic tradition.

Arkoun's search for authenticity can be understood as a search for foundations in the reconstructed collective memory of the community. It is a search to be carried on in languages equipped with the requisite social-scientific terminology and concepts—hence, not Arabic, the language of the Qur'an, much less Berber. It must be conducted in an atmosphere of intellectual freedom, beyond the reach of governments whose authority depends in part upon the defense of Islamic orthodoxy.[15] "The emotion-charged atmosphere prevailing in modern Muslim societies rules out the possibility of scientific study of a large number of sensitive problems."[16] Not surprisingly, Arkoun's methodology directly reflects the influence of Westerners such as Max Weber, Emile Durkheim, and Jacques Derrida, and indirectly, the work of Nietzsche and Heidegger.[17] Arkoun roams the frontiers of social scientific thought in a quest for inner passage between East and West, modernity and tradition.

Arkoun's peregrinations are both physical and intellectual. Since retirement from the Sorbonne in the early 1990s, he has taught in Amsterdam and London, and he continues to carry his message to all the continents, without, perhaps, being convinced of its full acceptance anywhere. In the West, he still thinks of himself as an opponent of lingering Orientalist tendencies, and in the Middle East, he finds himself uncomfortable (or unwelcome) in countries where official versions of Islam or strong fundamentalist movements prevent discussion of the issues he raises. His early work was all in French, much of it in scholarly journals and relatively inaccessible by virtue of both location and style. Some of his books are now available in Arabic; one is in English, and one in Italian.[18] All reflect his dedication to scientific endeavor, to scholarship, to empirical investigation. At the same time, he writes and speaks with the conviction of someone who is campaigning for what he sees as right and true: a conception of Islam large enough to accommodate all those who see themselves as Muslims, an idea of the Mediterranean region that brings together all the societies of the Book, and a liberalism that forecloses exclusive claims to truth without sacrificing the possibility or the necessity of truthfulness. He ventures to the very edge of postmodernism but then pulls back to the modernist camp in his embrace of truth.

Particularity

Arkoun distinguishes himself from writers such as Qutb or Iqbal by his concern for methodology. Iqbal revived old literary forms to assert the preeminence of human will over orthodoxy and reason, attempting, like Nietzsche and Pascal,[19] to avoid a scholastic critique of scholasticism. Qutb tried to cloak his radical interpretations of the Qur'an in the garb of orthodoxy,[20] claiming in effect that transhistoric revelation authorizes the historicization of itself. For Arkoun, the epistemological question precedes all others: *"How must one proceed to know what is in ancient and contemporary societies?"* [italics in original][21] He would ask Iqbal and Qutb how one can verify the primacy of revelation or of the autonomous individual. The answer, of course, is that one cannot verify those assumptions by the rules of science.

Phenomena constitute Arkoun's point of departure. "The absolute is not thought anywhere except in a phenomenal world, in contact with positivities such as matter, life, work, language, power, possessions, value."[22] The statement, a truism, does not foreclose the possibility of absolutes, nor does it deny the power of abstract ideas over human behavior. It merely rejects the possibility that universals can be brought to mind somewhere outside of human experience.

If, then, Muslims seek the truth about themselves, they must reexamine not simply the "truths" of revelation but all the particular ways in which those "truths" have been felt, understood, elaborated, justified, fashioned into orthodoxy, and experienced in context, over time and within geographical space. They must comprehend, among other things, the modern revivalist use of Islam *"as a refuge, a den, a springboard for all kinds of opposition, social protest, psychological reactions, cultural expressions"* [italics in original].[23] Such an enterprise would require the methods of modern anthropology, psychology, sociology, semiotics, linguistics, economics, philosophy, and perhaps other disciplines.

Arkoun calls for interdisciplinary investigation of the process by which revelation became orthodoxy in Islam. The Qur'an is (1) a set of revelations reported orally by Muhammad to his followers, (2) a diverging set of recitations in the newly emergent Arab Empire, (3) a written text developed in an effort to reduce diversity and solidify Arab rule, (4) a foundation for a corpus of codified law designed to unify the judicial practice of a multiethnic, multilingual empire, and (5) a reflection of universal truth as revealed to the Arabs.[24] For Arkoun, understanding Islam means comprehending how and why the fourth and fifth conceptions of the Qur'an ultimately predominated, whereas alternative understandings disappeared from the collective consciousness of Muslims. He asks why certain ideas gained currency and earned inclusion in orthodoxy, whereas others, earnestly advanced and defended, lost legitimacy. One hypothesis, derived from observation of the contemporary scene, is this: The state always seeks to reduce Islam to a single set of symbols.[25]

Following the logic of Nietzsche and Weber, Arkoun sees the first centuries of Islam as similar to those of every charismatic religion in its efforts to transcendentalize events, actors, and scriptures. Muhammad the Leader became Muhammad the Prophet-Model-for-all-men. Judicial practice based on pragmatic efforts to combine Qur'anic precepts with local custom gradually lost ground to the discipline of *fiqh*. The companions of the Prophet, themselves innovators by necessity, became exponents of orthodoxy through the corpus of hadith, which was sorted, selected, and elevated in status, supplementing the Qur'an as a source of the *shari'a*. And from the Qur'an reciters and the students of the hadith, divided on many critical matters (such as the status of a Muslim who had committed grave sins),[26] emerged the Sunni ulema to claim discovery of a fixed and unchanging law from which honest dissent was not possible. Arkoun emphasizes Shafi'i's role in sacralizing the sunna and empowering the ulema to maintain the transcendental nature of the law in the name of science.[27]

These changes occurred under identifiable historical, sociological conditions. Every dispute reflected a struggle for power.[28] The codification of the *shari'a* helped legitimize the role of both political leaders and the ulema. The transformation of positive law into divine law broadened the authority of the ulema and, inevitably, benefited some groups while penalizing and excluding others. Saints, mystics, and marabouts gradually extended the domain of the sacred to almost every aspect of life,[29] solidifying the power of the country against the city. Even Abu Hamid Muhammad al-Ghazali's (1059–1111) effort to reconcile the rationalism of the Mu'tazila with the mysticism of the Sufis *"speaks to the human conscience from a given sociocultural situation"* [italics in original],[30] Arkoun reminds us. Yet this historicity of the *shari'a* and of Sunnism more generally is, for him, an "unthought of Islamic thought."[31] The particularistic diversity of Islamic thought has faded in the collective memory by dint of the temporal success of all-too-human advocates of transcendental doctrine.

This observation leads Arkoun to a position of ambivalence toward the Mu'tazila and the *falāsifa,* the rationalist tendencies within the Islamic tradition. As one who pleads for the use of reason in understanding the Islamic past, he necessarily admires those tendencies and regrets their marginality. At the same time, a convinced historicist, he argues that Greek rationalism, by its emphasis on original substance and unchanging essence, reinforced the logocentrism of the Islamic tradition.[32] Reason and revelation together produced a medieval mentality that prevailed in the Islamic world through the nineteenth century, long after an analogous mindset had, he says, undergone erosion in Christian Europe.

Islamic logocentrism resulted from the imposition of philosophy on religion. The Greek concept of reason (which Arkoun terms "dogmatic") as leading mankind toward Being and pointing toward the True, the Good, and the Beautiful helped define the attributes of God. The logical search for first cause led to proofs of his existence and logical, schematic accounts of the creation. From the nature of reason, the attributes of God, and consequent deduction from revelation came the essential axioms for the codification of Islamic law: The Prophet cannot lie, the community cannot agree on error, the companions were reliable authorities on the life of the prophet, and so on. Once extracted and developed, these definitions and codes supported the Qur'anic claims of universality and diminished the status of ethnicity.[33] The search for meaning became identified with the application of logic to text; done right, it is done forever. Only the result need be repeated. Repetition becomes equated with truth.

According to Arkoun, logocentric discourse masks reality and represses the deeper, creative impulses of human beings. "In place of searching for reconciliation with that which is unavoidable in the human condition, it seeks to compensate for the weaknesses of this condition with the promise of future Happiness."[34] The "unavoidable" would seem to include differences of perception and language, diversity of economic, social, and political condition, conflict among groups of Muslims, and all the particular problems of living and dying. In the logocentric vision, those problems appear irrelevant or resolved once and for all; for example, Muslims cannot fight other Muslims, even though they do. The "truth" as it is felt and lived in all its particularity disappears behind the universal as a result of the sacralization of scripture and the transcendentalization of the formative period of Islam. Nietzsche made a similar point about Paul's role in the development of Christianity:

> The life, the example, the teaching, the death, the meaning and the right of the entire Gospel—nothing was left once this hate-obsessed false-coiner had grasped what alone he could make use of. Not the reality, not the historical truth! . . . The Church subsequently falsified even the history of mankind into the pre-history of Christianity.[35]

Far from permitting himself such intemperate language, Arkoun cloaks his assault in social-scientific jargon but, like Nietzsche, he aims to critique rationalism in the name of history. He does it by emphasizing the intent of Islamic thinkers rather than their impact. For example, the arguments of the Mu'tazila that both God and the Qur'an could not be outside of time, that is, "uncreated," if there were only one God constituted a step toward the historical understanding of Islam. It also provided an opening wedge for the use of reason in the elaboration of ethical judgments; this opening was pursued by the philosophers,[36] who sought to engage in "independent, rigorous and critical reflection," even though their work ultimately served, like that of the Mu'tazila, to reinforce an orthodox view. Similarly, Ibn Khaldun can be admired for his attempt at a sociology of belief and power, even though he did not manage to apply his critical methods to the emergence of Islam itself. As a consequence, his dynamic model reflects the substantialist immobility of medieval Islam.

Arkoun argues that Muslims escaped the constraints of logocentrism only in love and death, which were the special preserve of mystics, prophets, and some poets, as opposed to the domain of the theologians, philosophers, jurists, moralists, and great literary figures.

> It is there [in some interior space] that there occurs the ultimate struggle between an interior discourse, coincident in fleeting fashion with the feeling of a different and original truth, and an exterior, conventional discourse, which, in order to assure communication, is obliged to depend upon repetition. . . . It is in the light of that distinction that one can understand the meaning and significance of all the conflicts that have marked religious and philosophic thought.[37]

Like others searching for authenticity, Arkoun identifies with the "different" and "original" truth against the conventional, with the interior against the exterior, with that which is felt against that which is thought,

with ethnic and sectarian minorities against orthodoxy, with the particular against the universal. Particularity constitutes for him the richness of
Islamic culture and the proper focus of the modern historian, who must
study the production of universalizing myths and values and the subsequent interplay of myth and reality, universal and particular.

Radicalism

From this notion of Islam as a vast concatenation of particular impulses
and feelings, Arkoun derives his radical opposition to all forms of conventional ideology: democratic, nationalist, socialist, or fundamentalist.
Each selects abstract postulates from the tradition and erects upon them
an exclusivist claim to legitimacy. Arkoun denies all such exclusivist
claims for their ahistoricism, their neglect of felt realities past and present,
and their willingness to propagate false consciousness. "It is a question of
subverting all types of traditional discourse about the truth," he has written.[38] Like Nietzsche, Arkoun means to attack assertions about essence
and substance, whether those assertions are in the theological or philosophical mode. He seeks to undercut what he calls Islamic Reason,[39] the
foundation of the Islamic tradition, as a condition for the reconstruction
of an authentic (my term) way of being Muslim in the twentieth century.

Although Arkoun sees his own task as intellectual rather than political,
his work represents a commitment to, even if not a call for, revolution.
"The struggle for the emancipation of human beings from the kinds of
servitudes they fashion for themselves is inseparably intellectual and political."[40] Regimes depend on ideologies, ideologies utilize and cultivate
myths that bind and constrain, and these myths depend on the traditional
conception of truth for their plausibility. Arkoun's assault on Islamic Reason and on the false consciousness it perpetuates is necessarily an attack
upon the regimes, including all existing Arab governments, whose ideologies exploit this consciousness in any fashion whatsoever. It is a plea
to hear those muted voices and overlooked experiences that are casualties
of the official and scholarly preference for orthodoxy. "Only those scholars who harmonize their thought with their concrete engagement and
their engagement with their thought are engaged in the continuous fight
to create new spaces of freedom, to give new intellectual articulations to
the silent voices."[41]

Consciousness is false, for Arkoun, when it does not reflect critical reason and sociological reality. The notion of a transhistoric *shari'a*, essential
to the position and appeal of the establishment ulema as well as to groups
such as the Muslim Brotherhood, cannot be sustained against evidence of
painstaking efforts of the jurists to transcendentalize scripture, sayings,
and practice. Similarly, the effort to portray Islam either as opposed, in

essence, to secular authority or as supportive by nature of any and all governments ignores parts of the historical record, since Islam has at various times and places been both. The transformation of the "Medina experience" into the "Medina model" of Islamic government further obfuscates the truth. Finally, any vision of Islam as abstract, rational, monotheistic, and universalistic—the Islam dear to reformers of the *salafī* movement—neglects the enormous diversity in the way Islam has been lived over the centuries. It denies the sociological reality of popular Islam.

Arkoun's radicalism carries him a step beyond Iqbal, Shari'ati, and Qutb. Neither Shari'ati nor Qutb was less hesitant than Arkoun to attack existing regimes, but for them the standard for judgment could be found in the *shari'a*, viewed as a set of transhistoric principles ready for implementation according to the needs of time and place. Authentic Muslims not only believe in those principles but, like the founding generation of Muslims, interpret them and act upon them in accordance with historical circumstances. This is the sociological condition for truth. But unlike Arkoun, Shari'ati and Qutb do not expose the principles themselves to the critique of modern historical research. Qutb, for example, does not ask how and to what extent the principles he enunciates in *Social Justice in Islam* reflect the worldly conditions of the scholars who elaborated them; he accepts the existence of abstract, universal ideas, even if human beings can never fully understand or implement them. Arkoun rejects that position as indistinguishable from the apologetics of the ulema. "The true truth is thus in a structural situation of tension, of conflict, of mutual exclusion with the official truth," he has written.[42]

This demand for the "true truth," valid by both epistemological and sociological standards, secures Arkoun's position among those in search of authenticity. At moments, Arkoun speaks of the need to know the "objective" content of the Qur'an to utilize the "positivities" of all modern social scientific findings.

> We must undo the intolerable amalgamations, the abusive simplifications, the emotional formulations, the arbitrary demands, the neurotic obsessions that feed false consciousness, which is utilized nonetheless to raise the consciousness of the masses for the realization of an historic mission; we must at the same time reinsert in the area thus liberated the positive findings of a critical reexamination of the whole Islamic tradition in the light of the most recent conquests of scientific understanding.[43]

Science has usually meant externality and abstraction, and modern social science has dedicated itself to rendering external—hence, comprehensible at a different time and place—that which is initially internal and time-bound. Arkoun calls upon social science to understand *l'imaginaire*—that sedimentation of consciousness and conviction that governs so much be-

havior in any society—and to achieve "if possible . . . a direct and totalizing reading of the real."[44] But how can Arkoun believe it is possible? Why
is not science itself, built as it is on transhistoric procedures and axioms,
equally vulnerable to critical examination of the historicist sort? Where
does one seek verification of this truth as the subverter of all others? In
the face of such questions, Arkoun backs off from the dichotomy of true
and false: "One can only speak of a continuous epistemological critique to
reduce to a minimum the error factor of the consciousness. In this sense,
one can say that false consciousness is . . . [the form of consciousness
that] is not concerned with turning criticism back upon itself."[45]

He resorts to a disclaimer: There is no such thing as innocent discourse
or innocent method, which is to say that he, too, works from a particular
perspective in history. Yet there reverberates through Arkoun's work an
underlying faith in the truth-producing capacities—if not at this stage,
then at the next—of modern social science.[46] His revolutionary fervor
stems from a faith that the pursuit of knowledge will liberate human beings from the strictures imposed by the coincidence of state, party, religion, and national culture—a coincidence he calls "heavy with threat for
the quality of the civilization that Muslims wish to found."[47] He would
free human beings from the realm of myth generated by the purposeful
propagation of exclusivist, arbitrary visions of the past by exposing them
to "true truth" and "true reality."

Arkoun suggests that the contemporary revival movement seeks to replace one sort of alienation with another.[48] It combats the inroads of Western idealism with a reassertion of Islamic essentialism; it fosters a widen-
ing of the gap between the realm of mythical reality (*le réel imaginaire*) and
the pluralistic, particularistic realm of popular belief, which is a part of
the realm of lived reality (*réel vrai*).[49] For Arkoun, the scientific study of Islamic history would eliminate alienation by validating all dimensions of
collective memory and undercutting the capacity of any one dimension to
advance itself as the proprietor of truth. As the totality of the Islamic experience—thought and unthought, external and internal, learned and
popular—the truth frees Muslims to be themselves.

It is also possible that science, by according legitimacy to a vast range
of behavior and identifying truth with the understanding of that totality,
effectively isolates every individual, save the scholar, from truthful behavior. If there exists no truth divorced from the social circumstances in
which it is formulated, what is the significance of liberating the human
will? One is "free" to will anything one's circumstances permit (perhaps
one should say "compelled" not to will anything but that which is sociologically true) or one is "free" to will the scientific truth either by an act of
faith (false consciousness?) or because one is "compelled" by reason.
Where, then, lies the domain for autonomous human action that under-

lies Arkoun's radical attack on the strictures of Islamic Reason and the regimes that exploit those strictures?

Autonomy

As a radical, Arkoun believes in the capacity of human beings to reshape their world. As a historicist, he takes all truth to be a product of human mediation. As a philosopher-historian, he understands history as a product not simply of material circumstances but of the ways in which human beings have understood those circumstances and sought to manipulate them. He believes intellectuals have a duty to be committed because they have the capacity to make a difference. But as a critic of substantialism in both its Greek and Islamic versions, he rejects the notion of the autonomous individual, endowed by nature with reason and free will, and as a social scientist, he regards human beings as less free than they would like to think they are.[50] He is, in short, ambivalent about the ability of human beings to shape their own destiny.

Arkoun's understanding of the role of intellectuals in history accounts for at least some of this ambivalence. Like others, he is critical of the traditional Orientalist enterprise of squeezing from the great texts the essence of Islamic civilization—not so much because the Orientalists overestimated the impact of ideas and neglected the material factors but because they did not emphasize the human origins of the ideas, the development of the doctrines, the gradual transcendentalization of certain notions, and the delegitimization of others. Concrete human beings mediate truth. Thus, to understand Islamic truth one must understand the actions of its mediators from the Prophet through the companions to the Qur'an reciters, the ulema, the Mu'tazila, the philosophers, the great Sufis, and the rest. It was the mediators, the intellectuals, who generated orthodoxy, and it was they who, both intentionally and unintentionally, closed off the escape from a "medieval mentality."

They did not, of course, spin out ideas in disinterested fashion. Arkoun notes the degree to which ideas emerged to cover dynastic solidification, the bid for influence of the ulema, the popular effort to undercut religious authority, and the effort to lift Islam from its position as creed of the Arabs to that of universal religion. Ideas reflect circumstances imperfectly; as a result, the "collective conscience" to which they give rise may diverge significantly from both the original and subsequent historical circumstances. This is the origin of false consciousness, seen as affecting the behavior of the masses more than that of the elites, whose critical reason can and should carry them beyond. The vital question, for Arkoun, is why the efforts of the Mu'tazila, the philosophers, and Ibn Khaldun to rethink the truth in the light of experience withered for lack of pursuit. He accepts the judgment of Gustave von Grunebaum[51] and others about the stagnation of medieval Islamic thinking, but he wants to explore avenues of escape, by searching for reasons. That is what he means by "applied Islamology"[52]— an Orientalism that is both scientific and practical, rather than an Orientalism in which "one is more and more content to note the differences in mentalities and the uselessness of any effort to reduce them."[53]

For Arkoun, the Mu'tazila took a first step toward historicism. By bringing the Qur'an into the created realm, they opened the way to understanding the hadith as the imperfect efforts of human beings, starting with the Prophet, to elaborate and interpret God's will as expressed in the Qur'an—efforts necessarily subject to the critique of human reason. They challenged the efforts of the ulema to solidify their own power at the expense of the caliphs by posing as the guardians of a fixed, eternal *shari'a*, unamenable to amendment through human reason, and they opened the way toward innovation, which, by the emerging standards of mainstream theologians, constituted blasphemy.

Arkoun applauds this radical, historicizing thrust of the Mu'tazili but notices both sides of the sword. He has written: "Reason must intervene independently of revelation, as is established by the existence of aesthetic judgments outside the Islamic framework. In this case, reason is based upon natural, necessary—and therefore universal—knowledge: that is how the Mu'tazilite method . . . relates to that of the philosophers."[54]

By imbibing Greek essentialism, they located the foundations of reason beyond history, even as they were attempting to bring the understanding of revelation more thoroughly within it. They sacralized and desacralized at the same time, a fact that made it possible for someone like Abul Hasan al-Ash'ari (d. 935) to strengthen orthodoxy by incorporating aspects of the reasoning developed by the Mu'tazila, while rejecting most of their doctrine. The Mu'tazili effort ultimately contributed to the reinforcement of the "medieval mentality," antithetical to human autonomy and to a complete understanding of the Islamic tradition.

Like Gramsci (and like Said, who cites Gramsci), Arkoun sees human action mainly as a product of a hegemonic collective consciousness,[55] whose roots lie both in unreflected adherence to immemorial ways and in essentialist, rationalist dogmas that serve to legitimate those mores. For most individuals, and even for most intellectuals, the collective consciousness (*l'imaginaire*) guides action, but he calls upon the few capable of critical reason to undertake the Mu'tazili enterprise of separating the power structure of the Islamic world from "all the theology of serf-will [*serf-arbitre* as opposed to *libre-arbitre* (free will)] developed during the centuries in the societies of the Book."[56] The question modern intellectuals must ask is this: "*Under what verifiable conditions does the idea of truth acquire such strength as to command the destiny of an individual or produce a collective his-*

tory?" [italics in original][57] By inquiring about the origins of truth and understanding the mechanisms by which it is propagated, they escape the clutches of both the Islamic tradition and Cartesian visions of modernity. By asking why one version of truth prevailed over another and why certain avenues of thought were traveled while others were not, the intellectuals reconstruct the Islamic past as a series of human actions and inactions in which further episodes are possible but not necessary.[58] It is the intellectuals who rescue human autonomy from essentialism and determinism via an understanding of the totality of the Islamic experience.

Unicity

One is tempted to say that Arkoun thinks the intellectual can step outside the stream of Islamic history and then, enriched by a complete picture of its meanderings, walk purposefully back into it without fear of being carried away. Yet Arkoun would reject that analogy for its similarity to Plato's Allegory of the Cave and the suggestion that the shadowy multiplicity of life is mere illusion, to be stripped away if essential truth is to be understood. For Arkoun, the very idea of escaping shadows and illusions is itself illusory. In fact, every trip outside the cave constitutes a historical event, identifiable in space and time, and every intellectual who reenters to preach the truth contributes to division and even anarchy. There is no innocent discourse. There is no stepping outside history. But is there then no escape from anarchy? Does Islam explode under the pressure of historicist criticism into a thousand fragments, all deprived of truth value? Arkoun's commitment to particularity and autonomy leads him (and other authentics) to the brink of nihilism, from which he must fashion a retreat if he is to seek solutions to the problem of false consciousness as he promised in undertaking practical Islamology. His commitment drives him toward the search for meaning within history.

Arkoun seeks to demonstrate the oneness of the Islamic experience. His critique of the manipulation of Islam for both conservative and radical purposes depends on an empirical confirmation that the Islamic reality is plural and on a historical account of the development of plurality out of a single tradition. The Islam of the Muslim Brotherhood and the Islam of revolutionary Islam are false not only because they are not what they pretend to be, that is, representatives of the only true Islam, but because they underrate the degree to which the Islamic tradition is one in all its diversity. Liberation comes from the reconstruction of wholeness. The problem, he has said, is to "put back together [*remembrer*] a domain of meaning that has broken up [*éclaté*]."[59] This invitation to reassemble the tradition is the key image of his unitarian impulse.

What is one to put back together? Arkoun speaks of the "Qur'anic fact" as the basis of, as something quite intellectually separate from, the "Islamic fact" to which it gives rise. For him, there exist certain axiological values articulated in the Qur'an that constitute the bedrock of Islamic discourse. The Qur'an distinguishes positive from negative values by sets of criteria. By the names it assigns to God, by its discussion of the need for witness, by its assertion of the concepts of community and law, it establishes a framework for thought and action.[60] Islamic history can be understood as the projection through time of this axiology.

Arkoun sets down ten propositions that help define such a projection. They deserve comment.[61]

1. The Qur'an is a set of meanings that give rise to many doctrines. In place of essentialist commonalities shared by all human beings, who are divided by experience, Arkoun suggests an experiential unity of all Muslims stemming from the "Qur'anic fact."

2. The Qur'an includes both transhistoric messages and practical, ideological advice. "Messages" necessarily suggests problems of transmission, decoding, and interpretation. The unity of the "Islamic fact," then, lies not in the truth-bearing content of the Qur'an but in the factual unity of all the messages and advice it has generated.

3. The interpretation of the Qur'an cannot be "closed." Arkoun refers to the efforts of the jurists to codify the *shari'a*, elevating selections of hadith to the level of Qur'anic revelation and declaring the season for interpretation "closed." Unlike reformists who tried to demonstrate the irrationality of closure in the light of the transhistoric rationality of the Qur'an, Arkoun's use of the word "cannot" represents an assertion that it is impossible to circumscribe factual multiplicity with essentialist rules. The perceived need to "close" itself demonstrates the openness and plurality of the tradition.

4. The Qur'an cannot be reduced to ideology. Ideology links ideas with action. But Arkoun has already said that Islam has been understood as sets of abstract ideas and sets of recipes for practical action or inaction. Puritanical, revolutionary Islam has periodically insisted upon tight linkage between principles and action in its assaults on both the abstract Islam of the Sunni establishment and the political passivism of Sufism and popular Islam. Reduction to ideology would constitute closure.

5. The totality of interpretations constitute the whole tradition. This seems to be a tautology if "tradition" is understood as a stream of history generated with reference to the Qur'anic fact rather than

as some fixed set of ideas or practices located in a single period and place. Yet there may be more: the assertion that a totality of particulars does in fact constitute something unitary and therefore whole. Wholeness connotes health, solidarity, community, lack of alienation, autonomy, authenticity.

6. The whole tradition deserves anthropological investigation. The focus must be on the human elaboration of the tradition—the material culture, the myths, the texts, the doctrines—in the totality of its manifestations, which constitute its wholeness. Why? Not just because the "Islamic fact" is there to be studied but because the salvation of the Islamic world depends upon a correct understanding of the tradition as a whole. The search for authenticity drives investigation.

7. Each part of the tradition has functioned as an exclusive system.

8. After reconstruction of the whole tradition, each particular tradition must get rid of its exclusivity, its intolerance. Here is the normative political message. Each group, confronted with knowledge of the whole historical tradition and understood with the tools of modern social science, must overcome its false consciousness as privileged purveyor of truth.

9. There is currently no privileged way to determine what is true Islam. This seems contradictory, for Arkoun has just proposed a proper way to understand Islam. He seems to mean that no essentialist argument, built upon unprovable assumptions about ultimate reality, can prevail over others, although social science, denying itself such assumptions, may eventually succeed in supplying a satisfactory alternative—perhaps not "true," and hence not exclusivist, but truthful in its portrayal of the human situation, hence authentic.

10. Disputes must get first attention; the corpus of selected, "authentic" hadith must be reexamined to understand temporal reasons for selection and deselection. Arkoun acknowledges that the process of reexamining the Islamic tradition may be a long one, even if many scholars—Arabs and non-Arabs, Muslims and non-Muslims—participate in the task. For one thing, Arkoun wants a survey of not just what has been thought but of that which has remained unthought, by which he means that which is unthinkable (e.g., atheism); that which is beyond the limits of scientific thought, hence not yet thought; that which is masked or hidden; that which is rejected in the course of scientific development; and that which is simply forgotten.[62] Burdened with this enormous task, applied Islamology must begin at points where need is most acute. Scholarship must be imaginative and committed to the re-

duction of conflict through scientific elaboration of a unitary "Islamic fact." That is his project.

Does the project lie within or outside the Islamic fact? If it lies within, then how can it qualify to provide a privileged truth? If the truth is not privileged, how can it be used as a weapon against false consciousness? If it is privileged, must not its claim precede and exclude all others? Must it not be intolerant of intolerance? If the project lies outside the experience it describes, then it seems not to differ substantially from European Orientalism. Enhanced, perhaps, in its ability to produce privileged truth by virtue of distance, it is also diminished in its capacity to transform by persuading those within the tradition to adopt a perspective of understanding.[63]

In recent work, Arkoun suggests ever more insistently that a satisfactory understanding of Islam must go beyond the "Qur'anic fact" to reflect upon the religious impulses that gave rise to all three "societies of the Book."

> And because the Bible had already introduced these same figures [found in the Qur'an] with the same dialectical opposites and the same intention of ontological fixation, we can say that human unity is rooted in a religious imagination that goes beyond the strict [Qur'anic] formulation. Thus we are referred to a more radical unity—that of the myths and symbols that have nourished and produced the entire history of man in the realm of what can be called societies of the Book, that is those subject to the phenomenon of Revelation, handed down in the Holy Scriptures.[64]

He laments the historical movement of Islam, through the development of legalism and orthodoxy, away from this sense of unity. Even the introduction of philosophy pushed in quite a different direction, toward an "imagined unity," which ultimately served to further separate revelation from history. Only the mystics, and especially Ibn 'Arabi, preserved a feeling for "man as religious subject," drawn toward the immersion of self in God.[65] It is not surprising that the modern revival movement has used mysticism to rally its troops. But Arkoun finds this an inadequate shortcut through the forest of divisive traditions of the Islamic world. Unity comes not from mysticism but from a critical, anthropological understanding of mysticism as well as all other manifestations of religion in the societies of the Book.

Arkoun's project seems to lie both inside and outside the Islamic experience: It seeks to reconcile within and without, understanding and explanation, particularity and unity, sociological and epistemological truth. The starting point must be from within—from the side of understanding, particularity, and sociological truth: Islam as it is felt and practiced. But reflexive thought necessarily seeks explanation of such a particularistic understanding and its sociological validity; it moves beyond its own limits to see itself as one aspect of the particularistic chaos of Islamic life and to see Islam as one example of a scripture-dominated society, one of the societies of the Book. Then, fortified with a persuasive account of its place in the world, the project eliminates the exclusivist claims of its initial, internal belief structure. Internal truth, thus reformed, coincides with external reality. Epistemology reinforces sociology as grounds for legitimacy, and explanation coincides with understanding, theory with practice, thought with action. The drive for authenticity, seemingly particularistic in its thrust to discover the true Arab-Muslim personality, ends up pulling Muslims toward a unified perspective without universals.[66] Such is the difficult path Arkoun tries to walk.

The commonalities between Arkoun's ideas and those of a committed revivalist such as Sayyid Qutb stem from their common dedication to the problem of authenticity. Confronting the inadequacy of either faith or abstract reason as a basis for action, they ask how Muslims can reshape their world without abandoning either reason or faith. The reformists (*salafī*) such as Muhammad 'Abdu tried to bring together reason and faith, but Qutb and Arkoun both impose a further requirement: the reconciliation of reason and faith with sociological realities. They work within the same field, though from different premises with different methodologies and different approaches to concrete political problems.

Modernization

The call for authenticity arises from a rejection of both tradition, as the legitimation of customary behavior, and modernity, understood as belief in a rational, secular truth producing economic and social progress. Arkoun's position fits that conception of authenticity. Yet, unlike Qutb, Arkoun identifies with the modernist, Westernizing camp by arguing that modernism has been misunderstood. In the Islamic world, Mustafa Kemal, who applied Enlightenment ideas in Turkey, has been identified with modernism. But he did not understand, any more than had the Enlightenment itself, "the real game of social forces at work"[67] behind the ideas, the relationship between ideas and context. For Arkoun, modernism itself (or perhaps one should call it postmodernism for the sake of clarity) has come to reject the essentialist understanding, characteristic of both the theological perspective and Enlightenment philosophy.

For Arkoun, the most advanced, progressive elements in the West no longer espouse any version of essentialism, whether it be Cartesian rationalism, liberal secularism, or Marxist determinism; as a consequence, the zealots need not "exhaust themselves" in polemics against values no longer held in the West, that is, against Kemalism.[68] Instead, the East must join the West in an effort, barely begun, to achieve historical understanding of human hopes, fears, myths, truths, and action. Historicism constitutes the core of what Arkoun thinks is the modern (or postmodern) attitude, and defined in that way, modernity becomes a global impera- tive, as it seemed to be in the *nahḍa*, the Arab renaissance of the nine- teenth and early twentieth centuries. The Enlightenment, like Islam, be- comes not just a source of values but an object of inquiry: What does it owe to all three major monotheistic religions? To what extent is it an acci- dental, internal product of the West? To what extent does its secularism constitute a phase of human maturation in society?[69]

This unambiguous endorsement of modernity, and even of elements of postmodern methodologies, seems to put Arkoun in quite a different camp from Qutb and, to a lesser extent, from Iqbal and Shari'ati. His faith in social science, his language, his frank distaste for those who repeat old wisdom in defense of their positions, his contempt for "integralism,"[70] his image of himself as a part of a scientific community rather than a reli- gious one—all these factors set him apart from Qutb and apart from the contemporary revival movement as a whole. Yet this apparent distance narrows as one compares visions of the future.

Qutb and Arkoun both contemplate new beginnings. Arkoun deplores the efforts of Qutb to search for first principles, saying that the origins of these truths must be reexamined, if human beings are to be rediscovered in all their potential. In a sympathetic critique of Ibn Tufayl's *Hayy ibn Yaqzan*, he discerns an intuition that *"la table rase* or the radical beginning of knowledge is possible"[71]—a hint, for him, of Ibn Tufayl's incipient modernity. Arkoun himself seems to believe in attempting a *table rase* through the reconstruction of history. "Still today we are witnessing fresh vigor in the demand for a radical beginning: not only on the terrain and with the means of philosophy, but in the more and more rigorous practice of all the human sciences."[72] For him, the starting point for a new "Founding Action" must be an anthropological conception of the state of nature rather than a return to the principles of revelation—man as essen- tially nothing rather than something (such as "self," as Iqbal suggests.) "Radical thinking refers to the biological, historical, linguistic, semiotic condition shared by people as natural beings."[73] Yet Arkoun's belief in the possibility of a radical recommencement remains just that: a belief, like others. Although its character is derivative of human knowledge rather than revealed, it is the basis of the knowledge from which it derives. Al- though it liberates, it cannot liberate from the burden of that first princi- ple, which is a problem for him but not for Iqbal, Shari'ati, or Qutb, who all acknowledge the necessity of faith as a point of beginning.

All four writers contemplate a coming together of Muslim and even non-Muslim worlds. Arkoun calls for the immediate participation of all scholars in a grand campaign to understand the particularistic nature of all truths, including those passed on by Islam. For him, social science will increasingly permit the interpretation of particularity as a function of totality and enable Muslims to be at one with themselves and with the rest of the world. The overcoming of the gulf between East and West through the common endorsement of scientific methodology paves the way toward reconciliation within Islam. Qutb, on the other hand, foresees a world increasingly subdued by a newly triumphant, regenerated Islam. Unity comes from action rather than reflection.

All four authors seem to believe in progress, despite distrust of Enlightenment ideas in which the Western notion of progress has been based. For Arkoun, part of what is lacking in the "medieval" understanding characteristic of the Islamic world until the nineteenth century is the idea of progress. God dominated all levels of existence, science, and thought were confined to sacred space and time, observation and experiment were contested, and knowledge was seen as a kind of intellectual dreaming about essential truth.[74] Yet Arkoun, like the others, finds neither idealistic nor materialist thought an adequate foundation for a doctrine of progress. What has made the West surge forward, according to Arkoun, is not just the victory of reason over faith but the triumph of science over reason. Western science moved beyond its essentialist foundations, whereas Islamic philosophy and science, ensnared in a theological ambience, lost its critical impulse and the capacity to reexamine its own assumptions. Ibn Khaldun, empiricist and social scientist though he was, could see no escape from universal necessity. Neither could Sir Isaac Newton or Karl Marx, but the West moved beyond Newton and Marx, and the Islamic world did not rethink the conclusions of Ibn Khaldun or even pay much attention to them.

Can progress, then, represent any more than a possibility? Iqbal, Qutb, Shari'ati, and Arkoun all try to demonstrate the capacity for human improvement. For Arkoun, like Shari'ati, it comes from reflection about the historical generation of human culture. Both insist that human beings are responsible for making what they will of themselves; improvement appears problematic, accidental, and possible, though scarcely inevitable. Both thinkers, products of the twentieth century, nonetheless insist upon the inevitability of progress among human beings free to choose it.

That apparent contradiction hangs especially heavy over Arkoun. Social science cannot establish unambiguous definitions without resort to "false bourgeois universalism,"[75] he has warned. Its vocabulary "depends on the social dialectic characteristic of each society and each historical phase."[76] How then can one define in an unambiguous way a pattern of evolution one might call "progress"? He speaks of the inevitable march of science and the concomitant decline in the ability of religion to monopolize the production of truth. But I see neither what makes that march inevitable nor how one could call that march "progress," if one eschews an essentialist definition of the concept. He says the task of social science is to "articulate the multiplicity of human discourse by means of the constantly revised principles and methods of objective knowledge."[77] But if principles and methods are constantly revised, whence comes the unchanging standard by which one may judge whether revision constitutes progress or retrogression? And why does ever greater knowledge of human diversity free human beings from the perceived necessity of going in any particular direction, including the way in which science is presumably marching?

Arkoun sees reality as the standard. Science produces ever more accurate images of reality, which is itself changing. Science must change to keep up and to respond to its own self-critique, constantly abandoning the standards it creates. But as Nietzsche observed, such an exercise demobilizes and demoralizes. Arkoun prefers to retain the doctrine of progress through a double act of faith: a belief that science can within historical time elaborate a truth that goes beyond history and a belief that such a truth will be followed. Iqbal, Qutb, and Shari'ati at least acknowledge an unverifiable belief in an enduring standard. They are, however, no more explicit than Arkoun in recognizing as mere conviction the belief that human beings, reexposed to the truth, will choose it with greater consistency in the future than in the past.

Every society depends to some degree on myth, *l'imaginaire*; there can be no complete escape. Perhaps Arkoun would say that the myth of progress constitutes the prerequisite for constructive action in the twentieth century. Is not the myth of progress a fixed part of the modern world, like the scarcity of oil or the existence of atomic weapons? Can one compete in a progress-oriented world without embracing the myth and behaving as if it mattered? The myth of progress necessarily perpetuates an element of false consciousness insofar as it offers images of a lifestyle that may well be unachievable; it represents compromise of the radical historicist project to subvert all inherited values; it cannot be guaranteed without sacrificing human responsibility. Yet it must for practical reasons be preserved as a foundation for hope and an incentive for group action. Such might be Arkoun's response.

Equality and Group Action

As a revolutionary strategy, Arkoun's position suffers not just from its relative lack of utopian lure. It also depends upon free speech as the condition for intellectual activity, upon the intellectuals as a force for mobilization of the society, and upon the legitimation of all subgroup identities as a means of generating unity. However logical and laudable these presuppositions, they tend to further diminish the plausibility of group action. Free speech guarantees argument about what should be done, intellectuals have rarely been able to mobilize mass support, and equal status for subgroups creates a plurality from which unity must be painstakingly constructed.

Arkoun has written admiringly of Abu Hayyan al-Tawhidi (d. 1018), who expressed bitterness against a society that, despite Qur'anic injunctions, continued to value individuals more for their backgrounds than for their actions.[78] Tawhidi showed interest in some of the questions Arkoun deems vital: Why do societies tend to reject those who are different? How do standards of conventionality emerge? How can one jurist declare illicit that which another permits? Arkoun sees Tawhidi as a defender of equal human subjectivity.

For Arkoun, Tawhidi's instincts push modern historians toward an extended range of interests. They must look at all ethnic and professional groups, at the forgotten as well as the renowned, at those who were not guardians of high Islam as well as those who were. Equal subjectivity means each national and subnational area deserves historical, sociological, and anthropological analysis, with the aim of understanding how norms were imposed and how values lived.

Equality means, from Arkoun's perspective, the equal right to speak and be heard, but such a right can only be exercised if free speech is permitted: "To let all sectors of the society speak is a new demand that can in reality be satisfied only under political regimes won over to freedom of thought, of expression, and of publication."[79] For this reason, existing regimes in Muslim countries constitute, by their intolerance of dissidence and scientific research, double obstacles to the achievement of group identity with the totality of the Islamic experience: By their heavy propaganda on behalf of a mythical past, they render dangerous the position of a scientific historian bent upon reexamining the inherited wisdom, and they repress in the name of national unity all popular expressions of minority culture. Opposition groups are no less dedicated than the government to the utilization of Islam for political purposes and no less opposed to all critical study of Islamic issues.[80] Minority groups seldom speak for themselves, and intellectuals are not free to explore the historical terrain in which minorities and majorities diverged, the terrain from which genuine, authentic unity might be reconstructed.

As one would expect from an intellectual, Arkoun asks more from himself and his colleagues than from the masses. It is they, the intellectuals, who must examine the whole of the Islamic tradition and communicate the result to the "undivided and naive consciousness of the believers."[81] For that reason, they must work from within that consciousness, avoiding excessive intellectualization; they cannot ignore popular belief, as did the exponents of *nahḍa*, whether salafī or liberal, in the late nineteenth and early twentieth century.[82] They cannot dismiss the whole of the Islamic tradition as irrelevant to the present, as did the exponents of Arab revolution in the 1950s and 1960s. Nor, conversely, can they steep themselves in the tradition, neglecting both critical epistemology and sociological realities, as have the establishment ulema. For Arkoun, citing Weber and sounding like Gramsci, it is the intellectuals who must elaborate meaning for a society. But where are those intellectuals in the Arab-Islamic world today? Too many "false intellectuals" have accepted co-optation by repressive regimes in return for all too hasty training, he has said.[83]

In an early work, Arkoun joined Iqbal in emphasizing the role of modern poets in portraying the Arab-Muslim condition in concrete, comprehensible terms.

> One is justified in saying that it is in and through the new poetry that the most radical revolution has been accomplished in the Arab-Islamic milieu since the 1950s: not a destructive revolution (*haddāma*), as the opponents claim, but a transmutation of the collective sensibility, an enlarging and reanchoring of the imaginary.[84]

He saw poetry as a critical link between the intellectuals and the masses: "It is in modern poetry, much more than in official pronouncements, that marginal persons and low-income groups can, to the extent that they have access to it, find the most adequate expression of the deaths, births and renaissances of which they have been more or less confusedly the subjects."[85] Even if such poetry explicitly rejected religious belief and propounded Marxist ideology, it nonetheless put Arab Muslims in touch with themselves and their past. The poets represented those who, themselves capable of getting outside the Islamic experience and gaining perspective, could potentially move the public imagination from within.

The passage of but a few years, marked by the sharp successes of the Islamic revival movement, seems to have undermined Arkoun's optimism about the role of the poets. It is the followers of Qutb, cloaking a revolutionary message in traditional terms, who have won the ear of the masses, not the secular, revolutionary poets. The revivalists have successfully mobilized group action on the basis of "true faith" against believers and nonbelievers alike. In Arkoun's view, such groups are bent on injecting a new sort of false consciousness, a new source of alienation to replace older ones, further complicating the task of demythification, which falls to the "genuine" intellectual. It is not clear from Arkoun's later work how under these conditions he thinks the "true" intellectuals might be able to generate an effective political movement to compete with either the establishment or the revivalists. His own work is largely inaccessible to anyone outside the community of scholars.[86] It seems that a crevasse of Himalayan proportions isolates his conception of the Islamic "totality" from the mobilization of a popular consciousness around that "fact."

Institutions

Institutions constitute the key to authenticity and the great stumbling block for Arkoun as for other authentics. Amid repressive institutions, intellectuals cannot perform their essential roles. Under the barrage of propaganda emitted by the authorities, the masses seem unlikely to escape false consciousness. Shored up by fragments of Islamic revelation and elements of Western reason, institutions depend upon coercion as a substitute for constitutional solidity. They must eventually crumble. But on what grounds can more durable institutions be constructed in the absence of essential truth?

Arkoun says constitutional fragility characterizes both East and West. In the Islamic world, power is traditionally seen as derived from the caliph, but divine authority lies in texts. In the Sunni community, the caliph can and must apply a universal *shari'a* to an enormous diversity of peoples attached to differing statutes and differing versions of the *shari'a*. If he seeks to unify by coercion, as did the Umayyads, he appears illegitimate; if he concerns himself with a highly abstract law, far removed from the diversity of Islamic life, he consigns himself to the dustbin of history, as did the later 'Abbasids. The Islamic attachment to text puts authority in the hands of the ulema, who have fashioned not one truth but many of them in time and space. Contemporary historical analysis portrays the ulema as creators of the texts they have come to guard, defenders of both orthodoxy and dissent, partisans of order and, occasionally, advocates of revolt.[87] Yet, without the caliph, the ulema lack power, just as the caliph without the backing of the ulema lacks authority.[88] Only the Shi'i belief in the imams, direct inheritors of the spiritual powers of Muhammad, avoids such a dilemma by bestowing divine sanction upon an institution, the imamate.[89]

In the West, according to Arkoun, the problem is different but analogous. Power lies with mere human beings, but legitimacy depends upon Divine Reason. Popular sovereignty conflicts with self-evident truths. Liberalism proposes a secularization of authority that, if ever completed, would deprive the liberal faith of its certainty and authority. Western institutions stand, in fact, upon a contradictory mixture of faith and reason that may be no less precarious as a foundation for contemporary government than is Islamic theory. Legitimacy depends upon processes based on a presumption of absolute truth that has been eroded, leaving the processes themselves hanging without visible support.

Arkoun sees a threat in this generalized crisis of legitimacy. "Paradoxically, the more the foundations of authority are contested, the more the hold of the State is strong and omnipresent."[90] In both East and West, says Arkoun, the state has used propaganda as well as force to compensate for inadequate legitimacy. In the West, the propaganda overemphasizes the discreteness of religious and political domains, whereas equivalent propaganda in the Islamic world often presumes their identity. For Arkoun, no state has ever forgone the use of religion, heroes, and historical memories in seeking to justify its authority; even so, in contrast with most advocates of revival, he believes that no state could utterly obliterate the distinction between religion and politics. No state could command complete devotion.

> We should not forget that man agrees to obey, to be devoted, and to obligate his life when he feels a "debt of meaning" to a natural or supernatural being. This may be the ultimate legitimacy of the state understood as the power accepted and obeyed by a group, community, or nation. The crisis of meaning started when each individual claimed himself as the source of all or true meaning; in this case, there is no longer any transcendent authority. Relations of power are substitutes for relations of symbolic exchanges of meaning. To whom do we owe a "debt of meaning?"[91]

Although Arkoun criticizes existing Muslim states for their manipulation of Islam and the Islamic opposition for its ideological use of religion for secular purposes, he sees both the personal and political need for religion as a source of ultimate meaning in East and West alike.

The question is whether religion is central or marginal to political life. It has been central in the Islamic world, he says, because the bourgeoisie has not been sufficiently strong to impose separation and because the clergy, steeped in theology, has exercised judicial power.[92] Centrality comes from historical development rather than revelation; the societies of the Book, despite similarities in revelation, have taken rather different paths. Arkoun favors marginality because it leaves more room for a plurality of meanings and personal freedom.

> What happens to the real status of the person when the right to think, to self-expression, to publish, sell and buy all kinds of writings is strictly controlled by the ministry of information or "national guidance?" . . . For a Muslim . . . *the struggle for the right of the mind to truth* has always been waged from within a closed dogmatic system. [italics in original][93]

Commenting upon the efforts of the contemporary Islamic movement to construct model constitutions and to formulate an Islamic declaration of the rights of man, Arkoun wrote:

> Thus the political vision of these great texts is directed more toward the propagation of a mobilizing vision of utopia in response to the Western challenge than toward proposing precise programs for institutional reform, for

the conquest of citizen rights, for an emancipation of civil society such that the State would lose its "monopoly of legitimate violence."[94]

That statement may well sum up Arkoun's own agenda by default. He shuns mobilization, but how does one set about the "emancipation of civil society" without mobilization, and how does one mobilize without myth? The ability of the intellectuals to articulate a comprehensive understanding of the Islamic past and to liberate the masses from false consciousness depends upon their ability to work and think freely; it presupposes institutional reform of a revolutionary sort, which seems implausible as long as the state uses false consciousness to bolster its monopoly over the legitimate use of violence. Intellectuals on the outside, operating from safe, liberal, Western redoubts, must lead the way. "The emotion-charged atmosphere prevailing in modern Muslim societies rules out the possibility of scientific study of a large number of sensitive problems."[95] For Arkoun, Western-style political institutions, permitting Western-style social scientists to function, seem to be a prerequisite for the achievement of Islamic authenticity.

Such a formulation of Arkoun's argument is unfair in at least one respect. Arkoun sees Western social-scientific methodology as the route toward comprehension of the Islamic experience, and he appears to regard elements of the Western political tradition as fundamental to the process of reconstruction. In neither case, however, does he believe this because of, or in spite of, their being Western. Authenticity means moving beyond negative identification and retaliation,[96] beyond the "ideology of combat."[97] The freedom to rethink one's past depends upon freedom of speech and freedom of the press. The validation of all aspects of the Islamic experience implies tolerance, group autonomy, mutual respect of rights—polyarchy, to use Robert Dahl's term, rather than the millet system.[98] The rejection of essentialism and exclusivism necessarily drives religion toward marginality and the state toward a secular paradigm. In short, Arkoun appears to endorse the findings of Western political science, not for their origins in the West but for their basis in science. Social science conducts the search for Islamic authenticity, and social science directs construction of new institutions consistent with that tradition.

↩⌐

From the failure of social science to either describe or prescribe the course of development, Arkoun deduces not the need to abandon social science but a caveat for its improvement. His quest for authenticity depends upon a social science that is both objective and subjective, capable of understanding the world as it is and as it has been, capable of founding judgments about what should or should not be done, yet mindful of the "cognitive respect"[99] due all human beings and the possibility of ultimate meaning. He attempts to reconcile truth as feeling with truth as understanding.[100] The task is perhaps impossible, yet the alternative is a choice between utter relativism, in which every felt "truth," however objectionable, enjoys equal status, and the elevation of an abstract truth, whether Islamic or Western, to a position from which all others can be criticized and excluded. In the first case, social science has a large audience and nothing to say; in the second, it proclaims with conviction to the believing few, without regard (or perhaps with disdain) for those who disagree and disobey. As a social scientist, I share with Arkoun a distaste for such a choice and am compelled, therefore, to empathize with his endeavor.

A part of the attractiveness of his proposal resides in its relatively low propensity for generating violence compared with other theories of authenticity. By showing why history belies the claim of any group to a monopoly on Islamic truth, he wishes to dampen the fires of sectarian conflict. By defending popular Islam as a sociological truth deserving of the same respect as Sunnism, he puts himself at odds with the impulses of the *salafī* movement and of secular, nationalist thought, both of which are dedicated to the unification of belief and the centralization of power. By suggesting that the totality of the Islamic experience constitutes the truth from which reconstruction can begin, he hopes to forge unity without the kind of conflict engendered by claims of exclusivism. "One would try not to defend the truth of a faith but to understand faith as truth."[101] Moreover, Arkoun speaks little of struggle (jihad), with its violent overtones, and has backed away from poetry, with its tendency to focus on the individual search for authenticity even unto death, as the vehicle by which the masses could come to comprehend the true Islamic past. It is the intellectuals who, by reckoning scientifically with past and present alike in an atmosphere of tolerance, free speech, and free publication, must open the way for Muslims to come to terms with themselves. Unlike Qutb, and perhaps more like Nietzsche, Arkoun extols not the will to act but the will to think.

There may nonetheless lurk behind Arkoun's project a latent potential for violence. While he opposes all groups who proclaim their version of utopia, he speaks of discovering the truth about Islamic history. How all portions of the community would shuck their false consciousness—that is, their confidence in the truth-value of their beliefs—and embrace this reconstructed truth he does not explain. Who are the intermediaries between intellectuals and masses? If not the poets and if not the clerics, then who? By failing to lay any plausible basis for group action, he avoids both potential conflict and any chance for realizing goals. Although it might be plausible to argue that the truth would prevail within liberal institutions—themselves almost entirely foreign to the totality of the Islamic experience—his case for those institutions does not go beyond the need for freedom of expression. That they could emerge everywhere in the Islamic world without a group to champion and defend them seems unlikely, at least as unlikely as Qutb's conflict-avoiding idea that true Muslims will submit voluntarily to the sovereignty of God, after revolting against the sovereignty of mere mortals.

The problem with Arkoun's formulation lies with its rejection, on the one hand, of any and all privileged truths, and its espousal, on the other, of the superior truth-generating capacity of social science. Critical of those who start from an act of faith in the "true Islam" and exhort believers to struggle on its behalf, Arkoun nonetheless evinces a faith of his own, qualified though it is by acknowledgment that social science has not yet achieved truth and that no discourse is innocent. Yet he seems to believe the truth can be found and false consciousness overcome. Although he is not yet prepared to do battle for the glimmer of truth-to-come and although he himself might well have scruples about doing so in any case, why would others show such restraint? His all-encompassing tolerance could scarcely afford to brook the intolerance of those who regarded it as just another truth among many. Such status would transform its character, just as it would entirely alter the nature of Qutb's Sunnism, maraboutism in the High Atlas, Ismailism, or any of the other variants of the Islamic tradition Arkoun sees as mere fractions of a total truth. Exclusivism is intrinsic to the truths they represent, just as it is intrinsic to the idea of social science he advocates.

Arkoun appears overly sanguine in his hope for more general tolerance and understanding. His starting point for common understanding among Muslims is the "Qur'anic fact." He directs us to turn back still further—to the religious instincts common to societies of the Book—for a more general framework of mutual comprehension. "One must hope that gratuitous sermons, false promises, and calls for struggle among men will be less and less important obstacles to the return of creative and liberating expression, in the domain of culture as in that of religious testimony on behalf of the Absolute."[102] But does not Arkoun's insistence upon radical beginnings—man as nothing before the onset of culture—necessarily presuppose particularity and division? Even if one begins from the societies of the Book, the question is still how common experience distinguishes this group of human beings from another—from East Asians or Africans, for example. To see Muslims as fundamentally shaped by the "Qur'anic fact" is to see them as different from non-Muslims, as well as diverse in their historical experience with the Qur'an. Starting with particular aspects of human experience, can one ever build a persuasive case for the oneness of Islam, much less for the societies of the Book or for humanity as a whole? Can one ever demonstrate that the human species is united in its experience, though not in its essence? The aspiration may be more flawed than Arkoun's pursuit of it in the study of Islamic history.

Notes

1. An earlier version of this chapter appeared as "Arkoun and Authenticity" in *Peuples méditerranéens* 50 (January-March, 1990), pp. 75–106. It is reprinted with permission.

2. Mohammed Arkoun, *Pour une critique de la raison islamique* (Paris: Maisoneuve et Larose, 1984), p. 303, note 6.

3. Ibid., pp. 303–304.

4. Ibid., pp. 111–112.

5. Mohammed Arkoun, "Rethinking Islam Today," Occasional Papers Series, Center for Contemporary Arab Studies, Georgetown University, 1987, p. 2.

6. Trilling's distillation of the romantic view. See Lionel Trilling, *Sincerity and Authenticity* (Cambridge: Harvard University Press, 1972).

7. My shorthand for the Heideggerian idea.

8. Friedrich Nietzsche, *The Anti-Christ, in Twilight of the Idols/The Anti-Christ,* trans. R. J. Hollingdale (Middlesex: Penguin, 1987), p. 122.

9. Arkoun, *Critique*, p. 374.

10. Ibid.

11. Ibid.

12. Ibid.

13. Ibid.

14. See Arkoun's "Discours islamiques, discours orientalistes et pensée scientifique," in *As Others See Us: Mutual Perceptions, East and West,* ed. Bernard Lewis, special issue of *Comparative Civilization Review,* nos. 13–14 (1985–1986).

15. Arkoun argues that most academic scholarship has tended to serve the interests of new regimes by portraying a unified, unchanging, Arab-dominated Islam. See his "Society, State and Religion in Algeria (1962–1985)," in *The Politics of Islamic Revivalism,* ed. Shireen T. Hunter (Bloomington: Indiana University Press, 1988), p. 184.

16. Mohammed Arkoun, "The Topicality of the Problem of the Person in Islamic Thought," *International Social Science Journal* (August 1988), p. 414.

17. See Allan Bloom, *The Closing of the American Mind* (New York: Simon and Schuster, 1987), part 2, on this point. It seems strange for this reason that Arkoun himself uses "authenticity" as a derogatory label for opponents he deems essentialist rather than existentialist.

18. Many of the themes evoked in this chapter appear in Arkoun's *Rethinking Islam: Common Questions, Uncommon Answers* (Boulder: Westview, 1994), trans. and ed. Robert D. Lee. For a bibliography of Arkoun's writing, see that volume, pp. 135–138. The book is a translation of Arkoun's *Ouvertures sur l'Islam* (Paris: J. Grancher, 1989 and 1992), a work in which he sought to bring together his ideas and to express them in terms more accessible to a broad public.

19. Geneviève Léveillé-Mourin, *Le langage chrétien, antichrétien de la transcendance: Pascal-Nietzsche* (Paris: J. Vrin, 1978), part 3.

20. See, for example, Gilles Kepel's analysis of Qutb's definition of jihad in *Le prophète et pharaon: Les mouvements islamistes dans l'Egypte contemporaine* (Paris: La Découverte, 1984), chap. 2.

21. Arkoun, *Critique*, p. 206.

22. ("L'absolu ne se pense pas ailleurs que dans un monde phénoménal.") Mohammed Arkoun, *L'Islam: Morale et politique* (Paris: Desclée de Brouwer, 1986) p. 174.

23. Arkoun, "Society, State and Religion in Algeria (1962–1985)," p. 183.

24. See Mohammed Arkoun, *La pensée arabe* (Paris: Presses Universitaires, 1975), pp. 5–7, for a succinct treatment of this theme, which he develops in various ways in many of his works.

25. Arkoun, "Society, State and Religion in Algeria (1962–1985)," p. 23.

26. See W. Montgomery Watt, *The Formative Period of Islamic Thought* (Edinborough: Edinborough University Press, 1973).

27. Arkoun, *Critique*, chap. 2.

28. Discussing contemporary Algeria, Arkoun has written: "Islam is thus shared, used, disputed, manipulated at many levels, by all social actors with various ambitions, through different cultural tools. The game is social, political, secular; the instruments of the game are found in Islam because it is a rich stock, an illuminated legacy of symbols, signs, signals. That is why I speak about a mimetic competition for the control and exploitation of the symbolic capital, without which no group can gain, keep or exercise power." Arkoun, "Society, State and Religion in Algeria (1962–1985)," p. 184.

29. Arkoun, *Morale et politique*, p. 51.

30. Mohammed Arkoun, *Essais sur la pensée islamique*, 3d ed. (Paris: Maisonneuve et Larose, 1984), p. 234.

31. The "unthought" is a theme that recurs in Arkoun's work. For one of the most thorough discussions, see *Critique*, pp. 307ff. See also *La pensée arabe*, pp. 88–89.

32. Arkoun, *Essais sur la pensée islamique*, chap. 5; see also *La pensée arabe*, pp. 36–45.

33. Arkoun, *Essais sur la pensée islamique*, p. 195.

34. Ibid., p. 231.

35. Nietzsche, *The Anti-Christ*, p. 155.

36. Arkoun, *Morale et politique*, p. 100.

37. Arkoun, *Essais sur la pensée islamique*, p. 195.

38. Arkoun, *Critique*, p. 33.

39. See ibid., chap. 2, "Le concept de raison islamique."

40. Ibid., p. 38.

41. Mohammed Arkoun, "The Concept of Authority in Islamic Thought: La hukma illa lillah," prepared for *Islam: State and Society* (London: Curzon, 1988), p. 31 in typescript. This is my reworking of the typescript: "But the only scholars engaged in a continuous fight to create new spaces of freedom, to give new intellectual articulations to the silent voices, are those who harmonize their thought with their concrete engagement and their engagement with their thought."

42. Arkoun, *Critique*, p. 33.

43. Ibid., p. 111.

44. Mohammed Arkoun, *Lectures du Coran* (Paris: Maisonneuve et Larose, 1982), pp. 24–25.

45. Arkoun, *Critique*, p. 150.

46. In talking about his concept of committed Orientalism, "Islamologie appliquée," he has written: "Le problème se pose, ici, de savoir comment l'islamologie peut et doit intervenir. Il ne suffit sûrement pas de s'en tenir à la méthode 'neutre' descriptive, non engagée de l'islamologie classique; mais on ne saurait non plus opposer aux postulats de l'attitude croyante ou aux certitudes agressives du discours idéologique, la marche 'assurée' de la pensée scientifique. Il nous semble indispensable d'assumer à la fois toute la complexité de la situation historique vécue par les musulmans et toutes les inquiétudes de l'intelligence contemporaine en quête de vérité." Arkoun, *Critique*, p. 50. Is he warning here against arrogance and contempt, or is he expressing reservations about the reliability of modern social science?

47. Arkoun, *Essais sur la pensée islamique*, p. 303.

48. Arkoun argues that the current movement of Islamic resurgence continues the reformist mode of thinking rather than reexamining the genesis of that thinking and its role in Islamic history. Arkoun, "Rethinking Islam Today," p. 8.

49. Mohammed Arkoun, "Imaginaire social et leaders dans le monde musulman contemporain," *Arabica* 35 (1988), p. 28.

50. He speaks of achieving liberation from the Cartesian mode and softening Marxism. Arkoun, *Essais sur la pensée islamique*, p. 306.

51. See ibid., chap. 8.

52. Arkoun, *Critique*, chap. 1.

53. This is judgment about what he sees as "retrogression" in French Orientalism. Arkoun, *Essais sur la pensée islamique*, p. 306.

54. Arkoun, *Morale et politique*, p. 100.

55. Arkoun, *Critique*, chap. 3.

56. Ibid., p. 38.

57. Ibid., p. 33.

58. Arkoun, *Essais sur la pensée islamique*, p. 306.

59. Arkoun, *Critique*, p. 7.

60. Arkoun, *Morale et politique*, p. 40.

61. Arkoun, *Critique*, pp. 132–133. I have paraphrased.

62. Ibid., chap. 10.

63. See his reproach to von Grunebaum, in Arkoun, *Essais sur la pensée islamique*, chap. 8.

64. Mohammed Arkoun, "The Unity of Man in Islamic Thought," trans. R. Scott Walker, in *Diogène* 140 (1987), p. 54.

65. Ibid., p. 58.

66. The reference is again to the two impulses Arkoun says have guided his intellectual quest: "(1) to understand the Arab-Muslim personality claimed the nationalist movement, and (2) to determine the extent to which the modern civilization, represented by the colonial power, should be considered a universal civilization." Arkoun, "Rethinking Islam Today," p. 2.

67. Mohammed Arkoun, "Positivisme et tradition dans une perspective islamique: Le cas du Kémalisme," *Diogène* 127 (July–September, 1984), p. 92.

68. Arkoun, *Morale et politique,* p. 180.

69. Arkoun, "Positivisme," pp. 93–94.

70. See his discussion of al-Jundi in *Critique,* pp. 105–112.

71. See Arkoun, *Critique,* chap. 11.

72. Ibid., p. 347.

73. Arkoun, "Rethinking Islam Today," p. 8.

74. Arkoun, *Essais,* chap. 1.

75. Arkoun, "Positivisme," p. 106.

76. Arkoun, *Critique,* p. 208.

77. Ibid., p. 121.

78. Arkoun, *Essais sur la pensée islamique,* p. 108.

79. Arkoun, *Critique,* p. 215.

80. Arkoun, "Society, State and Religion in Algeria (1962–1985)," p. 184.

81. Arkoun, *Critique,* p. 112.

82. See Arkoun, *La pensée arabe,* for a discussion of the evolution of modern thought.

83. Arkoun, *Critique,* p. 239.

84. Mohammed Arkoun and Louis Gardet, *L'Islam: Hier. Demain.* (Paris: Buchet/Chastel, 1978), p. 244.

85. Ibid., p. 245.

86. His most readable work is *Ouvertures sur l'Islam* (Paris: Grancher, 1989, 1992), which I have translated as *Rethinking Islam: Common Questions, Uncommon Answers* (Boulder: Westview, 1994).

87. See Arkoun, *Morale et politique,* chap. 2.

88. Arkoun defines orthodoxy as "official religion resulting from the collaboration of a majority of the so-called 'ulama with the state." "Authority," p. 11 in typescript.

89. Arkoun, *Morale et politique,* pp. 134–146.

90. Arkoun, *Critique,* p. 156.

91. Arkoun, "Rethinking Islam Today," p. 24.

92. Arkoun, *Critique,* p. 210.

93. Arkoun, "Topicality of the Problem of the Person," p. 414.

94. Arkoun, *Morale et politique,* p. 162.

95. Arkoun, "Topicality of the Problem of the Person," p. 414.

96. The reference is to Nietzsche.

97. Arkoun, *Pensée arabe,* p. 117.

98. Robert Dahl, *Polyarchy* (New Haven: Yale University Press, 1976).

99. Peter Berger, *Pyramids of Sacrifice* (Garden City, N.Y.: Anchor, 1976).

100. See Jean Duvignaud, *Change at Shebika,* trans. Francis Frenaye (Austin: University of Texas Press, 1970), for an interesting discussion of that problem in the analysis of a Tunisian village.

101. Arkoun, *Lectures du Coran,* p. 21.

102. Mohammed Arkoun, "Islam: Les expressions de l'Islam," in *Encyclopedia Universalis* (Paris: Encyclopaedia Universalis France, Supplement for 1983), p. 212.

seven

◈

The Elusiveness
of Authenticity

TO SEEK AUTHENTICITY MEANS to search for what "really is" rather than what appears to be, what is fundamental rather than superficial, what is original rather than additional, what is genuine rather than false. For an action of mine to be authentic, it must reflect me, my own choices, my own circumstances, and therefore who I am—nay, who I "really" am and not what I may wish to think I am or what I would wish others to think I am.

It is not easy to apply such criteria to phenomena of everyday life. What is meant by "authentic Italian cuisine?" Surely it means something more than "Da Luigi" or "Da Antonio" over the front door and more than a bit of pizza or pasta on the menu. Does it mean that the chef must be Italian, or only of Italian descent? Must the ingredients all come from Italy, or is it sufficient that the wine, olive oil, and pasta be imported? Can there exist "authentic Italian cuisine" outside of Italy, where the decor, the products, and the clientele are often not Italian? Is it enough that such cuisine reproduce age-old recipes, or does "authentic Italian cuisine" imply the presence of an Italian chef, who is constantly experimenting and inventing, exploiting the best of local products in conjunction with an expanding variety of foreign ones to satisfy the most discriminating of evolving Italian palates?

Authenticity implies a standard that is more rigorous than some other standard. "Authentic Italian cuisine" implies that there must be some Italian cuisine that is inauthentic. The search for an "authentic" way of acting in the Islamic world means that other paths, such as just being a Muslim or embracing Western values, are deficient or insufficient. The search for authenticity targets a set of standards that go beyond previously existing foundations for judgment or implies a frame of reference in which standards themselves can be validated or rejected. It is a quest for new foundations upon which political institutions can be constructed and ideologies designed.

The four writers considered in this study all seek to reestablish foundations upon which meaningful, effective, modern lives can be built and societies constructed. All build upon a religious tradition, but none finds mainstream Islamic theology, either Sunni or Shi'i, adequate to the task. All criticize the mainstream for its rigidity, its fragmentation, its inattention and insensitivity to the problems of modern life. All four draw upon reason to guide the design of the new foundation, but none finds reason itself, the bedrock of Enlightenment philosophy, sufficient to supply meaning in a non-European culture. None accepts the propositions of theological reformists (some would say apologists) that a mere merger of reason and theology can provide a modern standard. In reformist thinking of the sort linked to the name of Muhammad 'Abdu, universal reason grounded in Western culture is necessarily the victor and further alienation of non-Europeans the result. If theology remains either subordinate to reason or to nationalist directives, as it has in most Middle Eastern countries, then it cannot provide direction. If it concerns itself only with theological questions or with mystical intercourse with God, quite divorced from modern life, then it cannot provide a standard, either. The quest for authenticity means looking for a firm foundation for personal well-being, knowledge of the world, and action in the world.

This is a tall order. That which is authentic and genuine must necessarily be essential to a person and a culture, but philosophical essentialism tends to negate the concreteness and particularity that authenticity requires. A theory of authenticity necessarily focuses upon that which is unique to each individual; it must find the *essential* elements of uniqueness without negating the obvious need of individuals to live in larger societies, of groups to live in a larger world. It must identify existential commonalities without lapsing back into the despised essentialism, seen as destroying the very inwardness and ownness to which authenticity aspires. It must give primacy to culture as the fundamental force shaping human beings, but it must also demonstrate some ground for human autonomy sufficient to justify a belief in human ability to shape life in this world. Without sufficient human autonomy to make choices, the need for new foundations is irrelevant. Only with the capacity to make choices, which cannot therefore be utterly a product of culture, can human beings escape the determinism that these writers tend to associate with certain brands of Islamic theology and certain kinds of Western social science. Finally, the effort to establish new foundations seeks to establish something to which one can cling in the maelstrom of contemporary living; it cannot therefore ignore the vicissitudes of history as have the rationalists of both the Western and Islamic sort, these writers would say. They are seeking new foundations because history has eroded the old ones. The new ones must thus supply a fixed orientation, a reliable posture, or at least a reliable methodology in an ever more turbulent environment.

It would be presumptuous to say that Iqbal, Qutb, Shari'ati, and Arkoun have all failed in their endeavors. If new foundations emerge, their contributions may well appear to have been critical. All of them have already had some success in winning an audience and shaping the thought of others. An independent Pakistan might never have emerged without Iqbal. Shari'ati clearly contributed to the revolutionary atmosphere of Iran in the 1970s, even if he did not live to see the revolution. Militant Sunni Islam continually reevokes the memory of Qutb, either explicitly or implicitly. And Arkoun has acquired increasing attention in the Arab world as well as in Europe.

Still, it would be difficult to argue that any of their individual efforts to put themselves at the forefront of modernity, without lapsing into skepticism, has entirely succeeded. However stunning many of the insights and however inspiring some of the language, the balance sheet necessarily tips toward conundrums, apparent contradictions, and inadequacies. These four writers ultimately fail to achieve their own objectives, but this failure reflects the intractable nature of the problem they are seeking to resolve, not the nature of Islam itself. In fact, although their success or failure will ultimately depend on the reaction of Muslims and although these writers have written in an Islamic context, using Islamic terminology and appealing to knowledge of Islamic history, Islam is not itself an issue. Their failure would not mean that a more successful formulation of authenticity could not emerge from the Islamic experience. It certainly does not mean that formulations based in the agnostic or Christian experiences are likely to enjoy more success. Their failure would necessarily reverberate in the global context, just as any eventual success would be a triumph for efforts to establish fresh, authentic foundations the world over.

This is, of course, to offer judgment from a rationalist standpoint that all would agree cannot be rationally defended, one of the points Nietzsche made with such force. My critique comes from the social scientific perspective, which is itself at stake in this literature, and from a comparativist who harbors serious reservations about comparativism but who also mistrusts proclamations of difference and otherness whether they come from Orientalists or Islamic militants.

The claim of difference necessarily accompanies any theory of authenticity, but to acknowledge that claim in every case is to accept ontological and political anarchy, hence utter relativity, which every quest for authenticity would wish to avoid. Uncritical embrace of such a theory turns out to be an unfriendly reaction.

To say that these writers have not entirely succeeded in their enterprise does not mean that they have all failed in the same ways or that they have not enjoyed greater success in one domain or another. They have advanced four perspectives that lead toward rather different recommendations. By reviewing differences and similarities, it may not only be possible to evaluate successes and failures but also to understand the shape of an ongoing, world-wide conversation about authenticity.

Particularity and Unicity

Authenticity implies, above all else, that the search for truth began with human experience in its infinite particularity. For Iqbal, that means first and foremost that each individual consciousness is unique. The unique consciousness may be a result of unknowable, internal factors but is surely a product, as well, of a set of social circumstances experienced in a window of time. Iqbal and Arkoun are especially cognizant of the pitfalls in speaking of Muslim particularity, or even Sunni Muslim particularity. Every village in every Muslim country is different from every other, and no two individuals are identical within even one. Moreover, although villagers may pretend life has never changed from what it was for their ancestors, historical scholarship readily demonstrates variation in experience. Storytelling often confirms this observation.

As Theodor Adorno has observed, the quest for authenticity embraces localism. If women in Deh Koh, a village in the mountains of western Iran, have long put amulets on their babies to keep evil spirits away, does this not constitute an element of an authentic local lifestyle?[1] Do such women not have a right to be suspicious of religious militants who tell them that they should seek protection through prayer to God? The Islamic Republic of Iran has demonstrated hostility to this sort of "authentic" peasant behavior in the name of a revolution propelled in some considerable measure by appeals to "authentic" Iranian values against the godless, materialistic, scientistic "universalism" of the West. The shah tried to demonstrate the authenticity of his regime by linking it to the pre-Islamic Iran; the new regime prefers to focus on the Islamic experience, particularly on the post-1500, Shi'i period of Iran's Islamic experience, as the essence of Iran's unique identity. But how does one demonstrate that the examples of 'Ali and Fatima are essential to Iranian culture, although neither spoke Persian or lived in Iran, whereas those who praise Cyrus the Great or champion the use of amulets are not?

The search for essence thus intrudes upon an investigation dedicated to the study of concrete particulars, an investigation dead set against the essentialist assumptions about human nature so characteristic of the rationalist tradition. Empirical investigation of experience evolves into a process of abstraction for the sake of finding what is "authentic." Arkoun attempts to avoid this dilemma by arguing that the new foundation must not be some arbitrary selection of experiences to buttress convenient ideologies but, instead, an understanding of the entire Islamic tradition in all its richness and particularity, starting from the "Qur'anic fact." Thus he takes revelation to be fundamental but would have us examine the Islamic tradition in the context of the phenomenon of revelation in general and, more specifically, revelation as given to peoples of the Book.

The method is induction; from the plethora of factual information about Islamic history and the overwhelming variety of experience, one concludes that the study of revelation as a process is fundamental to an understanding of the totality of the Islamic experience. Particulars become subsumed in a totality, the essence of which may reside in the phenomenon of revelation. Localism disappears into globalism or into something very close to it. All aspects of Islam acquire the stamp of "authenticity," provided that they abjure claims to exclusivity.

Of course, exclusivity normally follows from claims of certainty, which therefore have to be abandoned or at least subordinated to a greater certainty, which resides in the broadest grasp of the history of revelation. This knowledge of the totality necessarily relativizes all the beliefs contained within it, although they are all legitimate, authentic components of the totality. "The human sciences," a term Arkoun prefers to "social science," emerge supreme in their ability to understand belief systems without denying validity to any of them. The benefit comes not from an infinite list of human particularities but from a set of abstractions. For example, Arkoun argues that a reading of the Qur'an necessarily reflects the power and position of those who are engaged in the reading. He further asserts that all peoples make choices grounded in the way they imagine their own history and the history of others; by understanding what they imagine, students of the human sciences can comprehend their choices, even though those choices may often reflect nonrational and even irrational beliefs. Such abstractions, in turn, necessarily reflect the work of other scholars, many outside the field of Islamic studies altogether, who are constantly in the process of developing and refining a set of universal propositions about human behavior.

The question is how to distinguish between such propositions and those that the search for authenticity seeks to avoid. All these writers resist the determinism of Marx, who insists that the social scientist can know history with complete certainty by examining the "essential" elements of it, namely, the evolution of class structures in response to changes in the means of production. All resist generalizations in which economic, social, and political variables drive development processes without regard for cultural differences. They deny the fundamental sameness of human beings that would permit abstract reasoning about behavior in a "state of nature" à la Rousseau or Locke or about development using the Western model as a base. Such propositions conflict with their assertions about the concrete particularity of human existence as well as with the postulated autonomy of all human beings. Yet Arkoun, too, would push toward universal propositions, abandoning concrete particularities (such as amulets) in favor of global statements about the importance of *l'imaginaire.*

He is not alone in this regard. Qutb seeks to convince us not that all human beings are utterly different from one another, or even that all Muslims are necessarily distinctive, despite apparent differences in custom, practice, and attitude. Rather, he seeks to identify the essential elements of the Islamic experience so that Muslims can rise above their differences and passivity and act upon the newly discovered foundation. For him, Islam is a method—a system, as Shepard calls it. By studying the example of Muhammad and his companions, Qutb abstracts a method: identifying the *jāhilīya*, gathering one's faith and support within the society, moving outside of that society and building a new community, and finally attacking the old society and bringing it to its knees. In each age and in every locale, the challenges would be different and the means of approaching those challenges different; for these reasons, he does not specify the sort of institutions a Muslim community ought to create. Yet he appears to be articulating a model for "authentic" Muslim behavior just as universal as Arkoun's propositions or Weber's observations about bureaucracy. In fact, the model, though derived from concrete Muslim experience, is not intrinsically Islamic. If the message transmitted by Muhammad was aimed at all mankind, then Qutb's model must also be seen as universal, or at least as applicable to all those who choose to declare themselves "Muslim." Since there are no cultural requirements for who can be a Muslim, this constitutes universality, though not of the sort Arkoun would embrace.

Shari'ati's propositions stem less from his analysis of Muhammad than from historical study of 'Ali and Fatima or of events such as the hajj. In his essay on Fatima, he shows how she does not represent a typical woman in either Western or Middle Eastern terms. She is unique, he says at every possible opportunity. Hence her ultimate particularity should serve as a model for women; they must "be themselves." Similarly, Shari'ati calls for more intense study of 'Ali and other important characters in Shi'i history so that Iranians may have more detailed, more nuanced models for "authentic" behavior. Shari'ati devotes many essays to suggesting that Shi'ism is, in essence, revolutionary, not static, passive, clergy-dominated, and inegalitarian as he thought it had become under centuries of Safavi, Qajar, and Pahlavi rule. He sought to define the "essence" of Shi'ism by looking at the defining events and personalities of the Shi'i tradition. His masterful account of the hajj uses the most minute details of the rites as a springboard for soaring thoughts about the human condition. It is an experience, he tells us, in which human beings find themselves by losing themselves in humanity. The method is inductive, but the result is once again highly abstract, highly general.

For Iqbal each human being is utterly unique, but the discovery of that uniqueness leads toward the source of all individuality, which is God. Islam emerges as a path by which one may make this dual discovery of self and God, which also happens to be the discovery of particularity and universality. In finding the essence of our "selves," we find being, which we share with God and all other creatures. Non-Muslims may pursue other routes toward this goal. The oneness of all things (*tawḥīd*) guarantees that possibility, and the realization of the possibility, however implausible, would constitute the ultimate assertion of both unicity and particularity.

Iqbal starts from a sharp sense of "ownness" and otherness. The poet starts from concrete images to build a sense of his own consciousness and personality. The poetic tools permit him to search for that which is felt as well as that which is reasoned and to express an utterly personal view of the world. But Iqbal writes about the self not as a mere exercise in personal discovery but in a way he hopes will inspire others to find themselves as Muslims. In fact, perhaps more clearly than Shari'ati, Qutb, and Arkoun, Iqbal sees "being" as the ultimate discovery. Individuals learn through the exploration of the self to see themselves not just as discrete beings. In fact, once Iqbal has worked his way toward the "essence" of things, it is difficult to argue that Muslims are different from others in any fundamental sense. Abstraction comes to dominate concreteness, oneness prevails over diversity, being over becoming, and universality over particularity—even though the quest for authenticity proclaims the need to escape these very things!

The erosion of particularity that marks the thought of Iqbal as it does the work of Qutb, Shari'ati, and Arkoun results from forces that are intrinsic to the search for authenticity. Authenticity requires foundations, and foundations must be broad and general. They must at least reflect some minimum common denominator in a universe dominated by diversity. If the authentic individual is unique to the point that no measure of the uniqueness can be explained, then the search for authenticity experiences a postmodernist defeat. Authenticity requires modification of particularistic assumptions, because the word itself demands standards, and particularity cannot provide standards. The force at work is one of intellectual proclivity.

A second force is one of practical proclivity. These writers have sought new foundations in the hope that human beings will act on them. All write not merely to inform or amuse but to incite. They all hope for significant social change, even revolution. But revolutions do not occur from the self-realizing actions of unique individuals. Revolutions require ideologies to bring people together. Ideologies help people understand what is common to many of them as well as, perhaps, what sets them apart from others. Insofar as ideologies must be built on philosophical foundations, the foundations must provide a basis for common human endeavor. As a practical matter, even though all these writers might not see themselves as ideologues and might even detest ideology (as does Arkoun, for example), they need to account for some common ground upon which human beings can act. Radical individuality and extreme cultural particularity do not provide such a ground. Arkoun, for instance, would put the Mediterranean world back together again, and his desire to compare the historical impact of revelation in Islam, Christianity, and Judaism constitutes the ground for that coming together. For him, the recognition of the rich diversity in the Islamic tradition constitutes a ground for acting against any single group's effort to impose one strand.

Ideologues destroy particularity even as they claim to save it, and this is one of Arkoun's objections to them. An ideologue of Iranian nationalism may be willing to overlook differences between male and female, villager and city dweller, Turkish speaker and Persian, Shi'i Muslim and Bahai and must also overlook commonalities between Iranians and other peoples. Certain particularities must be congealed and consolidated; localisms become folklore; others must be obfuscated in the interest of commonality. Islam assumes a single face, to the detriment of all other practices and versions. Such an ideological construction might well succeed in "saving" particularity, but surely many within and even without the boundaries of its appeal would not see it as their own. Such a reification of particularity becomes dehumanizing and inauthentic. Arkoun would therefore say that the foundation can only come from a totalizing of all particularities. The result, though, is necessarily an absolute: All particularities suffer relativization.

To know the truth about an entire historical movement, by grasping the totality of particulars from which it has been constituted, requires some perspective beyond that of history, just as complete knowledge of the self cannot come before a life is complete, which is at death. At death, one cannot be anyone else but an authentic person, for in that instant one can see all that one has been or has not been, all that one has imagined and all that one has not imagined. Such knowledge would provide a firm platform for action, because it would provide an authentic understanding of the self. This is why Heidegger speaks of authentic living as living with awareness of death.

Iqbal, Qutb, and Shari'ati all write mainly about life in this world, not the next, but they all share a romantic-mystical fascination with death as fulfillment of the quest for authenticity. If authenticity means being one-self in all its particularity, then the achievement of authenticity may require death. Iqbal returns time and again in his poetry to the mystical unity of the self and the absolute, a unity completed at death. No one can rob death of its personal, inward character. Shari'ati emphasizes the importance of martyrdom in the Shi'i tradition; the annual celebration in Iran of the death in 680 of Husayn, the second son of 'Ali (ibn abī ṭālib) has always been a moment of community identification and renewal. For Shari'ati, it symbolizes the revolutionary character of the Shi'i tradition, a tradition willing to encounter death on the path toward authentic life. Qutb emphasizes jihad, a struggle that might be spiritual at one point and violent at another. If authentic action to protect and expand the Islamic community requires violent action, then one cannot shy from the possibility of death. If death is the result of action deemed appropriate for the welfare of the community, it must necessarily be a thoroughly authentic outcome.

Arkoun's thought does not contain this same fascination with death as a step toward authenticity, yet his notion of grasping the totality of the Islamic experience appears to require an end to history. How can one capture the totality if it is not complete? If the experience itself continues to expand and change, does this mean that the foundation itself will change? And if that is the case, is one not required to advance yet another level and attempt to describe the dynamics of history in order to find firm footing? It is difficult to see how the footing could be firm unless the procedure were deductive, rather than inductive, and then one is back to the sort of essentialism that Arkoun and all the others resist.

To know the Islamic experience in its totality so that the resulting perspective can be regarded as a foundation for authentic action would appear to mean the cutting, drying, and mounting of all its particular dimensions. It appears to require a perfection of the anthropological-historical-semiotic craft capable of generating reliable information about every aspect of the Islamic past. Arkoun seems to have something like this in mind when he speaks about working from the Qur'anic fact and about trying to understand its path through history; he writes as if one needs to rethink all of Islamic history in some definitive way. If the "rethinking" is not definitive and must necessarily be repeated ad infinitum, then Islam itself is constantly changing and the worries of many Islamists are correct: There is nothing solid to grasp. Arkoun himself would topple over into a kind of

postmodern relativism where he does not wish to be. But a definitive outcome of "rethinking" would be synonymous with the reification of tradition by the army of scholars Arkoun would mobilize for the intellectual
battle. This is exactly what Arkoun has accused the ulema and the Islamists
of doing—of using a combination of faith and reason to buttress a single, albeit limited and partial, view of the Islamic experience in the name of a political ideology. Arkoun proposes liberalism as a response to the complexity
and multiplicity of the tradition viewed in its totality. Only if the totality
can be definitively characterized in this way can his liberalism enjoy firm
footing.

Adorno seems correct. Although the "jargon of authenticity" commits
itself to concreteness and particularity, its need for foundations drives it
toward a search for totality, abstraction, and essence.[2] To understand totality, the quest for authenticity must examine life when it is complete,
which is at death, and the totality of an experience, which is perhaps the
end of its history—the death of history—even though the search for authenticity brings with it an effort to expose old foundations and truths to
the movement of history. The fascination with death is not peculiar to Islam but to the search for authenticity.[3] The pursuit of essence and abstraction draws the adventure away from its starting point in particularity toward a sort of idealism that is precariously close to the kind of
essentialism and universalism it criticizes so heartily. The search for new
foundations means a new idealism, with all the hopes and disappointments that always accompany an optimistic approach. Of course, as has
often proved true, when hopes are dashed and disappointments begin to
multiply, such idealism often seeks scapegoats, and the specter of violence again rears its head. Such tendencies lurk within all idealistic religions, especially young and expanding ones, and thus they lurk not so
much within establishment Islam or mainstream Christianity as within
the search for authenticity.

Autonomy and History

The search for authenticity harbors another, related contradiction. Its
maxim that I must "be true to myself" implies that I am something before
I am just one more human being. I am the product of concrete circumstances and a moment in history. But the search also insists that I am a
product of my own choices. Something is mine because I choose it, and if
I choose in a manner consistent with who I am, I have made an authentic
choice. Authentic choice would thus appear, at first glance, to be highly
conservative, a way of preserving who I am. But the quest for authenticity
is anything but conservative; it asks people to rethink who they are and to
choose a new identity, a new form of political action, and a new society. It

calls for transformation by virtue of autonomous human action. This means, of course, that I can and must choose to be what I have not yet been.[4] I must confront my circumstances and my moment in history as they present themselves to me.

Acutely aware of the problem, Sayyid Qutb noted that it can be eliminated only in a genuinely Islamic community, which he said did not exist in his day. In such a genuine community, the circumstances of each individual would naturally encourage choices consistent with the circumstances, and these choices, if authentic, would merely reaffirm the direction of the community. Since Qutb declined to specify any specific institutions for such a community and instead seemed to think of Islam as a system or process for making decisions, the availability of such choice may be tautological: The individual is free to choose anything because that is the nature of the community, and anything the individual chooses will, by definition, be consistent with the open-ended nature of the community. But surely this is not what Qutb meant; the foundations he sought to restore would appear vulnerable to human assault. The other interpretation is that Qutb foresaw no conflict in an Islamic community because human beings have no choice but to choose authentic behavior. They would have been born into circumstances that would force them to make such "authentic" choices. The flavor of this interpretation is distinctly totalitarian.

Neither interpretation may be entirely fair. Qutb thought authentic choice is limited by God's instructions, of which some are universal in their applicability. The early Muslims chose to obey those instructions and to implement them in a new community, which resembled the older Arab society in an overwhelming number of particulars but differed in a few fundamental ways. The founders overcame their circumstances, and in founding a new community, they made it much easier for their progeny to follow the path of righteousness. The subsequent degradation of the Islamic community under the Umayyads and the 'Abbasids shows, however, that even leaders reared in an Islamic setting could err. The circumstances created in the initial Islamic community were not sufficient to prevent error. Individual autonomy continued to characterize Muslims. This would suggest that the conflict between circumstances and autonomy can never be definitively resolved, even in an "authentic" Islamic community.

If that is so, then an individual must dispose of a standard that permits decision about which elements of circumstance are essential to authentic living and must be preserved, which elements must be abandoned, and which are neither helpful or harmful. Islamic revelation would appear to be the standard, but not as it has been interpreted by the mainstream of Islamic discourse. Rather, one must adhere to a Qutbian view of things and abandon the culture of traditional Islam in the name of "true Islam." Much of what most believers have deemed essential turns out to be unimportant and even harmful (obedience to authority, for example). Qutb seems to propose a standard but then backs off from making concrete recommendations; a new Islamic community must establish institutions and standards consistent with the abstract principles enunciated in the Qur'an. The "true" believer is asked at one moment to abandon the living tradition of Islam in favor of Qutb's reading of that tradition and then, at a second moment, to support a newly founded community of Islam, even against individual conscience or a new Qutb. The first position squares well with human autonomy but badly with the idea that human beings are products of particular circumstances that define authentic action. The second position reverses the priorities and puts circumstance ahead of autonomy.

Qutb saw faith as the key ingredient of a "true believer"; the exercise of reason without underlying belief leads one astray. The sort of understanding Qutb himself exhibited can only come from the grace of God, and yet the presumption of choice postulates belief as an act of individual will. Qutb wrote books in the apparent hope that he could persuade others to join him in the path he was mapping. Unless he believed that human beings could rally others to form a group capable of political action, there would be little hope of human beings transforming their own circumstances. This is precisely what Qutb insists early Muslims did and what he expects of "true believers" now. If faith comes before reason and reason before action and if faith depends upon the grace of God, then human beings can do nothing worthwhile on their own. Such an assumption protects the omnipotence of God and helps explain why it is that not every person—Muslim or non-Muslim, even when confronted with the evidence Qutb lays out—will join his group. If God creates faith as a product of historical circumstances, such as Qutb's trip to America, his experience in Nasir's prisons, or the secularizing, Westernizing climate of the modern Middle East, one has an existentialist explanation for the Islamist movement that confutes Qutb's emphasis on human autonomy. Yet without help from God or circumstance, Qutb would have difficulty accounting for the formation of a group of true believers to transform the condition of Muslims.

Iqbal and Shari'ati provide somewhat more consistent accounts of individual autonomy. They speak frankly of the culture and history shaping the choices available for human choice. They both draw upon elements of their own culture to show that it opens possibilities rather than foreclosing them, but they seem much less concerned than Qutb with demonstrating that a set of choices will necessarily lead in a particular direction, such as the formation of a new Islamic community. Shari'ati certainly never claims that everyone must be Shi'i Muslim to lead an authentic life, nor does Iqbal ever suggest that Islam is the only possible religion. They see other religions as possible launching platforms for genuine, authentic individual personalities, and therefore it is ironic that both contributed, in effect, to the formation of two rather narrow and sectarian nation-states. It is difficult to imagine that either would be content with the way regimes that have emerged limit individual identity and volition.

For Iqbal and Shari'ati, Islam emerges as a path toward authenticity rather than the exclusive formula for authentic living. One who is born a Muslim must confront it, consider its formidable history, and seize upon the options it offers; in doing so, a Muslim chooses his or her own life and thereby exercises the godliness within. Non-Muslims might do similar things, because God has, after all, created a world that is one, and awareness of that fact might logically cause one to identify with that singular wholeness, rather than with the narrower circumstances into which one was born. Human beings are not autonomous unless God permits them to be free to rise above circumstance, and both Shari'ati and Iqbal, men who did precisely that, seem much more comfortable with that conclusion than Qutb, who was seeking to create and defend a new Islamic community.

For Qutb, Islam is a system by which human beings have been able to renew themselves through the formation of a group and the founding of a new community. It provides a method for this transformation. It is a tool, but it also defines the ultimate end, a community in which individuals can be true believers without conflict, in a way that Qutb does not thoroughly specify. The secularization of Islam is even more pronounced in Iqbal and Shari'ati, who see it as one means for individuals to transcend their own circumstances, including Islam itself. God has left human beings completely free to make their own destiny, and therefore there cannot be any necessary outcome, such as the formation of a specific Islamic community. Autonomy defeats necessity, whether that necessity is Marxist, developmental, or religious.

Whereas Qutb, Shari'ati, and Iqbal all see human autonomy as exercised within a set of given constraints, Arkoun sees the constraints themselves as chosen. All human beings make decisions in the light of the images they hold of themselves, their surroundings, and other peoples. The images themselves are a product not just of physical circumstances and social setting but of previous thoughts and choices. Myths necessarily constitute important elements in all these images, but the myths are themselves a product of the human imagination. Decisions also reflect social, economic, and political situations. Thus, when Arkoun approaches the question of human rights in Islam or the understanding of human autonomy, he examines the development of these ideas as a product of human choices under given circumstances of geography and power and within the prevailing "imaginary" of the time and place. Insofar as one comes to understand how and why choices have been made, the realm of choice expands to include many understandings and practices, many practical attitudes toward Islam; and one also understands that there cannot be any way of legitimating any single set of choices. Every person has a right to "own" his or her choices, and no one therefore has a right to impose his or her "own" choices on others. For Arkoun, liberal democracy reemerges not because the Qur'an recommends it or because the West has enjoyed some success with it but because it protects human autonomy, which is itself rooted in the ability to study and discuss the choices human beings have made. Liberalism protects scholarship, and scholarship enables choice.

Arkoun's idealism shines through in his defense of scholarship conducted in a liberal democratic atmosphere, which he sees not just as another culturally conditioned choice but as an avenue to conserving and preserving choice. It constitutes the foundation, the criterion for authentic living and decision, the defense against arbitrary, exclusive definitions of truth (he would put Qutb's definition in that category) and against postmodern relativism. The Muslim world can be itself, in Arkoun's view, by understanding and respecting all of what it has been and by permitting all Muslims to choose what they want to be.

The plausibility of Arkoun's view depends on an insistence among all advocates of authenticity that one's experience must be one's "own." "Ownness" must either reflect what one is as a product of circumstances or what one chooses. It may be both, if one chooses to keep at least elements of one's circumstances and past. To make that choice intelligently, one must know everything possible about one's past, and that means, for Muslims, the sort of Islamology that Arkoun advocates. Islamology leads to an understanding of the entire Muslim experience; all Muslims own the whole tradition, and hence authentic decision requires a choice of what is "mine" that respects all other choices. His ideal is "ownness" based on free and enlightened choice.

If there is necessity in Arkoun's understanding of things, it comes from the progress of scholarship. The human sciences produce an ever more sophisticated understanding of revelation, text, images, economics, society, and history, and such progress expands the range of effective human choice. Recent history is a story of increasing human autonomy. Knowledge of history generates some capacity for guidance and control.

But knowledge may also, quite to the contrary, undermine several sorts of necessity—religious, economic, geographical—and reveal history as a set of semiarbitrary choices, later sanctified by doctrine. Arkoun would certainly concur with that judgment, and acknowledge that the Arkounian foundation does not provide much impulse, much direction, much practical guidance for those who would make their way. Autonomy leaves human beings free to go just about anywhere they wish. If Muslims come to understand their ties to other societies of the Book and their links to Mediterranean culture, these changes might occasion practical political consequences in the long run.

The new foundation that Arkoun attempts to construct does not appear to owe anything to Islam. When he observes that Westerners have exaggerated the secular nature of Western democracies, which in fact continue to pay heavy debts to the Christian religion, he prepares the way for a democracy that is heavily dependent on Islam. But his defense of choice, scholarship, and democracy is not Islamic. He discovers a new foundation not in the Sunna or the Qur'an but in knowledge of the development of the Sunna and the Qur'an. In seeking to expand our understanding of revelation and the importance of symbolism in human behavior, he makes Islam the object of study and reflection and not the source of ultimate wisdom or even methodology, as Iqbal, Shari'ati, and Qutb do in varying degrees. But he does attempt to specify how a Muslim, the product of the Islamic tradition, can live in a truthful, authentic way. As with Iqbal and Shari'ati, the path itself need not be Islamic; Arkoun would not exclude non-Muslims from the possibility of authentic existence.

As for democracy, Arkoun defends it not as a good but as a means of preserving another good, which is choice. Scholarship in a liberal environment expands the array of available choices by providing a nuanced view of the entire Islamic experience. Democracy is the means by which a people then exercise choice within the limits imposed by liberalism. Neither democracy nor liberalism comes from the Islamic tradition, in his view, but they are not the possessions of the Western tradition, either. In fact, he notes quite accurately that the erosion of essentialist liberal thought in the West has undermined the foundations of liberal democracy. Cut loose from their moorings, liberal institutions must be defended everywhere in pragmatic terms, as Arkoun proposes. Such institutions permit the achievement of authentic living in every cultural setting and are unique to none. They are neither the product of Western essentialism, for this would violate Arkoun's wish to begin from existence and particularity, nor a product of historical necessity, which would violate his assumption about human autonomy. Neither necessary nor essential from that perspective, they turn out to be fundamental to what Arkoun regards as the construction of new foundations. But can one defend ideals in a world without ideals? Arkoun raises this issue in his observations about the West, where idealism has fallen on hard times, and again when he argues for liberal democracies in a broader cultural setting.

What is the proper scale of such democracies? Arkoun expresses concern for the welfare of subnational groups, acknowledges the contemporary power of nation-states, works actively to revive the concept of Mediterranean culture, advocates analysis of the impact of revelation on societies of the Book and, of course, speaks of the totality of the Islamic experience. All five levels constitute foundations, and he does not unambiguously endorse one at the expense of all others.

The other writers examined here are only somewhat less ambivalent about the scale of politics. Iqbal's "sense of self" carried him from the scale of the individual to that of all Muslims and even all humanity; he criticized nation-states and then embraced the emerging idea of a separate Muslim community in India. Qutb wrote extensively about the creation of the *umma* but in fact probably aimed his ideas at the Egyptian community. Shari'ati extolled the qualities of Iranian Shi'ism but saw Islam as a route toward the realization of human potential.

Unlike liberal thought, which tends to begin from a hypothesis about human beings in a "state of nature," unscathed by culture, the advocates of authenticity all insist that human beings are products of a past that reflects a variety of collective experiences. Identities depend upon these ethnic, linguistic, social, economic, and political experiences of the past. In the liberal scheme of things, political communities appear to be natural and beyond analysis; a group of people gets together, considers the common welfare, and forms a civil society, as Locke would say. (Locke acknowledges that they could be quite divided on the point of religion.) In the logic of authenticity, people choose that which is "theirs," a part of their cultural experience; certain sorts of political groupings necessarily take precedence over others. Iqbal, Qutb, Shari'ati, and Arkoun all demonstrate the plausibility of bonds. All imply the need for fresh political foundations that would reflect the quest for authenticity.

In this they follow a pattern established elsewhere. The early articulations of "authentic" German culture sought to diminish the universality of the French Enlightenment and to extol "natural" German affinities. Rousseau certainly saw himself as a champion of politics on a smaller scale. Senghor's theory of *négritude*, Fanon's advocacy of violence as a means of restoring identity, and Gutierrez's notion of liberation theology are all, in part, arguments about the proper scale of politics. As Adorno has said, the jargon of authenticity embraces localism.[5]

Yet by virtue of the complications inherent in the case for authenticity, no scale is preemptive of all others. No author studied here makes an unambiguous case for the nation-state, which is, after all, a European concept. No one vaunts the Islamic community above all else, a concept that tends to ignore the contemporary ethnic, political, and socioeconomic solidarities most likely to spark the group action Qutb wants. No one ignores either the individual or humanity as a whole as relevant political units. The logic of authenticity does not—perhaps cannot—specify an "authentic" scale for politics, however much it purports to speak about questions of scale.[6]

Most liberal theory assumes political communities are naturally occurring phenomena to be discovered by observation. Little is said about the groups of people who come together to form them. Theories of nationalism supply support for such notions, and these theories hark back to some of the same ideals, such as "self-realization" and "self-determination," that the logic of authenticity invokes, but these ideas of naturalness never did square well with the realities of the Middle East. The efforts of Husayn, sharif of Mecca, to found an "Arab state" (without Egypt) at the end of World War I rang almost as hollow as European efforts to use and abuse the idea of self-determination. The logic of authenticity underlay all these machinations; the logic was not convincing then, and it is not convincing now.

On the one hand, the quest for authenticity requires a scale of politics that conforms to what is legitimately ours rather than theirs, a part of our experience, a reflection of what is local and meaningful. On the other hand, it requires that a political community reflect choice. The first criterion implies naturalness, but the second does not. The first could be used to incite revolt against imperialism and the nation-states imperialism established in the Middle East. The second implies any scale as long as it is ratified by choice. Liberal theory coupled with nationalism suffers from the same malady. The logic of authenticity provides no solution but may, indeed, complicate the problem by emphasizing particularity at the expense of "national" groupings, nationalism at the expense of internationalism, localism at the expense of universalism. Of course, these tendencies also constitute a part of the appeal.

Islam, Authenticity, and Modernity

In a world where uniformity threatens local customs and identities, the call for authenticity reverberates with some success. In response to the superficiality of modern life, authenticity offers the promise of penetrating to what is primal. Where modern life seems a product of forces beyond the control of individual human beings and small, impotent political entities, authenticity evokes self-determination and choice. Against the forces of science and reason so dominant in the contemporary world, authenticity reelevates the irrationalities of condition and belief to determinant roles. The call to authenticity, whether issued by Jean-Jacques Rousseau or Sayyid Qutb, constitutes a response to the dilemmas of modernity. Authenticity carries no meaning except in a context in which modernity has eroded cultures, values, and identities without repairing what has been damaged. The advocates of authenticity would attempt a repair.

If this analysis is correct, then Islam cannot be regarded as either the primary cause of the problem or a necessary source of solutions. The

problem has afflicted Christian, Muslim, and other cultures rather indis-
criminately, and the proposed solutions have ranged from the explicitly
religious to the Nietzschean diatribes against established religion. Islam
becomes an issue by virtue of its domination of cultural patterns in certain countries and by virtue of the propensities for particularism inherent
in the search for authenticity. It therefore becomes both a part of the problem and, potentially, a part of the solution at this secondary level.

Much of the contemporary Islamist movement can be interpreted as a
particularistic effort to solve a general problem in a manner that is faithful
to Islamic particularism. Kierkegaard sought to do something analogous
within the Christian context, whereas other European philosophers have
sought to solve the problem of particularism in a manner faithful to any
and all particularisms simultaneously. Of course, none of the Muslim proponents is entirely indifferent to the more general problem, and Arkoun,
most prominently, is quite acutely aware of it.

The four writers studied here do not represent all the strands of the
contemporary Islamist movement. It would be difficult to gather sufficient data to demonstrate that the entire Islamist movement can be con-
strued as a reaction to modernism and a part of the search for authenticity, although some writers have become even more explicit than Shari'ati
in articulating the need to define authenticity. From Iqbal to Hasan
Hanafi, there would appear to be a rather clear progression of thought.

If this is so, then much of the so-called Islamic revival finds its explanation not in Islam but in a set of modern circumstances that Islam has been
called upon to address. The Islamist movement should perhaps inspire
fear, not because it is Islamic but because it is wrestling with the same
problems as Nietzsche and Heidegger and coming up with some analogous remedies. It should inspire respect precisely because it is providing,
albeit with mixed success or even failure, not one solution but a set of solutions that may conceivably come to guide Muslims and non-Muslims
alike as they confront these problems. To read Iqbal, Qutb, Shari'ati, and
Arkoun is not just to read about Islam; it is to read about the human condition, even though the vocabulary is unfamiliar to many Westerners. In
fact, these writers alert us to issues of religion and politics that have often
been ignored in a West where secularism is said to prevail, although the
empirical study of politics demonstrates the hypocrisy of that view. Unlike many moderns, these writers take religion seriously; their religion
happens to be Islam, and therefore Islam is their vehicle in the search for a
new politics.

It may well turn out that these writers and others have, by looking to Islam as a solution to current psychological, social, economic, and political
problems, contributed to the secularization of the religion. Insofar as Islam
constitutes a realm of the sacred preserved by the ulema and used by indi-

viduals seeking inner fortitude, it may be largely irrelevant to political life. (This is the Western notion of secularism, which has never been fully realized.) But insofar as Islam has come to constitute the very terms of debate in the search for new foundations in political life, it may increasingly find itself sacrificing the notion of the sacred to questions of power.[7] What does the majority say on these matters? Postrevolutionary Iran appears to be in this position, and some members of the clergy are uneasy. Religion is a factor in almost every political debate, even more than in the West. The arguments these four writers advance are not, in the end, religious arguments; their persuasiveness depends not on the intrinsic nature of Islam but on whether they help Muslims with problems engendered by modernity, problems encapsulated in the word "authenticity." Religion, for all of them, is a positive or negative force, depending on its impact on the society. The religion of the ulema gets bad reviews because it props up an evil regime and condones laws deemed unhealthy; the religion of the peasants, steeped in superstition, could disappear without regret for its passivity toward politics and its de facto embrace of the status quo. Only Arkoun finds room for every conceivable variant of Islam within his tent, but he sees a more thorough knowledge of Islam not just as a value in itself but as a vehicle for remaking the map of the world through the reformulation of collective imaginaries. All four writers see Islam as a means toward a set of collective goals they deem desirable.

Their goals include the refounding of political life. The quest for authenticity is a search for foundations, or perhaps it is, more precisely, an effort to create foundations. The presumption of human autonomy means that political foundations necessarily reflect human effort, but the need for solidity implies that human efforts must necessarily be cloaked so that they rise above ordinary human actions and become the bases of subsequent human decisions. These theories of authenticity need authentication, if they are to become foundations and influence the course of affairs, and Islam cannot provide that authentication as long as the parameters within which these writers work are not altered: They all concur that God does not intervene in the unfolding of human affairs. They propound timebound propositions about how human beings should understand their condition and act to alter those specific conditions. These authors would not suppose that the timeless, unchanging, eternal God would violate those characteristics to prefer one or another approach to authenticity. Authentication must therefore come from the human sphere. Iqbal and Arkoun appear to seek it primarily from the cultural and intellectual elites; Qutb and Shari'ati look to the masses. However, the quest for authenticity springs from confusion among both elites and masses about identity, values, and goals. The perpetual shortage of political legitimacy in the Arab world reflects this confusion, which the search for authenticity would seek to remedy. Instead, it can be a remedy only if these very groups, divided and confused, can be rallied to authenticate one or another theory of authenticity. To judge by the number of groups inspired by his thought, Sayyid Qutb has had the most success, but those he has inspired have found themselves at odds with the mainstream in Egypt and elsewhere. How does one prove that a minority is right? Would a majority be sufficient to ratify his ideas? How does one ratify that proposition? Arkoun's ideas seem unlikely to muster general support in an academic community where idealism is suspect and skepticism widespread. He would surely prefer scientific to popular validation, but the notion that science is somehow self-validating disappeared with logical positivism.

The search for authenticity ultimately founders on this point of validation, which Islam cannot provide. Islam cannot validate a particular reading of Islam. God cannot provide validation without becoming something other than the transcendent God these writers describe. Philosophy is the only means by which these ideas can be sustained, but, like European advocates of authenticity, these authors have doubts about adopting reason and logical coherence as the sole criterion for philosophical reflection; they entertain the possibility that the irrational may enjoy equal truth status with the rational, and as a result, they find themselves struggling to avoid subjectivism. This struggle is not peculiar to either East or West, Islam or Christianity, Buddhism or agnosticism. It is a general human problem of the twentieth century. It would be as wrong to disregard these attempts at solution because they invoke Islam (and therefore speak in a way many see as irrelevant, if not hostile, to non-Muslims) as it would be to take them at face value merely because they invoke Islam (and therefore speak "truth" or at least a language most Muslims can understand and some will inevitably embrace.) Yet many in the East and the West alike assume one or the other of these attitudes, losing sight of the broader search for authenticity in which much of the world is engaged. To the contrary, by taking the quest for authenticity as a condition of politics the world over, one may uncover common ground that might be used to bridge the great cultural chasms that some writers[8] (including proponents of authenticity) now assert are fundamental to the human condition.

Notes

1. See Erika Friedel, *Women of Deh Koh: Lives in an Iranian Village* (New York: Penguin, 1991).

2. Theodor W. Adorno, *The Jargon of Authenticity*, trans. Knut Tarnowski and Frederic Will (Evanston, Ill.: Northwestern University Press, 1973), p. 93.

3. See Adorno's discussion of Heidegger in ibid., p. 152, "Authenticity is death."

4. See ibid., p. 60.

5. Ibid., p. 59. Mehrzad Boroujerdi has written about the nativistic tendencies of Shar'iati and others in *Iranian Intellectuals and the West: The Tormented Triumph of Nativism* (Syracuse, N.Y.: Syracuse University Press, 1996).

6. Hasan Turabi, speaking about the Sudan, has expressed precisely the same sort of ambivalence, saying, for example: "The elites are moving away from nationalist to Islamist slogans and aspirations. . . . Already, we are moving toward a synthesis. Islam does not transcend completely and absolutely one's allegiance to the immediate involvement. You are entitled as a Muslim to relate to your neighborhood, to your family, to your people, to your nation, provided you don't become introverted, and you don't become chauvinistically nationalist. . . . As long as you are open, Islam is not necessarily against that measure of nationalism or that measure of loyalty to one's place, one's country, one's fatherland, as long as you also relate to the *Dar al-Islam*, to all the Muslims and then to the whole earth on which all of us live." In Hasan Turabi, *Islam, Democracy, the State, and the West: A Round Table with Dr. Hasan Turabi*, ed. Arthur L. Lowrie (Tampa, Fla.: World and Islam Studies Enterprise, 1993), p. 78.

7. See Dale F. Eickleman and James Piscatori, *Muslim Politics* (Princeton: Princeton University Press, 1996), for an excellent treatment of these issues.

8. Samuel Huntington, for example.

Selected Bibliography

Abedi, Mehbi. "Ali Shariati: The Architect of the 1979 Islamic Revolution of Iran." *Iranian Studies* 19 (1986), pp. 229–234.

Abubaker, Muhammad A. "Sayyid Qutb's Interpretation of the Islamic View of Literature." *Islamic Studies* 23, 2 (Summer 1984), pp. 57–65.

Adorno, Theodor W. *The Jargon of Authenticity.* Translated by Knut Tarnowski and Frederic Will. Evanston, Ill.: Northwestern University Press, 1973.

Ahmed, Akbar S. *Postmodernism and Islam: Predicament and Promise.* London: Routledge, 1992.

Ajami, Fouad. "The Impossible Life of Moslem Liberalism: The Doctrines of Ali Shariati and Their Defeat." *New Republic,* June 2, 1986.

Ajami, Fouad. *The Arab Predicament.* Cambridge: Cambridge University Press, 1981.

Akhavi, Shahrough. "Shari'ati's Social Thought." In *Religion and Politics in Iran,* edited by Nikki R. Keddie. New Haven: Yale, 1983.

Almond, Gabriel, and G. Bingham Powell, Jr. *Comparative Politics: A Developmental Approach.* Boston: Little, Brown, 1966.

Anderson, Benedict. *Imagined Communities: Reflections on the Origin and Spread of Nationalism.* London: Verso, 1983.

Ansell-Pearson, Keith. "Nietzsche on Autonomy and Morality: The Challenge to Political Theory." *Political Studies* 39 (1991), pp. 270–286.

Apter, David E. *The Politics of Modernization.* Chicago: University of Chicago Press, 1965.

Arkoun, Mohammed. "The Concept of Authority in Islamic Thought." In *The Islamic World from Classical to Modern Times: Essays in Honor of Bernard Lewis.* Princeton: Darwin Press, 1989.

Arkoun, Mohammed. "Discours islamiques, discours orientalistes et pensée scientifique." In *As Others See Us: Mutual Perceptions, East and West,* edited by Bernard Lewis. Special issue of *Comparative Civilization Review,* nos. 13–14 (1985–1986).

Arkoun, Mohammed. *Essais sur la pensée islamique.* 3d ed. Paris: Maisonneuve et Larose, 1984.

Arkoun, Mohammed. "Imaginaire social et leaders dans le monde musulman contemporain." *Arabica* 35 (1988), pp. 18–35.

Arkoun, Mohammed. "Islam: Les expressions de l'Islam." In *Encyclopaedia Universalis,* pp. 108–212. Paris: Encyclopaedia Universalis France, Supplement for 1983.

Arkoun, Mohammed. "Islamic Culture, Modernity, and Architecture." In *Architecture Education in the Islamic World.* Geneva: The Aga Award for Architecture, 1986.

Arkoun, Mohammed. *La pensée arabe.* Paris: Presses Universitaires, 1975.

Arkoun, Mohammed. *Lectures du Coran.* Paris: Maisonneuve et Larose, 1982.

Arkoun, Mohammed. "Les fondements arabo-islamique de la culture maghrébine." In *Gli interscambi culturali e socio-economici fra l'Africa settentrionale e l'Europa Mediterranea,* Atti del Congresso Internazaionle de Amalfi, December 5–8, 1983, pp. 741–759.

Arkoun, Mohammed. *L'humanisme arabe au IVᵉ/Xᵉ siècle: Miskawayh philosophe et historien.* 2d ed. Paris: J. Vrin, 1982.

Arkoun, Mohammed. *L'Islam: Morale et politique.* Paris: Desclée de Brouwer, 1986.

Arkoun, Mohammed. "The Notion of Revelation: From Ahl al-Kitab to the Societies of the Book." *Die Welt des Islams* 28 (1988), pp. 62–81.

Arkoun, Mohammed. "Positivisme et tradition dans une perspective islamique: Le cas du Kémalisme." *Diogène* 127 (July-September 1984), pp. 89–107.

Arkoun, Mohammed. *Pour une critique de la raison islamique.* Paris: Maisonneuve et Larose, 1984.

Arkoun, Mohammed. "Rethinking Islam Today." Occasional Papers Series, Center for Contemporary Arab Studies, Georgetown University, 1987.

Arkoun, Mohammed. *Rethinking Islam: Common Questions, Uncommon Answers.* Translated and edited by Robert D. Lee. Boulder: Westview, 1994. (*Ouvertures sur l'Islam.* Paris: J. Grancher, 1989 and 1992.)

Arkoun, Mohammed. "Society, State and Religion in Algeria (1962–1985)." In *The Politics of Islamic Revivalism,* edited by by Shireen T. Hunter. Bloomington: Indiana University Press, 1988.

Arkoun, Mohammed. "The Topicality of the Problem of the Person in Islamic Thought." *International Social Science Journal* 117 (August 1988), pp. 407–422.

Arkoun, Mohammed. "The Unity of Man in Islamic Thought." Translated by R. Scott Walker. *Diogenes* 140 (1987), pp. 50–69.

Arkoun, Mohammed, and Louis Gardet. *L'Islam: Hier. Demain.* Paris: Buchet/Chastel, 1978.

Barakat, Halim. *The Arab World: Society, Culture, and State.* Berkeley: University of California Press, 1993.

Bastide, Georges. "La notion d'authenticité." *Diotima* 9 (1981), pp. 134–136.

Bauer, P. T. *Dissent on Development.* Cambridge: Harvard University Press, 1976.

Beaufret, Jean. *Introduction aux philosophes de l'existence.* Paris: Denoël, 1971.

Bell, Linda A. *Sartre's Ethics of Authenticity.* Tuscaloosa: University of Alabama Press, 1989.

Bellamy, Richard, and Darrow Schecter. *Gramsci and the Italian State.* Manchester: Manchester University Press, 1993.

Bennabi, Malek. *Vocation de l'Islam.* Paris: Seuil, 1954.

Benot, Yves. *Qu'est-ce que le développement?* Paris: François Maspero, 1973.

Benson, Steven R. "Islam and Social Change in the Writings of 'Alī Sharī'atī: His *Hajj* as a Mystical Handbook for Revolutionaries." *Muslim World* 81 (1991), pp. 9–26.

Berger, Peter. *Pyramids of Sacrifice.* Garden City, N.Y.: Anchor, 1976.

Berman, Marshall. *The Politics of Authenticity.* New York: Atheneum, 1970.

Berque, Jacques. *L'Islam au défi.* Paris: Gallimard, 1980.

Berque, Jacques. *Langages arabes du présent.* Paris: Gallimard, 1980.

Binder, Leonard. *Islamic Liberalism: A Critique of Development Ideologies*. Chicago: University of Chicago Press, 1988.

Bloom, Allan. *The Closing of the American Mind*. New York: Simon and Schuster, 1987.

Boggs, Carl. *Gramsci's Marxism*. London: Pluto, 1976.

Boisard, Marcel A. *L'humanisme de l'Islam*. Paris: Albin Michel, 1979.

Bonino, Jose Miguez. *Doing Theology in a Revolutionary Situation*. Philadelphia: Fortress, 1975.

Boroujerdi, Mehrzad. *Iranian Intellectuals and the West: The Tormented Triumph of Nativism*. Syracuse, N.Y.: Syracuse University Press, 1996.

Bouhdiba, Abdelwahab. *A la recherche des normes perdues*. Tunis: Maison Tunisienne de l'Edition, 1973.

Boullata, Issa J. *Trends and Issues in Contemporary Arab Thought*. Albany: SUNY Press, 1990.

Bourdieu, Pierre. *L'ontologie politique de Martin Heidegger*. Paris: Editions de Minuit, 1988.

Broccoli, Angelo. *Antonio Gramsci e l'educazione come egemonia*. Firenze: La Nuova Italia, 1972.

Brubaker, Rogers. *The Limits of Rationality: An Essay on the Social and Moral Thought of Max Weber*. London: Allen and Unwin, 1984.

Carré, Olivier. *La légitimation islamique des socialismes arabes*. Paris: Fondation Nationale des Sciences Politiques, 1979.

Carré, Olivier. "Le combat-pour-Dieu et l'état islamique chez Sayyid Qotb, l'inspirateur du radicalisme islamique actuel." *Revue française de science politique*, 33, 4 (August 1983), pp. 680–703.

Carré, Olivier. *Mystique et politique: Lecture révolutionnaire du Coran par Sayyid Qutb, frère musulman radical*. Paris: Editions du Cerf, 1984.

Charmé, Stuart Zane. *Vulgarity and Authenticity: Dimensions of Otherness in the World of Jean-Paul Sartre*. Amherst: University of Massachusetts Press, 1991.

Chehabi, Houchang Esfandiar. "Modernist Shi'ism and Politics: The Liberation Movement of Iran." Ph.D. diss., Yale University, 1986.

Cockcroft, James D., André Gunder Frank, and Dale L. Johnson. *Dependence and Underdevelopment*. Garden City, N.Y.: Doubleday, 1972.

Crowther, Paul. "Autonomy and Authenticity: A Prelude to Educational Hermeneutics." *Educational Philosophy and Theory* 13 (March 1981), pp. 15–22.

Dahl, Robert. *Polyarchy*. New Haven: Yale University Press, 1976.

Dar, Bashir Ahmad. *Iqbal and Post-Kantian Voluntarism*. Lahore: Bazm-Iqbal, 1956.

Dar, Bashir Ahmad. *A Study in Iqbal's Philosophy*. Lahore: Ghillam Ali, 1971.

Deutsch, Karl. "Social Mobilization and Political Development." *American Political Science Review* 55 (September 1961), pp. 493–514.

Djaït, Hichem. *La personnalité et le devenir arabo-islamiques*. Paris: Seuil, 1974.

Djaït, Hichem. *L'Europe et l'Islam*. Paris: Seuil, 1978.

Duverger, Maurice. *Political Parties: Their Organization and Activity in the Modern State*. 2d rev. ed. Translated by Barbara and Robert North. London: Methuen, 1959.

Duvignaud, Jean. *Change at Shebika*. Translated by Frances Frenaye. Austin: University of Texas Press, 1977.

Eickleman, Dale F., and James Piscatori. *Muslim Politics*. Princeton: Princeton University Press, 1996.

Eisenstadt, S. N. *Modernization: Protest and Change*. Englewood Cliffs, N.J.: Prentice-Hall, 1966.

Emerson, Rupert. *From Empire to Nation*. Boston: Beacon, 1960.

Esposito, John. *The Islamic Threat: Myth or Reality?* New York: Oxford, 1992.

Esposito, John, ed. *Voices of Resurgent Islam*. New York: Oxford University Press, 1983.

Etienne, Bruno. *L'islamisme radical*. Paris: Hachette, 1987.

Ferrara, Alessandro. *Modernity and Authenticity: A Study in the Social and Ethical Thought of Jean-Jacques Rousseau*. Albany: SUNY Press, 1993.

Friedel, Erika. *Women of Deh Koh: Lives in an Iranian Village*. New York: Penguin, 1991.

Gellner, Ernest. *Muslim Society*. Cambridge: Cambridge Uuniversity Press, 1981.

Gellner, Ernest. *Nations and Nationalism*. Ithaca: Cornell University Press, 1983.

Gellner, Ernest. *Postmodernism, Reason, and Religion*. London: Routledge, 1992.

Germino, Dante. *Antonio Gramsci: Architect of a New Politics*. Baton Rouge: Louisiana State University Press, 1990.

Gramsci, Antonio. *Il materialismo storico e la filosofia di Benedetto Croce*. Torino: Edizioni Riuniti, 1975.

Gramsci, Antonio. *The Modern Prince and Other Writings*. New York: International Publishers, 1978.

Gramsci, Antonio. *Note sul Machiavelli, sulla politica e sullo stato moderno*. Torino: Edizioni Riuniti, 1979.

Grimm, Ruediger H. *Nietzsche's Theory of Knowledge*. Berlin: W. de Gruyter, 1977.

Gruppi, Luciano. *Il concetto di egemonia in Gramsci*. Roma: Editori Riuniti, 1972.

Gutierrez, Gustavo. *A Theology of Liberation*. Maryknoll, N.Y.: Orbis, 1973.

Haddad, Yvonne. *Contemporary Islam and the Challenge of History*. Albany: SUNY Press, 1982.

Haddad, Yvonne Yazbeck. "The Qur'anic Justification for an Islamic Revolution: The View of Sayyid Qutb." *Middle East Journal* 37, 1 (Winter 1993), pp. 14–28.

Haim, Sylvia G. "Sayyid Qutb." *Asian and African Studies* 16 (1982), pp. 147–156.

Halpern, Manfred. *Social Change in the Middle East and North Africa*. Princeton: Princeton University Press, 1963.

Hanafi, Hasan. *Al-turāth wal tajdīd*. Cairo: Al-markaz al-'arabī lil bahth wal nashr, 1980.

Hanafi, Hassan. *Religious Dialogue and Revolution: Essays on Judaism, Christianity, and Islam*. Cairo: Anglo-Egyptian Bookshop, n.d.

Hanafi, Hasan. "Una nuova tendenza dell'Islam sunnita." *Le monde diplomatique*, 281 (1977). Reprinted in *Islam, politica e società*. Torino: Tirrenia, 1979, pp. 71–86.

Haq, Mahbub ul-. *The Poverty Curtain: Choices for the Third World*. New York: Columbia University Press, 1976.

Harper, Ralph. *The Seventh Solitude: Man's Isolation in Kierkegaard, Dostoevsky, and Nietzsche*. Baltimore: Johns Hopkins University Press, 1965.

Heckle, Patrizia Longo. *The Statue of Glaucus: Rousseau's Modern Quest for Authenticity*. New York: Peter Lang, 1991.

Heidegger, Martin. *Being and Time*. Translated by John Acquarrie and Edward Robinson. New York: Harper, 1962.

Heidegger, Martin. *The Question Concerning Technology*. Edited and translated by William Lovitt. New York: Harper and Row, 1977.

Herf, Jeffrey. *Reactionary Modernism*. Cambridge: Cambridge University Press, 1984.

Hirsch, Fred. *Social Limits to Growth*. Cambridge: Harvard University Press, 1976.

Hitti, Philip. *Islam: A Way of Life*. Chicago: University of Minnesota Press, 1970.

Hourani, Albert. *Arabic Thought in the Liberal Age, 1798–1939*. Cambridge: Cambridge University Press, 1983.

Hourani, Albert. *Islam in European Thought*. Cambridge: Cambridge University Press, 1991.

Hudson, Michael C. *Arab Politics: The Search for Legitimacy*. New Haven: Yale University Press, 1977.

Huntington, Samuel. "The Clash of Civilizations." *Foreign Affairs* 72, 3 (Summer 1993), pp. 22–49.

Huntington, Samuel. *Political Order in Changing Societies*. New Haven: Yale University Press, 1968.

Ibn Khaldun. *The Muqaddimah: An Introduction to History*. Translated by Franz Rosenthal. Princeton: Princeton University Press, 1967.

ILO International Labour Office. *Employment, Growth, and Basic Needs*. New York: Praeger, 1977.

Iqbal as a Thinker. Lahore: Ashraf, 1944.

Iqbal, Mohamed. *Thoughts and Reflections of Iqbal*. Edited by Syed Abdul Vahid. Lahore: Ashraf, 1964.

Iqbal, Mohammad. *Secrets of the Self: A Philosophical Poem*. Translated by R. A. Nicholson. New Delhi: Arnold-Heinemann, 1978.

Iqbal, Muhammad. *The Development of Metaphysics in Persia: A Contribution to the History of Muslim Philosophy*. Lahore: Bazm-Iqbal, 1959.

Iqbal, Muhammad. *Javid-Nama*. Translated by Arthur J. Arberry. London: Allen and Unwin, 1966.

Iqbal, Muhammad. *The Mysteries of Selflessness*. Translated by Arthur J. Arberry. London: Murray, 1953.

Iqbal, Muhammad. *Poems from Iqbal*. Translated by V. G. Kiernan. London: Murray, 1955.

Iqbal, Muhammad. *The Reconstruction of Religious Thought in Islam*. Lahore: Ashraf, 1982.

Iqbal, Muhammad. *Shikwa and Jawab-i-Shikwa: Complaint and Answer, Iqbal's Dialogue with Allah*. Translated by Khushwant Singh. Delhi: Oxford, 1981.

Jansen, Johannes J. G. *The Neglected Duty: The Creed of Sadat's Assassins: Islamic Resurgence in the Middle East*. New York: Macmillan, 1986.

Juergensmeyer, Mark. *The New Cold War? Religious Nationalism Confronts the Secular State*. Berkeley: University of California Press, 1993.

Kautsky, John H. *The Political Consequences of Modernization*. New York: John Wiley and Sons, 1972.

Keddie, Nikki, with a section by Yann Richard. *Roots of Revolution*. New Haven: Yale University Press, 1981.

Keddie, Nikki R., ed. *Religion and Politics in Iran*. New Haven: Yale University Press, 1983.

Kedourie, Elie. "Minorities and Majorities in the Middle East." *Archives européenes de sociologie* 25 (1984), pp. 276–282.

Kedourie, Elie. *Nationalism*. London: Hutchinson, 1960.

Kemal, S. "Some Problems of Genealogy." *Nietzsche-Studien* 19 (1990), pp. 30–42.

Kepel, Gilles. *Le prophète et pharaon: Les mouvements islamistes dans l'Egypte contemporaine*. Paris: La Découverte, 1984. (*Muslim Extremism in Egypt: The Prophet and Pharaoh*, translated by Jon Rothschild. Berkeley: University of California Press, 1993.)

Kerr, Malcolm. *Islamic Studies: A Tradition and Its Problems*. Malibu, Calif.: Undena, 1980.

Kerr, Malcolm H. *Islamic Reform: The Political and Legal Theories of Muhammad 'Abduh and Rashid Rida*. Berkeley: University of California Press, 1966.

Khomeini, Ruhollah. *Islam and Revolution: Writings and Declarations of Imam Khomeini*. Translated and annotated by Hamid Algar. Berkeley: Mizan, 1981.

Khwaja, Jamal. *Authenticity and Islamic Liberalism*. New Delhi: Allied Publishers, 1987.

Kierkegaard, Sören. *Fear and Trembling: A Dialectical Lyric*. Translated by Walter Lowrie. Princeton: Princeton University Press, 1941.

Kierkegaard, Sören. *Philosophical Fragments or a Fragment of Philosophy*. Translated by David F. Swenson and Howard V. Hong. Princeton: Princeton University Press, 1962.

Kierkegaard, Sören. *Two Ages: The Age of Revolution and the Present Age*. Edited and translated by Howard V. Hong and Edna H. Hong. Princeton: Princeton University Press, 1978.

Kotb, Sayed [Sayyid Qutb]. *Social Justice in Islam*. Translated by John B. Hardie. New York: Octagon, 1953.

Krailsheimer, Alban. *Pascal*. Oxford: Oxford University Press, 1980.

Kuhry, Robert. *Authenticity: The Being of the Self, the World, and the Other*. Saratoga, Calif.: R and E Publishers, 1992.

La Spisa, Mauro. *Fede e Scandolo nei diari di S. A. Kierkegaard*. Firenze: GeG, 1970.

Laroui, Abdallah. "Antistoricismo ed egemonia culturale." In *La coscienza dell-altro*, edited by Liliana Magrini. Firenze: Cultura, 1974.

Laroui, Abdallah. *The Crisis of the Arab Intellectual*. Translated by Diarmid Cammell. Berkeley: University of California Press, 1976.

Laroui, Abdallah. *L'idéologie arabe contemporaine*. Paris: François Maspero, 1977.

Lehman, David, ed. *Development Theory: Four Critical Studies*. London: Frank Cass, 1979.

Lerman, Eran. "Mawdudi's Concept of Islam." *Middle Eastern Studies* 17, 4 (October 1981), pp. 492–509.

Lerner, Daniel. *The Passing of Traditional Society*. Glencoe, Ill.: Free Press, 1964.

Léveillé-Mourin, Geneviève. *Le langage chrétien, antichrétien de la transcendance: Pascal-Nietzsche*. Paris: J. Vrin, 1978.

Lipset, Seymour Martin. *Political Man*. Garden City, N.Y.: Doubleday, 1960.

Lukes, Steven. *Essays in Social Theory*. New York: Columbia University Press, 1977.

Lukes, Steven. *Individualism*. Oxford: Blackwell, 1973.

Macomber, W. B. *The Anatomy of Disillusion: Martin Heidegger's Notion of Truth*. Evanston, Ill.: Northwestern, 1967.

Malik, Hafeez, edr. *Iqbal: Poet-Philosopher of Pakistan*. New York: Columbia University Press, 1971.

Matthee, Rudi. "The Egyptian Opposition on the Iranian Revolution." In *Shi'ism and Social Protest*, edited by Juan R. I. Cole and Nikki R. Keddie. New Haven: Yale University, 1986.

Maudūdi, Abul A'lāa. *The Islamic Law and Constitution*. 3d ed. Translated by Khurshid Ahmad. Lahore: Islamic Publications, 1967.

Maududi, Abu-l 'Ala. *Conoscere l'Islam*. Roma: Mediterranée, 1973.

Maududi, Abu-l 'Ala. *Vivere l'Islam*. Ancona: SITA, 1979.

McClelland, David. *The Achieving Society*. Princeton: Van Nostrand, 1961.

McDonough, Sheila. "Iqbāl, Gāndhī, and Muhammad 'Alī." In *Essays on Islamic Civilization Presented to Niyazi Berkes*, edited by Donald P. Little. Leiden: Brill, 1976.

McKenzie, Charles S. *Pascal's Anguish and Joy*. New York: Philosophical Library, 1973.

Memmi, Albert. *The Colonizer and the Colonized*. Translated by Howard Greenfeld. New York: Orion Press, 1965.

Michels, Robert. *Political Parties: A Sociological Study of the Oligarchical Tendencies of Modern Democracy*. Translated by Eden and Cedar Paul. London: Jarrold and Sons, 1915.

Miller, James. *History and Human Existence: From Marx to Merleau-Ponty*. Berkeley: University of California Press, 1979.

Mitchell, Richard P. *The Society of Muslim Brothers*. London: Oxford, 1969.

Montesquieu. *Lettres persanes*. Paris: Garnier Frères, 1975.

Moussali, Ahmad S. *Radical Islamic Fundamentalism: The Ideological and Political Discourse of Sayyid Qutb*. Beirut: AUB, 1992.

Munson, Henry, Jr. *Islam and Revolution in the Middle East*. New Haven: Yale University Press, 1988.

Navabi, Abbas. "Reform and Revolution in Shi'i Islam: The Thought of Ali Shariati." Ph.D. diss., Indiana University, 1988.

Newell, W. R. "Heidegger on Freedom and Community: Some Political Implications of His Early Thought." *American Political Science Review*, 78 (1984), pp. 775–784.

Nietzsche, Friedrich. *Beyond Good and Evil*. Translated by R. J. Hollingdale. Middlesex: Penguin, 1983.

Nietzsche, Friedrich. *Thus Spoke Zarathustra*. Translated by Walter Kauffman. Middlesex: Penguin, 1981.

Nietzsche, Friedrich. *Twilight of the Idols/The Anti-Christ*. Translated by R. J. Hollingdale. Middlesex: Penguin, 1987.

Nietzsche, Friedrich. "The Use and Abuse of History." In *Thoughts out of Season*, Part 2. London: Allen, 1927.

Packenham, Robert A. *Liberal America and the Third World: Political Develoopment Ideas in Foreign Aid and Social Science*. Princeton: Princeton University Press, 1973.

Pala, Alberto. *Il rapporto uomo-natura in Antonio Gramsci*. Sassari: Polumbo, 1960.

Pascal, Blaise. *Lettres écrites à un provincial*. Paris: Flammarion, 1981.

Pascal, Blaise. *Pensées*. Text established by Leon Brunschwigg. Paris: Flammarion, 1976.

Pocock, John G. A. *Politics, Language, and Time: Essays on Political Thought and History*. New York: Atheneum, 1973.

Polk, William R., ed. *The Developmental Revolution: North Africa, the Middle East, and South Asia.* Washington, D.C.: Middle East Institute, 1963.

Poole, Ross. *Morality and Modernity.* London: Routledge, 1991.

Poster, Mark. *Existential Marxism in Postwar France.* Princeton: Princeton University Press, 1975.

Pye, Lucian W. "Political Modernization: Gaps Between Theory and Reality." *Annals of the American Association for Political and Social Science* 442 (1979), pp. 28–39.

Qara'i, Mahliqa, and Laleh Bakhtiar. *Iqbal: Manifestation of the Islamic Spirit. Two Contemporary Views: Ayatullah Sayyid Ali Khamene'i and Ali Shariati.* Albuquerque, N.Mex.: ABJAD, 1991.

Qutb, Sayyid. *In the Shade of the Qur'an.* Translated by M. Adil Salahi and Ashur A. Shamis. London: MWH, 1979.

Qutb, Sayyid. *Islam: The Religion of the Future.* Delhi: Markazi Maktaba Islami, 1974.

Qutb, Sayyid. *Islam and Universal Peace.* Indianapolis, Ind.: American Trust Publications, 1993.

Qutb, Sayyid. *This Religion of Islam.* Delhi: Markazi Maktaba Islami, 1974.

Qutb, Sayyid. "No God but God—The Program for Life." In *Milestones,* chap. 5, translated by William Shepard. Typescript.

Qutb, Syed. *Milestones.* Karachi: International Islamic, 1981.

Rahman, Fazlur. "Some Aspects of Iqbal's Political Thought." *Studies in Islam* 5 (1968), pp. 161–166.

Raschid, M. S. *Iqbal's Concept of God.* London: Kegan Paul, 1981.

Riggs, Fred. *Administration in Developing Countries: The Theory of Prismatic Societies.* Boston: Houghton Mifflin, 1964.

Rosenblum, Nancy L. *Another Liberalism: Romanticism and the Reconstruction of Liberal Thought.* Cambridge: Harvard University Press, 1987.

Rosenthal, Ervin J. *Islam in the Modern National State.* Cambridge: Cambridge University Press, 1965.

Rosenthal, Franz. "'I Am you'—Individual Piety and Society in Islam." In *Individualism and Conformity in Classical Islam,* edited by Amin Banani and Speros Vryonis. Wiesbaden: Harrassowitz, 1977.

Rosenthal, Franz. *The Muslim Concept of Freedom Prior to the Nineteenth Century.* Leiden: E. J. Brill, 1960.

Rostow, Walt W. *The Stages of Economic Growth: A Non-Communist Manifesto.* Cambridge: Cambridge University Press, 1960.

Rousseau, Jean-Jacques. *Du contrat social.* Paris: Garnier, 1962.

Rousseau, Jean-Jacques. *Emile ou l'éducation.* Paris: Garnier-Flammarion, 1966.

Rousseau, Jean-Jacques. *Julie, ou la nouvelle Héloïse.* Paris: Flammarion 1967.

Ruedy, John. *Modern Algeria: The Origins and Development of a Nation.* Bloomington: Indiana University Press, 1992.

Runciman, Steven. *A History of the Crusades.* Vol. 1. Cambridge: Cambridge University Press, 1951.

Runciman, W. G. *A Critique of Max Weber's Philosophy of Social Science.* Cambridge: Cambridge University Press, 1972.

Safi, Louay M. *The Challenge of Modernity: The Quest for Authenticity in the Arab World.* Lanham, Md.: University Press of America, 1994.

Said, Edward W. *Covering Islam*. New York: Pantheon, 1981.

Said, Edward W. *Culture and Imperialism*. New York: Vintage, 1994.

Said, Edward W. *Orientalism*. London: Routledge and Kegan Paul, 1978.

Sallis, John. "Nietzsche and the Problem of Knowledge." *Tulane Studies in Philosophy*, 18 (1969), pp. 105–122.

Salvatore, Armando, "The Rational Authentification of *turāth* in Contemporary Arab Thought: Muhammad al-Jābirī and Hasan Hanafī." Paper presented at the annual meeting of the Middle East Studies Association, Phoenix, November, 1994.

Sartre, Jean-Paul. *Réflexions sur la question juive*. Paris: Gallimard, 1954. (*Anti-Semite and Jew*. Translated by George J. Becker. New York: Schocken, 1965.)

Savory, Roger M. "Orthodoxy and Aberrancy in the Ithnā 'Asharī Shī'ī Tradition." In *Islamic Studies Presented to C. J. Adams*, edited by Wael B. Hallaq, pp. 169–181. Leiden: Brill, 1991.

Schiller, Friedrich. *On the Aesthetic Education of Man*. Translated by Reginald Snell. New York: Frederick Ungar, 1965.

Schimmel, Annemarie. *Islam in the Indian Subcontinent*. Leiden-Köln: Brill, 1980.

Shariati, Ali. *An Approach to the Understanding of Islam*. Translated by Venus Kaivantash. Houston: Free Islamic Literatures, 1980.

Shariati, Ali. *Art Awaiting the Saviour*. Translated by Homa Fardjadi. Houston: Free Islamic Literatures, 1980.

Shariati, Ali. *Culture and Ideology*. Translated by Fatollah Marjani. Houston: Free Islamic Literatures, 1980.

Shariati, Ali. *Fatima Is Fatima*. Translated by Laleh Bakhtiar. Tehran: Shariati Foundation, c. 1980.

Shariati, Ali. *Hajj*. Translated by Ali A. Behzadnia and Najla Denny. Houston: Free Islamic Literatures, 1980.

Shariati, Ali. *Histoire et destinée*. Translated by F. Hamèd and N. Yavari-d'Hellencourt. Paris: Sindbad, 1982.

Shariati, Ali. *Man and Islam*. Translated by Fatollah Marjani. Houston: Free Islamic Literatures, 1981.

Shari'ati, Ali. *Marxism and Other Western Fallacies: An Islamic Critique*. Translated by R. Campbell. Berkeley: Mizan, 1980.

Shariati, Ali. *On the Sociology of Islam*. Translated by Hamid Algar. Berkeley: Mizan, 1979.

Shariati, Ali. *One Followed by an Eternity of Zeroes*. Translated by Ali Asghar Ghassemy. Houston: Free Islamic Literatures, 1980.

Shariati, Ali. *Red Shi'ism*. Translated by Habib Shirazi. Houston: Free Islamic Literatures, 1980.

Shariati, Ali. *Reflections of Humanity: Two Views of Civlization and the Plight of Man*. Houston: Free Islamic Literatures, 1980.

Shariati, Ali. *Religion vs. Religion*. Translated by Laleh Bakhtiar. Albuquerque, N.Mex.: ABJAD, c. 1989.

Shariati, Ali. *Selection and/or Election*. Translated by Ali Asghar Ghassemy. Houston: Free Islamic Literatures, 1980.

Shari'ati, Ali. *What Is to Be Done*. Edited by Farhang Rajaee. Houston: Institute for Research and Islamic Studies, 1986.

Shepard, William. "The Development of the Thought of Sayyid Qutb as Reflected in Earlier and Later Editions of 'Social Justice in Islam.'" *Die Welt des Islams* 32, 2 (1992), pp. 196–236.

Shepard, William. "The Doctrine of Progress in Some Modern Muslim Writings." *Bulletin of the Henry Martyr Institute of Islamic Studies* 10, 4 (October-December 1991), pp. 51–64.

Shepard, William. "Islam as a 'System' in the Later Writings of Sayyid Qutb." *Middle Eastern Studies* 25, 1 (January 1989), pp. 31–50.

Shils, Edward. *Political Development in the New States.* The Hague: Mouton, 1965.

Sivan, Emmanuel. "The Islamic Republic of Egypt." *Orbis* 31, 1 (Spring 1987), pp. 43–53.

Sivan, Emmanuel. *Radical Islam: Medieval Theology and Modern Politics.* New Haven: Yale University Press, 1985.

Smith, Wilfred Cantwell. *Modern Islam in India: A Social Analysis.* London: Victor Gollancz, 1946.

Souriau, Christine. "La conscience islamique devant quelques oevres récentes d'intellectuels du Maghreb." *Revue de l'occident musulman et de la Méditerranée* 29 (1st semester 1980), pp. 69–107.

Spera, Salvatore. *Kierkegaard politico.* Roma: Istituto di Studi Filosofici, 1978.

Stern, J. P. *Nietzsche.* Transbridge, England: Harvester, 1978.

Streng, Frederick J. "Three Approaches to Authentic Existence: Christian, Confucian and Buddhist." *Philosophy East and West* 32 (October 1982), pp. 371–392.

Tamir, Yael. *Liberal Nationalism.* Princeton: Princeton University Press, 1993.

Taylor, Alan R. *The Islamic Question in Middle East Politics.* Boulder: Westview, 1988.

Taylor, Charles. *The Ethics of Authenticity.* Cambridge: Harvard University Press, 1991.

Taylor, Charles. *Sources of the Self.* Cambridge: Harvard University Press, 1989.

Thompson, John B. *Critical Hermeneutics: A Study in the Thought of Paul Ricoeur and Jürgen Habermas.* Cambridge: Cambridge University Press, 1981.

Tibi, Bassam. *The Crisis of Modern Islam: A Preindustrial Culture in the Scientific Age.* Translated by Judith von Sivers. Salt Lake City: University of Utah Press, 1988.

Tibi, Bassam. "Islam, Modern Scientific Discourse, and Cultural Modernity: The Politics of Islamization of Knowledge as a Claim to De-Westernization." Paper presented at annual meeting of the Middle East Studies Association of North America, San Antonio, Tex., November 10–13, 1990.

Trilling, Lionel. *Sincerity and Authenticity.* Cambridge: Harvard University Press, 1972.

Turabi, Hasan. *Islam, Democracy, the State, and the West: A Round Table with Dr. Hasan Turabi.* Edited by Arthur L. Lowrie. Tampa, Fla.: World and Islam Studies Enterprise, 1993.

Vahid, Syed 'Abdul. *Iqbal, His Art and Thought.* Lahore: Ashraf, 1944.

Vattimo, Gianni. *Al di là del soggetto: Nietzsche, Heidegger, e l'ermeneutica.* Milano: Feltrinelli, 1984.

Vattimo, Gianni. *The End of Modernity.* Translated by Jon R. Snyder. Baltimore: Johns Hopkins University Press, 1988.

Vattimo, Gianni. *Il soggetto e la maschera: Nietzsche e il problema della liberazione.* Milano: Bompiani, 1979.

Voll, John Obert. *Islam: Continuity and Change in the Modern World.* Boulder: Westview, 1982.

Watt, W. Montgomery. *The Formative Period of Islamic Thought.* Edinborough: Edinborough University Press, 1973.

Watt, W. Montgomery. *Islamic Fundamentalism and Modernity.* London: Routledge, 1988.

Weber, Max. *The Protestant Ethic and the Spirit of Capitalism.* Translated by Talcott Parsons. London: Allen and Unwin, 1930.

White, Stephen K. *Political Theory and Postmodernism.* Cambridge: Cambridge University Press, 1991.

Wiarda, Howard J., ed. *New Directions in Comparative Politics.* Boulder: Westview, 1985.

Yack, Bernard. *The Longing for Total Revolution: Philosophic Sources of Social Discontent from Rousseau to Marx and Nietzsche.* Princeton: Princeton University Press, 1986.

Zimmerman, Michael. "Socratic Ignorance and Authenticity," *Tulane Studies in Philosphy* 29 (1980), pp. 133–149.

Zubaida, Sami. *Islam, The People and the State: Political Ideas and Movements in the Middle East.* London: I. B. Tauris, 1993.

About the Book and Author

"Authenticity" has begun to rival "development" as a key to understanding the political aspirations of the Islamic world. Almost everywhere modernity has laid waste to tradition, those habits and practices deemed to be timeless and true. Imperialism carried European notions of progress into Muslim-dominated parts of the globe, and subsequently Muslims themselves espoused Western practices, techniques, and philosophies. Regimes calling themselves liberal, socialist, and Arab nationalist all embraced modernity as their principal objective.

Most of these regimes failed to create the promised better lives their citizens desired. Moreover, ordinary Muslims felt despair as modernity ripped apart families, exposed youngsters to the materialism and hedonism of Western entertainments, heightened social expectations, and undermined religious belief. Even though tradition has proved itself incapable of staving off modernity, the promises and premises of modern development literature have been called into question.

Where is the truth around which Muslims can rally? Does modernity require a rejection of tradition? Does the embrace of Islamic ideas necessitate turning away from modernity? Robert D. Lee explores these compelling questions by presenting four contemporary Muslim writers—Muhammad Iqbal, Sayyid Qutb, 'Ali Shari'ati, and Mohammed Arkoun—all of whom have refused to bow to such a dichotomy of modernity and tradition. This study examines their efforts, deeply influenced by European thinking, to find a truth beyond tradition and modernity—an "authentic" understanding of Islam upon which Muslims can build a future.

All four thinkers believe such an authentic understanding can serve as the foundation for a new politics. Lee argues, however, that each of these versions of authenticity suffers shortcomings and falters in its efforts to move from the particularity of culture onto a grander scale of political organization appropriate for the modern world.

Robert D. Lee is professor of political science at Colorado College.

Index